TOP **10**
PARIS

Top 10 Paris Highlights

The Top 10 of Everything

CONTENTS

Paris Area by Area

Streetsmart

Within each Top 10 list in this book, no hierarchy of quality or popularity is implied. All 10 are, in the editor's opinion, of roughly equal merit.

Title page, front cover and spine *The iconic Eiffel Tower at springtime*
Back cover, clockwise from top left *Pretty outdoor tables in Montmartre; the ornate Hall of Mirrors in the Palace of Versailles; Apollo Fountain at Versailles; Eiffel Tower; Sacré-Coeur*

The rapid rate at which the world is changing is constantly keeping the DK Eyewitness team on our toes. While we've worked hard to ensure that this edition of Paris is accurate and up-to-date, we know that opening hours alter, standards shift, prices fluctuate, places close and new ones pop up in their stead. So, if you notice we've got something wrong or left something out, we want to hear about it. Please get in touch at **travelguides@dk.com**

Welcome to
Paris

Paris, City of Light. Capital of romance and revolution. A heady mix of café philosophers and Coco Chanel couture. A foodie paradise. A culture-lover's dream. The focus of a thousand iconic movie images. Paris is all these things and more... so who could deny that it's Europe's most magical destination? With DK Eyewitness Top 10 Paris, it's yours to explore.

We love Paris: its culture, its charm, its *je ne sais quoi*. What could be better than exploring the chic shops of the **Marais** district or sniffing out the best cheeses in **Rue Montorgeuil**'s market; wandering through village-like **Montmartre** or browsing the bookstalls of the **Latin Quarter**; people-watching in the **Jardin du Luxembourg** or sauntering along **Boulevard St-Germain** for an early morning coffee at **Café de Flore** in the footsteps of Hemingway and Picasso? And what could be more fun than hopping on a Vélib' bike and cycling along the Seine from the **Eiffel Tower** to **Sainte-Chapelle**?

Paris is a city made for strolling, along its leafy boulevards and through its parks, against a backdrop of elegant Haussmann buildings and soaring contemporary structures. There's history in these cobblestoned streets, but Paris is also a striking 21st-century city, where cutting-edge art is displayed in the **Palais de Tokyo**, and a new generation of acclaimed chefs is experimenting and building upon Paris's reputation for gastronomic excellence.

Whether you're coming for a weekend or a week, our Top 10 guide brings together the best of everything that Paris has to offer, from the world-famous glories of the **Louvre** to the pretty lakes and waterfalls in **Bois de Vincennes**. The guide has useful tips throughout, from seeking out what's free to places off the beaten track, plus 11 easy-to-follow itineraries, designed to tie together a clutch of sights in a short space of time. Add inspiring photography and detailed maps, and you've got the essential pocket-sized travel companion. **Enjoy the book, and enjoy Paris**.

Clockwise from top: **Boulevard St-Germain, Sacré-Coeur, Versailles gardens, Centre Georges Pompidou, River Seine from Pont Alexandre III, Galeries Lafayette interior, Moulin Rouge**

Exploring Paris

Paris has an inexhaustible wealth of things to see and do. Here are some ideas for how to make the most of your time. The city is relatively compact, so you should be able to do most of your sightseeing on foot, and you're never far from a metro station.

Musée d'Orsay is housed in a former railway station.

Key
— Two-day itinerary
— Four-day itinerary

Two Days in Paris

Day ❶
MORNING

Cross **Pont Neuf** *(see p80)* over the River Seine to the Ile de la Cité and view the cathedral of **Notre-Dame** *(see pp20–23)*, partially damaged by fire in April 2019, or visit **Sainte-Chapelle** *(see pp36–7)*. Continue south into the lively **Latin Quarter** *(see pp124–7)* and pause for lunch in a classic Left Bank bistro *(see p133)*.

AFTERNOON

Meander through the stylish district of **St-Germain-des-Prés** *(see pp124–7)* to the **Musée d'Orsay** *(see pp16–19)* and admire its impressive collection of Impressionist paintings. From here it's a short walk to **Hôtel des Invalides** *(see pp38–9)* and the **Eiffel Tower** *(see pp24–5)*, stunningly lit up at night.

Day ❷
MORNING

Take in the views from atop the **Arc de Triomphe** *(see pp30–31)*, then stroll the **Avenue des Champs-Elysées** *(see p111)* and **Jardin des Tuileries** *(see p103)* to the **Musée du Louvre** *(see pp12–15)*.

AFTERNOON

Explore the hip **Marais** *(see pp92–5)*, stopping at the **Centre Georges Pompidou** *(see pp32–3)*. Rent a Vélib' bike and cycle to **Montmartre** *(see pp146–9)* and walk up to **Sacré-Coeur** *(see pp26–7)* for panoramic views.

Four Days in Paris

Day ❶
MORNING

Visit Montmartre's **Sacré-Coeur** *(see pp26–7)*, then head down through

Panthéon's awe-inspiring interior features elegant arches, which link the pillars that support the dome.

Montmartre's leafy Place du Tertre, where artists set up their easels, is full of life and colour.

Pigalle (see pp146–9) to Opéra National de Paris Garnier (see pp104–5) and elegant Place Vendôme (see p104).

AFTERNOON

Wander through Jardin des Tuileries (see p103) and visit Monet's Water Lilies at the Musée de l'Orangerie (see p52). Then stroll along the Avenue des Champs-Elysées (see p111) to the Arc de Triomphe (see pp30–31).

Day ❷
MORNING

Discover modern art at the Centre Georges Pompidou (see pp32–3), then explore the recently refurbished Musée Carnavalet (see p94). Enjoy a bistro lunch on Place des Vosges (see p93).

AFTERNOON

See the Marais district (see pp92–5) and Ile St-Louis (see pp78–81). Pass by Notre-Dame (see pp20–23) before enjoying Sainte-Chapelle (see pp36–7).

Day ❸
MORNING

Take a boat trip along the River Seine (see p170) before a visit to the great Impressionists at the Musée d'Orsay (see pp16–19).

AFTERNOON

Pay your respects to Napoleon at Hôtel des Invalides (see pp38–9) and then head to the Eiffel Tower (see pp24–5).

Day ❹
MORNING

You'll have time to see all the star exhibits of the Musée du Louvre (see pp12–15) before heading off for lunch in the Latin Quarter (see pp124–7).

AFTERNOON

Visit the Panthéon (see pp34–5), explore the lovely Jardin des Plantes (see p135) and end the day strolling, and dining, around Place de la Contrescarpe (see p136).

Top 10 Paris Highlights

Magnificent vaulting and stained-glass windows, Sainte-Chapelle

Top 10 Paris Highlights

From Notre-Dame to the Eiffel Tower, Paris holds some of the world's most famous sights. These ten attractions should be top of the list for any first-time visitor, and remain eternally awe-inspiring.

Musée du Louvre ①

The world's most visited museum also contains one of the world's finest collections of art and antiquities (up to 1848). To complete the superlatives, it was once France's largest royal palace *(see pp12–15)*.

② Musée d'Orsay

This former railway station is one of the world's leading art galleries and, for many, reason alone to visit Paris *(see pp16–19)*.

Notre-Dame ③

This great Gothic cathedral, founded on the site of a Gallo-Roman temple, is a repository of art and history. It is also the geographical "heart" of France *(see pp20–23)*.

④ Eiffel Tower

More than seven million visitors a year ascend to the top of this famous Paris landmark for the spectacular views. It was erected for the Universal Exhibition of 1889 *(see pp24–5)*.

Sacré-Coeur ⑤

The terrace in front of this monumental white-domed basilica in Montmartre affords one of the finest free views over Paris *(see pp26–7)*.

6 Arc de Triomphe

Napoleon's triumphal arch, celebrating battle victories, stands proudly at the top of the Champs-Elysées and, along with the Eiffel Tower, is one of the city's most enduring images *(see pp30–31)*.

7 Centre Georges Pompidou

Home to France's National Museum of Modern Art, the building itself is a fascinating work of contemporary art *(see pp32–3)*.

Panthéon 8

The great and the good of France, including Voltaire, are buried in the Panthéon *(see pp34–5)*

9 Sainte-Chapelle

Known as "a gateway to heaven", this exquisite church was built to house relics collected by St Louis on his Crusades *(see pp36–7)*.

10 Hôtel des Invalides

The glowing golden dome of the Hôtel des Invalides church is unmistakable across the rooftops of Paris. It houses Napoleon's tomb *(see pp38–9)*.

TOP 10 ★ Musée du Louvre

One of the world's most impressive museums, the Louvre contains some 35,000 priceless objects. It was built as a fortress by King Philippe-Auguste in 1190, but Charles V (1364–80) made it his home. In the 16th century François I replaced it with a Renaissance-style palace and founded the royal art collection with 12 paintings from Italy. Revolutionaries opened the collection to the public in 1793. Shortly after, Napoleon renovated the Louvre as a museum.

1 Venus de Milo
This iconic statue of Greek goddess Aphrodite – later known as Venus by the ancient Romans – is the highlight of the museum's Greek antiques. It dates from the end of the 2nd century BC and was discovered on the Greek island of Milos in 1820.

2 Marly Horses
Coustou's rearing horses **(above)** being restrained by horse-tamers were sculpted in 1745 for Louis XIV's Château de Marly. Replicas stand near the Place de la Concorde.

3 Mona Lisa
Arguably the most famous painting in the world, Leonardo da Vinci's portrait of a Florentine noblewoman with an enigmatic smile *(see p15)* has been beautifully restored. Visit early or late in the day.

4 Slaves
Michelangelo sculpted *Dying Slave* **(left)** and *Rebellious Slave* (1513–20) for the tomb of Pope Julius II in Rome. The unfinished figures seem to be emerging from their "prisons" of stone.

5 Glass Pyramid
The unmistakable glass and steel pyramid, designed by I M Pei, became the Louvre's new entrance in 1989. Stainless steel tubes make up the 21-m- (69-ft-) high frame.

6 Medieval Moats
An excavation in the 1980s uncovered the remains of the medieval fortress. You can see the base of the towers and the drawbridge support under the Cour Carrée.

7 The Winged Victory of Samothrace
This Hellenistic treasure (3rd–2nd century BC) stands atop a stone ship radiating grace and power. It was created to commemorate a naval triumph at Rhodes.

8 The Raft of the Medusa
The shipwreck of a French frigate three years earlier inspired this gigantic early Romantic painting **(left)** by Théodore Géricault (1791–1824) in 1819. The work depicts the moment when the survivors spot a sail on the horizon.

9 Perrault's Colonnade
The majestic east façade by Claude Perrault (1613–88), with its paired Corinthian columns, was part of an extension plan commissioned by Louis XIV.

Musée du Louvre

10 The Lacemaker

The Winged Victory of Samothrace **7**

The Raft of the Medusa **8**

Mona Lisa **3**

Marly Horses **2**

Dying Slave **4**

Perrault's Colonnade **9**

Glass Pyramid **5**

Key
- Ground floor
- First floor
- Second floor

Venus de Milo **1**

Medieval Moats **6**

10 The Lacemaker
Jan Vermeer's masterpiece **(above)**, painted around 1665, gives a simple but beautiful rendering of everyday life and is the highlight of the Louvre's Dutch collection.

NEED TO KNOW

MAP L2 ■ Musée du Louvre, 75001 ■ 01 40 20 53 17 ■ www.louvre.fr

Open 9am–6pm Mon, Thu, Sat & Sun (to 9:45pm Wed & Fri); closed Tue, 1 Jan, 1 May, 14 Jul, 25 Dec

Adm €17; free 1st Sun of month (except Apr–Sep); under-18s free; under-26s (EU only) free

■ For a light lunch, try Le Café Marly in the Richelieu Wing or the food court in Carrousel du Louvre. For a more special option, book at Alain Ducasse's Bistrot Benoit below the pyramid.

■ Pre-booking a timed entry slot is essential, even for visitors who benefit from free entry. Tickets can be booked on the Louvre website. Choose a date and a 30-minute window to access the museum.

Gallery Guide
The foyer is under the pyramid. Those with tickets are given priority access at the pyramid. Alternatively, buy tickets at the Carrousel du Louvre entrance *(99 rue de Rivoli)* or Porte des Lions. The Sully, Denon and Richelieu wings lead off from the foyer. Painting and sculpture are displayed by country, plus galleries for *objets d'art*, antiquities and prints. The Petit Galerie, in the Richelieu wing, is a temporary exhibition area aimed at children.

Louvre Collections

Ancient Egyptian vase

 French Paintings
This superb collection ranges from the 14th century to 1848 and includes works by such artists as Jean Watteau, Georges de la Tour and J H Fragonard.

 French Sculpture
Highlights include the Tomb of Philippe Pot by Antoine le Moiturier, the Marly Horses *(see p12)* and works by Pierre Puget.

 Egyptian Antiquities
The finest collection outside Cairo, featuring a Sphinx in the crypt, the Seated Scribe of Sakkara, huge sarcophagi, mummified animals, funerary objects and intricate carvings depicting life in Ancient Egypt.

 Greek Antiquities
The art of Ancient Greece here ranges from a Cycladic idol from the third millennium BC to Classical Greek marble statues (c.5th century BC) to Hellenistic works (late 3rd–2nd century BC).

5 Near Eastern Antiquities
A stunning collection includes a recreated temple of an Assyrian king and the Codex of Hammurabi (18th-century BC), mankind's oldest written laws.

6 Italian Paintings
French royalty adored the art of Italy and amassed much of this collection (1200–1800). It includes many works by Leonardo da Vinci.

7 Italian Sculpture
Highlights of this collection, dating from the early Renaissance, include a 15th-century *Madonna and Child* by Donatello and Michelangelo's *Slaves (see p12)*.

8 Dutch Paintings
Rembrandt's works are hung alongside domestic scenes by Vermeer and portraits by Frans Hals.

9 Objets d'Art
The ceramics, jewellery and other items in this collection span history and the world.

10 Islamic Art
This exquisite collection, which spans 13 centuries and 3 continents, is covered by an ultra-modern glass veil.

Louvre Collections

Key
- Basement
- Ground floor
- First floor
- Second floor

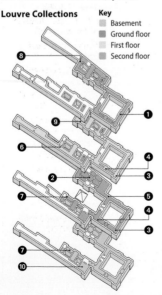

LEONARDO DA VINCI AND THE MONA LISA

Leonardo da Vinci, Renaissance man extraordinaire, was not only an artist but also a sculptor, engineer, architect and scientist. His many interests included the study of anatomy and aerodynamics.

Born in Vinci to a wealthy family, Leonardo da Vinci (1452–1519) took up an apprenticeship under Florentine artist Andrea del Verrocchio, then served the Duke of Milan as an architect and military engineer, during which time he painted the *Last Supper* mural (1495). On his return to Florence, to work as architect to Cesare Borgia, he painted his most celebrated portrait, the *Mona Lisa* (1503–06). It is also known as *La Gioconda*, allegedly the name of the model's aristocratic husband, although there is ongoing speculation regarding the identity of the subject. The work, in particular the sitter's mysterious smile, shows mastery of two techniques: *chiaroscuro*, the contrast of light and shadow, and *sfumato*, subtle transitions between colours. It was the artist's own favourite painting and he took it with him everywhere. In 1516 François I brought them both to France, giving da Vinci the use of a manor house in Amboise in the Loire Valley, where he died three years later.

Mona Lisa, da Vinci's enigmatic portrait

TOP 10 ARCHAEOLOGICAL TREASURES

1 Hammurabi's Code (1792–1750 BC)

2 Parthenon Marbles (5–4th century BC)

3 Assyrian Lamussa (713 BC)

4 Ain Ghazal Statue (7000 BC)

5 Chapel to Tomb of Akhethotep (2400 BC)

6 The Monzon Lion (12–13th century)

7 The Louvre Doll (3rd–4th century)

8 Frieze of Lions (510 BC)

9 Bull's head column capital (510 BC)

10 The Seated Scribe (2600–2500 BC)

TOP 10 ⭐ Musée d'Orsay

This world-class collection covers a variety of art forms from the years 1848 to 1914, and includes a superb Impressionist section. Its setting, in a converted railway station, is equally impressive. Built in 1900, in time for the Paris Exposition, the station was in use until 1939, when it was closed and largely ignored, although it was the location for Orson Welles' 1962 film, The Trial. It was later used as a theatre and as auction rooms, and in the mid-1970s was considered for demolition. In 1977, the Paris authorities decided to save the defunct station building by converting it into this striking museum.

3 The Building

The former railway station that houses this museum **(left)** is almost as stunning as the exhibits. The light and spacious feel on stepping inside, after admiring the magnificent old façade, takes one's breath away.

Van Gogh Paintings 4

The star of the collection is Vincent van Gogh (1853–90) and the most striking of the canvases on display is the 1889 work showing the artist's *Bedroom at Arles* **(right)**. Also on display are some of the artist's self-portraits, painted with his familiar intensity.

1 Le Déjeuner sur l'Herbe

Edouard Manet's (1832–83) controversial painting (1863) was first shown in an "Exhibition of Rejected Works". Its bold portrayal of a classically nude woman enjoying the company of 19th-century men in suits brought about a wave of criticism.

2 Olympia

Another Manet portrayal (1865) of a naked courtesan, receiving flowers sent by an admirer, was also regarded as indecent, and shocked the public and critics, but it was an important influence on later artists.

5 Blue Waterlilies

Claude Monet (1840–1926) painted this stunning canvas (1919) on one of his favourite themes. His love of waterlilies led him to create his own garden at Giverny in order to paint them in a natural setting. This work inspired many abstract painters later in the 20th century.

6 Degas' Statues of Dancers

The museum has an exceptional collection of works by Edgar Degas (1834–1917). Focusing on dancers **(left)** and the world of opera, his sculptures range from innocent to erotic. *Young Dancer of Fourteen* (1881) was the only one exhibited in the artist's lifetime.

7 Jane Avril Dancing

Toulouse-Lautrec's (1864–1901) paintings define Paris's *belle époque*. Jane Avril was a famous Moulin Rouge dancer and featured in several of his works, like this 1895 canvas **(left)**, which Toulouse-Lautrec drew from life, in situ at the cabaret.

8 Dancing at the Moulin de la Galette

One of the best-known paintings of the Impressionist era (1876), this work was shown at the Impressionist exhibition in 1877. The exuberance of Renoir's (1841–1919) work captures the look and mood of Montmartre and is one of the artist's masterpieces.

9 La Belle Angèle

This portrait of a Brittany beauty (1889) by Paul Gauguin (1848–1903) shows the influence of Japanese art on the artist. It was bought by Degas, to finance Gauguin's first trip to Polynesia.

10 Café Campana

Offering a rest from all the impressive art, the museum's café, renovated by the Campana Brothers, is delightfully situated behind one of the former station's huge clocks. A break here is an experience in itself and the food is good too.

NEED TO KNOW

MAP J2 ▪ 1 Rue de la Légion d'Honneur, 75007 ▪ 01 40 49 48 14 ▪ www.musee-orsay.fr

Open 9:30am–6pm Tue–Sun (to 9:45pm Thu); closed 1 May & 25 Dec

Adm €14 (under-18s free, under-26s EU only free); free first Sun of month; pre-booking a timed entry slot online is essential, even for visitors who benefit from free entry

▪ Café Campana, situated on the fifth floor, is open for lunch, snacks and drinks from Tuesdays through Sundays, plus dinner on Thursdays.

▪ Music concerts are often held. Concert tickets include free museum entry. Call 01 53 63 04 63.

Museum Guide
The museum is undergoing renovations until 2021, so works of art may be moved around. It's best to pick up a floorplan as soon as you enter the gallery to find out where the works or collections you want to see are on display. In general, the upper level is home to the Impressionist galleries, while the ground floor has works from the Academic, Realist and Symbolist movements. Decorative arts from the 1900s, including a fine Art Nouveau collection, are in the Pavillon Amont, on the ground floor as well as on floors 2, 3 and 4.

Musée d'Orsay Collections

 The Impressionists
One of the best Impressionist collections in the world. Admirers of Manet, Monet and Renoir will not be disappointed.

2 **The Post-Impressionists**
The artists who moved on to a newer interpretation of Impressionism are equally well represented, including Matisse, Toulouse-Lautrec and the towering figure of Van Gogh.

3 **School of Pont-Aven**
Paul Gauguin was at the centre of the group of artists associated with Pont-Aven in Brittany. His work here includes *Yellow Haystacks*, painted when the artist visited the region in 1889.

 Art Nouveau
Art Nouveau is synonymous with Paris, with many metro stations retaining entrances built in that style. Pendants and glassware by René Lalique (1860–1945) are among the examples on display here.

5 **Symbolism**
This vast collection includes works by well-known artists such as Gustav Klimt (1862–1918) and Edvard

Musée d'Orsay Collections

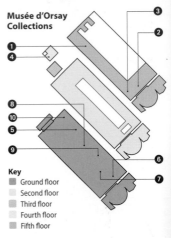

Key
- Ground floor
- Second floor
- Third floor
- Fourth floor
- Fifth floor

Munch (1863–1944), and James Whistler's (1834–1903) portrait of his mother, dating from 1871.

 Romanticism
The Romantics wanted to raise awareness about the spiritual world. One fine example is *The Tiger Hunt* (1854) by Eugène Delacroix (1798–1863).

7 **Sculpture**
The collection includes pieces by Rodin *(see p120)* and satirical carvings of politicians by Honoré Daumier (1808–79).

8 **Naturalism**
Naturalist painters intensified nature in their work. *Haymaking* (1877) by Jules Bastien-Lepage (1848–84) is a fine example.

9 **Nabis**
The Nabis Movement made art into a more decorative form. Pierre Bonnard (1867–1947) is one of its founding members.

10 **Architecture**
In addition to the 19th-century architectural etchings and drawings, there is a room dedicated to the creation of the Opéra Garnier *(see p104)*.

Blue Dancers (1890), Edgar Degas

THE IMPRESSIONIST MOVEMENT

Regarded as the starting point of modern art, the Impressionist Movement is the best-known and best-loved art movement in the world – certainly if the popularity of the Musée d'Orsay is anything to go by. It began in France, and almost all its leading figures were French. Impressionism was a reaction against the formality and Classicism insisted upon by the Académie des Beaux-Arts in Paris, which was very much the art establishment, deciding what would or would not be exhibited at the Paris Salon. The term "impressionism" was coined by a critic of the style, who dismissed the 1872 Monet painting *Impression: Sunrise*,

now on display at the Musée Marmottan (*see p157*). The artists themselves then adopted the term. The style influenced Van Gogh and was to have a lasting influence on 19th- and 20th-century art.

Cathedral at Rouen **(1892–3), Claude Monet**

TOP 10 IMPRESSIONISTS

1 **Claude Monet** (1840–1926)

2 **Edouard Manet** (1832–83)

3 **Auguste Renoir** (1841–1919)

4 **Edgar Degas** (1834–1917)

5 **Camille Pissarro** (1830–1903)

6 **Alfred Sisley** (1839–99)

7 **James Whistler** (1834–1903)

8 **Walter Sickert** (1860–1942)

9 **Mary Cassatt** (1844–1926)

10 **Berthe Morisot** (1841–95)

On the Beach **(1873), Edouard Manet**

TOP10 ⭐ Notre-Dame

The "heart" of the country, both geographically and spiritually, the Cathedral of Notre-Dame (Our Lady) stands on the Ile de la Cité. After Pope Alexander III laid the foundation stone in 1163, an army of craftsmen toiled for 170 years to realize Bishop Maurice de Sully's magnificent design. Almost destroyed during the Revolution, the Gothic masterpiece was restored in 1841–64 by architect Viollet-le-Duc. A devastating fire in 2019 toppled the cathedral's famous 96-m (315-ft) spire and caused part of the roof to cave in.

1 Portal of the Last Judgment

This central relief over the doors of Notre-Dame depicts the biblical Last Judgment – when the souls of humankind will stand before God. The good souls move to the right, towards paradise, while the souls of the condemned move to the left and are led to hell. Though completely damaged during the Revolution, the portal was restored brilliantly in the 19th century.

2 Point Zero

Roads in France are measured from this plaque in front of the church, making it the very center of the whole country – technically. Legend has it that any visitor who steps on it will inevitably return to Paris one day.

3 Portal of the Virgin

The splendid stone tympanum **(right)** was carved in the 13th century and shows the Virgin Mary's death and coronation in heaven. However, the statue of the Virgin and Child that stands between the doors is a modern replica.

4 Flying Buttresses

The striking flying buttresses supporting the cathedral's east façade are by Jean Ravy. The best view is from Square Jean XXIII.

5 West Front

The entrance to the cathedral **(right)** is through three elaborately carved portals. Biblical scenes, sculpted in the Middle Ages, depict the Life of the Virgin, the Last Judgment and the Life of St Anne.

6 Gallery of Kings

The west façade of Notre-Dame cathedral is adorned with the statues of the kings from the book of Judah. During the French Revolution the heads of these statues were chopped off, symbolically believed to be the kings of France. The missing heads were found nearly 200 years later at a construction site nearby and are now up on display.

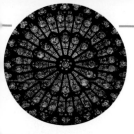

7 Rose Windows

Three great rose windows adorn the north, south and west façades, but only the north window **(left)** retains its 13th-century stained glass, depicting the Virgin surrounded by figures from the Old Testament. The south window shows Christ encircled by the Apostles.

8 Gargoyles

A key feature of the Gothic style of architecture, these grotesque statues stretch from the cathedral's roof and channel water off the roof, acting as waterspouts. On a rainy day, visitors can see the water pouring from their mouths.

9 Galerie des Chimères

Lurking behind the upper gallery between the towers are decorative sculptures or *chimères* **(above)**, placed here to ward off evil.

10 The Towers

The huge Gothic towers are 69 m (226 ft) high; 387 steps within the north tower lead to great views. In 2013, new bells rang here to celebrate the cathedral's 850th birthday.

NEED TO KNOW

MAP N4 ▪ 6 Parvis Notre-Dame – Pl Jean-Paul II, 75004 ▪ 01 53 10 07 00 (towers); 01 42 34 56 10 (cathedral) ▪ www.notredamedeparis.fr

The cathedral is currently closed to the public due to ongoing restoration work.

The Fire of Notre-Dame
On 15 April 2019, fire broke out near the cathedral's spire during renovation work. Watched by many onlookers, the fire quickly spread to the east and west along the roof, which was partially covered in scaffolding at the time. As the flames reached the Gothic towers, the spire collapsed and crashed through the vaulted roof. It took 500 firefighters more than 12 hours to extinguish the inferno. It is thought the cathedral was 30 minutes away from being all but destroyed had the fire engulfed the bell towers, causing them to fall. Many of the priceless treasures and artworks were rescued from the blaze; the 16 copper roof statues had already been removed due to the refurbishment. The vaulted stone ceiling and the cathedral's rose windows mostly survived. The government has set an ambitious goal to have the cathedral restored to its former glory by 2024 – including, after much public debate, a faithful reconstruction of the original spire.

Famous Visitors to Notre-Dame

 Joan of Arc
The patriot Jeanne d'Arc (1412–31), who defended France against the invading English, had a posthumous trial here in 1455, despite having been burned at the stake 24 years earlier. She was found to be innocent of heresy.

 François II and Mary Stuart
Mary Stuart (Mary Queen of Scots; 1542–87) had been raised in France and married the Dauphin in 1558. He ascended the throne as François II in 1559 and the king and queen were crowned in Notre-Dame.

 Napoleon
The coronation of Napoleon (1769–1821) in Notre-Dame in 1804 saw the eager general seize the crown from Pope Pius VII and crown himself emperor and his wife, Josephine, empress.

 Josephine
Josephine's (1763–1814) reign as Empress of France lasted only five years; Napoleon divorced her in 1809.

 Pope Pius VII
In 1809 Pope Pius VII (1742–1823), who oversaw Napoleon's Notre-Dame coronation, was taken captive when the emperor declared the Papal States to be part of France. The pope was imprisoned at Fontainebleau, 50 km (30 miles) south of Paris.

 Philip the Fair
In 1302 the first States General parliament was formally opened at Notre-Dame by Philip IV (1268–1314), otherwise known as Philip the Fair. He greatly increased the governing power of the French royalty.

 Henry VI of England
Henry VI (1421–71) became King of England at the age of one. Like his father, Henry V, he also claimed France and was crowned in Notre-Dame in 1430.

Statue of Joan of Arc inside Notre-Dame

 Marguerite of Valois
In August 1572, Marguerite (1553–1589), sister of Charles IX, stood in the Notre-Dame chancel during her marriage to the Protestant Henri of Navarre (1553–1610), while he stood alone by the door.

Henri of Navarre
As a Protestant Huguenot, Henri's marriage to the Catholic Marguerite resulted in uprising and many massacres. In 1589, he became Henri IV, the first Bourbon king of France, and converted to Catholicism, stating that "Paris is well worth a Mass".

Charles de Gaulle
On 26 August 1944, Charles de Gaulle entered Paris and attended a Magnificat service to celebrate the liberation of Paris, despite the fact that hostile snipers were still at large outside the cathedral.

Charles de Gaulle visits Notre-Dame

SAVING NOTRE-DAME

Novelist Victor Hugo

Paris's great cathedral has had a history of deterioration and restoration. When Victor Hugo's novel *Notre-Dame de Paris (The Hunchback of Notre-Dame)* was published in 1831, the cathedral was in a state of decay. Even for the crowning of Napoleon in 1804, the crumbling setting had to be disguised with ornamentation. During the Revolution, the cathedral was sold to a scrap dealer, though fortunately not demolished. Hugo was intent on saving France's spiritual heart and helped mount a campaign to restore Notre-Dame before it was too late; Eugène Emmanuel Viollet-le-Duc (1814–79) was chosen for the restoration. Repairs began again in 2019 before the cathedral was damaged by fire. Within 24 hours of the blaze, President Macron vowed to rebuild Notre-Dame and more than €800 million was raised. At the same time, sales of Hugo's iconic novel rocketed, prompting French booksellers to ask for profits from renewed sales to be directed towards the restoration.

TOP 10
EVENTS IN NOTRE-DAME HISTORY

1 Construction of the cathedral begins (1163)

2 St Louis places the Crown of Thorns here temporarily (1239)

3 Construction is completed (1334)

4 Retrial of Joan of Arc (1455)

5 Revolutionaries loot the cathedral and make it a Temple of Reason (1789)

6 Crowning of Emperor Napoleon (1804)

7 Restoration work is completed (1864)

8 Mass for the Liberation of Paris (1944)

9 New bells with a medieval tone mark the 850th anniversary (2013)

10 Fire destroys the spire and roof (2019)

***The Hunchback of Notre-Dame**, Hugo's 1831 novel, tells the story of Quasimodo, a hunchbacked bell-ringer at Notre-Dame, who falls in love with gypsy girl Esmeralda.*

🔟 ⭐ Eiffel Tower

The most distinctive symbol of Paris, the Eiffel Tower was much maligned by critics when it appeared on the city's skyline in 1889 as part of the Universal Exhibition, but its graceful symmetry soon made it the star attraction. A feat of engineering, at 324 m (1,062 ft) high, it was the world's tallest building until it was surpassed by New York's Chrysler Building in 1930. Despite its delicate appearance, it weighs 10,100 metric tons and engineer Gustave Eiffel's construction was so sound that it never sways more than 7 cm (2.5 in) in strong winds.

The iconic Eiffel Tower

3 Lighting

Some 20,000 bulbs and 336 lamps make the Eiffel Tower **(left)** a spectacular night-time sight. It sparkles like a giant Christmas tree for five minutes every hour from dusk until 1am.

4 View from the Trocadéro

Day or night, the best approach for a first-time view of the tower is from the Trocadéro (see p142), which affords a monumental vista from the Chaillot terrace across the Seine.

1 Gustave Eiffel's Office

Located at the top of the tower is Gustave Eiffel's office, which has been restored to its original condition. It displays wax models of Thomas Edison and Eiffel himself.

2 First Level

You can walk the 345 steps up to the 57-m-(187-ft-) high first level and enjoy a hearty meal at the all-day brasserie. This level also includes glass floors and educational displays.

5 Viewing Gallery

At 276 m (906 ft), the stupendous view **(right)** stretches for 80 km (50 miles) on a clear day. You can also see Gustave Eiffel's sitting room on this level.

7 Champ-de-Mars

The long gardens of this former parade ground stretch from the base of the tower to the École Militaire (military school).

8 Ironwork

The complex pattern of the girders (above), held together by 2.5 million rivets, stabilizes the tower in high winds. The metal can expand up to 15 cm (6 in) on hot days.

9 Hydraulic Lift Mechanism

The 1899 lift mechanism is still in operation and travels some 103,000 km (64,000 miles) a year. The uniformed guard clinging to the outside is a model.

10 Bust of Gustave Eiffel

This bust of the tower's creator (below), by Antoine Bourdelle, was placed below his achievement, by the north pillar, in 1929.

6 Second Level

At 116 m (380 ft) high, this level is the location of Le Jules Verne restaurant, one of the finest in Paris for food and views (see p123). It is reached by a private lift in the south pillar.

THE LIFE OF GUSTAVE EIFFEL

Born in Dijon, Gustave Eiffel (1832–1923) was an engineer and builder who made his name building bridges and viaducts, and helped in the design of the Statue of Liberty. Eiffel was famous for the graceful designs and master craftsmanship of his many wrought-iron constructions. He once said that his famous tower was "formed by the wind itself". In 1890 he became immersed in the study of aerodynamics, and kept an office in the tower until his death, using it for experiments. In 1889, when the Eiffel Tower was erected, its creator was awarded the Légion d'Honneur.

NEED TO KNOW

MAP B4 ■ Champ de Mars, 7e ■ 08 92 70 12 39 ■ www.toureiffel.paris

Open Lift 9:30am–11:45pm daily; last adm for top 10:30pm (Jul–Aug: 9am–12:45am; last adm 11pm); Stairs 9:30am–6:30pm daily; last adm 6pm (Jul–Aug: 9:30am–12:45am; last adm midnight)

Adm €10.40–€25.90 (stairs & elevators only); €2.60–€6.50 for 4–11s; €5.20–€13 for 12–24s

■ There are restaurants and snack bars on levels 1 and 2, along with a Champagne bar on level 3, plus food kiosks around the base.

■ Skip the queue and book the ticket online or opt for a tour (cultival.fr).

TOP 10 ★ Sacré-Coeur

One of the city's most photographed sights, the spectacular white basilica of Sacré-Coeur (Sacred Heart) watches over Paris from its highest point. The basilica was built as a memorial to the 58,000 French soldiers killed during the Franco-Prussian War (1870–71). It took 46 years to build and was finally completed in 1923 at a cost of 40 million francs (6 million euros). Priests still pray for the souls of the dead here, 24 hours a day, as they have since 1885. People flock here for the breathtaking panoramic views – at sunset, in particular, there are few sights in Paris more memorable.

1 Great Mosaic of Christ

A glittering Byzantine mosaic of Christ, created by Luc Olivier Merson between 1912 and 1922, decorates the vault over the chancel. It represents France's devotion to the Sacred Heart.

3 Bronze Doors

The doors of the portico entrance are beautifully decorated with bronze relief sculptures depicting the Last Supper and other scenes from the life of Christ.

4 The Dome

The distinctive egg-shaped dome of the basilica is the second-highest viewpoint in Paris after the Eiffel Tower. Reached via a spiral staircase, vistas can stretch as far as 48 km (30 miles) on a clear day.

2 Crypt Vaults

The arched vaults of the crypt **(above)** house a chapel that contains the heart of Alexandre Legentil, one of the advocates of Sacré-Coeur.

5 Statue of Christ

The basilica's most important statue shows Christ giving a blessing. It is symbolically placed in a niche over the main entrance, above the two bronze equestrian statues.

6 Stained-Glass Gallery

One level of the great dome is encircled by stained-glass windows **(right)**. From here is a beautiful view over the whole interior.

7 Bell Tower

The *campanile*, designed by Lucien Magne and added in 1904, is 80 m (262 ft) high. One of the heaviest bells in the world, the 19-ton La Savoyarde hangs in the belfry. Cast in Annecy in 1895, it was donated by the dioceses of Savoy.

8 Façade

Architect Paul Abadie (1812–1884) employed a mix of domes, turrets and Classical features in his design of this basilica. The Château-Landon stone secretes calcite when wet and so it keeps the façade **(left)** bleached white.

10 Equestrian Statues

Two striking bronze statues of French saints stand on the portico above the main entrance, cast in 1927 by Hippolyte Lefèbvre. One statue is of Joan of Arc, while the other is of Louis IX, who was later canonized as Saint Louis.

NEED TO KNOW

MAP F1 ■ 35 Rue du Chevalier-de-la-Barre, 75018 ■ 01 53 41 89 00 ■ www.sacre-coeur-montmartre.com

Basilica: open 6am–10:30pm daily, last entry 10:15pm

Dome: open Oct–Feb: 10am–5:30pm daily; Mar–May: 9:30am–7pm daily; Jun–Sep: 9am–8:30pm daily; adm €8

■ Grab a bite on the terrace at Le St-Jean on 23 Rue des Abbesses and watch the world go by.

■ An evocative sung Mass takes place on Sundays at 11am.

9 The Funicular

To avoid the steep climb up to Sacré-Coeur, take the *funiculaire* cable railway **(below)** and enjoy the views at leisure. It runs from the end of rue Foyatier, near Square Willette.

Following pages Arc de Triomphe illuminated at dusk

🔟⭐ Arc de Triomphe

The best day to visit the world's most familiar triumphal arch is 2 December, the date that marks Napoleon's victory at the Battle of Austerlitz in 1805. Work began on the 50-m (164-ft) arch in 1806 but was not completed until 1836, due, in part, to Napoleon's fall from power. Four years later, Napoleon's funeral procession passed beneath it, on its way to his burial in Les Invalides. Traffic is banned along the Champs-Elysées on the first Sunday of the month, making it easier to access and get that perfect photo of the Arc de Triomphe.

4 Tomb of the Unknown Soldier

In the centre of the arch flickers the eternal flame on the Tomb of the Unknown Soldier **(left)**, a victim of World War I buried on 11 November 1920. It is symbolically reignited every day at 6:30pm.

1 Museum

Within the arch is a small but interesting museum which tells the history of its construction and gives details of various celebrations and funerals that the arch has seen over the years. The more recent of these are shown in a short video.

2 Departure of the Volunteers in 1792

One of the most striking sculptures is on the front right base. It shows French citizens leaving to defend their nation against Austria and Prussia.

5 Viewing Platform

Take the elevator or climb 284 steps to the top of the Arc de Triomphe to get a sublime view **(below)** of Paris and a sense of the arch's dominant position in the centre of the Place de l'Etoile. To the east is the Champs-Elysées and to the west is the Grande Arche de La Défense (see p155). There are another 40 steps after the lift.

Arc de Triomphe

3 Triumph of Napoleon

As you look at the arch from the Champs-Elysées (see p111), J P Cortot's high-relief on the left base shows the restored *Triumph of Napoleon*. It celebrates the Treaty of Vienna peace agreement signed in 1810, when Napoleon's empire was in its heyday.

7 Battle of Austerlitz

Another battle victory is shown on a frieze on the arch's north side. It depicts Napoleon's heavily outnumbered troops breaking the ice on Lake Satschan in Austria, a tactic which drowned thousands of enemy troops.

6 Battle of Aboukir

Above the *Triumph of Napoleon* carving is this scene **(above)** showing Napoleonic victory over the Turks in 1799. The same victory was commemorated on canvas in 1806 by the French painter Antoine Gros and is now on display at the Palace of Versailles *(see p155)*.

8 Frieze

A frieze running around the arch shows French troops departing for battle (east) and their victorious return (west).

THE GREAT AXIS

The Arc de Triomphe is the central of three arches; together they create a grand vision of which even Napoleon would have been proud. He was responsible for the first two, placing the Arc de Triomphe directly in line with the Arc de Triomphe du Carrousel in front of the Louvre *(see pp12–15)*, which also celebrates the victory at Austerlitz. In 1989, the trio was completed with the Grande Arche de La Défense. The 8km-long (5-mile) *Grand Axe* (Great Axis) runs from here to the Louvre's Pyramid.

9 General Marceau's Funeral

Marceau died in battle against the Austrian army in 1796, after a famous victory against them the previous year. His funeral is depicted in a frieze located above the *Departure of the Volunteers in 1792*.

10 Thirty Shields

Immediately below the top of the arch runs a row of 30 shields, each carrying the name of a Napoleonic victory.

NEED TO KNOW

MAP B2 ▪ Pl Charles-de-Gaulle, 75008 ▪ 01 55 37 73 77 (enquiries) ▪ www.paris-arc-de-triomphe.fr/en

Open 10am–10:45pm daily; pre-booking a timed entry slot is essential

Adm €13 (under 18s, EU 18–25s free)

▪ An installation by environmental artist Christo will see the arch wrapped in recyclable fabric and rope from 18 September to 3 October 2021. Check christojeanneclaude.net for details.

▪ Enjoy the old-world charm of Le Fouquet *(99 Ave des Champs-Elysées)*.

▪ Arch access is via the underground tunnel only.

TOP 10 ★ Centre Georges Pompidou

Today it's one of the world's most famous pieces of modern architecture. When the Pompidou Centre opened in 1977, however, architects Richard Rogers and Renzo Piano startled everyone by turning the building "inside out", with brightly coloured pipes displayed on the façade. Designed as a cross-cultural arts complex, it houses the excellent Musée National d'Art Moderne (Modern Art Museum), as well as two cinemas, a library, shops and performance space. The outside forecourt is a popular gathering spot for tourists and locals alike.

1 Pipes

Part of the shock factor of the Pompidou Centre is that the utility pipes are outside the building **(below)**. Not only that, they are vividly coloured: bright green for water, yellow for electricity and blue for air conditioning.

5 Bookshop

The ground-floor bookshop sells a range of postcards, posters of major works in the Modern Art Museum and books on artists associated with Paris.

3 Escalator

One of the building's most striking and popular features is the external escalator **(right)** which climbs, snake-like, up the front of the Centre in its plexiglass tube. The view gets better and better as you rise high above the activity in the Centre's forecourt, before arriving at the top for the best view of all.

2 Top-Floor View

The view from the top of the Pompidou Centre is spectacular. The Eiffel Tower is visible, as is Montmartre in the north and the monolithic Tour Montparnasse to the south. On clear days views can stretch as far as La Défense *(see p155)*.

4 The Piazza

Visitors and locals gather in the open space in front of the Centre to enjoy a variety of street performers and the changing installations of sculptures, which are often related to shows at the Centre.

6 Stravinsky Fountain

This colourful fountain in Place Igor Stravinsky was designed by Niki de Saint-Phalle and Jean Tinguely as part of the Pompidou Centre development. Inspired by composer Stravinsky's ballet *The Firebird* (1910), the bird spins and sprays water.

8 Avec l'arc noir (With a Black Arch)

One of the pioneers of Abstract art, artist Vasily Kandinsky (1866–1944) promoted the use of non-naturalist geometric forms. His *Avec l'arc noir* (1912) features a black line that recalls the *douga* (wooden arch) of a Russian *troika* (carriage).

7 Man with a Guitar

Within the Modern Art Museum, this 1914 work **(above)** by artist Georges Braque (1882–1963) is one of the most striking of the Cubist Movement.

NEED TO KNOW

MAP P2 ▪ Pl Georges Pompidou 75004 ▪ 01 44 78 12 33 ▪ www.centrepompidou.fr

Museum: 11am–9pm Wed–Mon (to 11pm Thu); closed 1 May; adm €11–14; free 1st Sun of the month, under-18s free, under-26s (EU only) free

Brancusi's Studio: 2–6pm Wed–Mon

▪ The centre's café has free Wi-Fi access. For something grander, head to Georges, the rooftop brasserie.

▪ Pre-booking a timed entry slot online is essential.

Centre Guide

The Centre is home to various institutions. The Museum of Modern Art (Mnam) is on levels 4 and 5, and there is a cinema on level 1 and in the basement. Check at the information desk or on the website for details about the temporary shows (level 6), rehangs of works and the contemporary art "happenings". Displays at the Mnam often change and some works are now shared with its sister institution in Metz.

9 Brancusi's Studio

The Romanian sculptor Constantin Brancusi (1876–1957) left his entire studio to the state. It has been reconstructed **(left)** in the Piazza, and displays his abstract works.

10 Compositie n°3

Together with Piet Mondrian, Dutch painter Bart van der Leck (1876–1958) founded the De Stijl style, an abstract approach in which colours are limited and forms created with horizontal and vertical lines. The figurative basis for his work *Compositie n°3* is believed to have been harvesters.

TOP 10 ⭐ The Panthéon

Paris's Panthéon is a fitting final resting place for the nation's great figures. Originally built as a church at the behest of Louis XV, it was completed in 1790 and was intended to look like the Pantheon in Rome, but more closely resembles St Paul's Cathedral in London. During the Revolution it was used as a mausoleum. Napoleon returned it to the Church in 1806 and it became a public building in 1885.

1 Crypt
The crypt **(above)** is eerily impressive in its scale, compared to most tiny, dark church crypts. Here lie the tombs and memorials to worthy French citizens, including the prolific French writer Emile Zola (see p49).

2 Frescoes of Sainte Geneviève
Delicate murals by 19th-century artist Pierre Puvis de Chavannes, on the south wall of the nave, tell the story of Sainte Geneviève, the patron saint of Paris. She is believed to have saved the city from invasion in 451 by Attila the Hun and his hordes through the power of her prayers.

3 Façade
The Panthéon's façade **(right)** was inspired by Roman architecture. The 22 Corinthian columns support both the portico roof and bas-reliefs.

4 Dome
Inspired by Sir Christopher Wren's design for St Paul's Cathedral in London, as well as by the Dôme Church at Les Invalides (see p38), this iron-framed dome **(right)** is made up of three layers. At the top, a narrow opening lets in only a tiny amount of natural light, in keeping with the building's sombre purpose.

5 Dome Galleries
A staircase leads to the galleries immediately below the dome itself, affording spectacular 360-degree panoramic views of Paris. The pillars surrounding the galleries are both decorative and functional, providing essential support for the dome.

6 Women
One of five women buried in the Panthéon, Simone Veil, a Holocaust survivor and French politician, was the latest to be laid here in 2018.

7 Foucault's Pendulum

In 1851 French physicist Jean Foucault (1819–68) followed up an earlier experiment to prove the Earth's rotation by hanging his famous pendulum from the dome of the Panthéon. The plane of the pendulum's swing rotated 11° clockwise each hour in relation to the floor, thereby proving Foucault's theory.

LOUIS BRAILLE

One of the most influential citizens buried in the Panthéon is Louis Braille (1809–52). Braille became blind at the age of three. He attended the National Institute for the Young Blind and was a gifted student. He continued at the Institute as a teacher and, in 1829, had the idea of adapting a coding system in use by the army, by turning words and letters into raised dots on card. Reading Braille has transformed the lives of blind people ever since.

The Panthéon

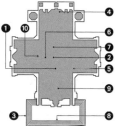

NEED TO KNOW

MAP N6 ■ Pl du Panthéon, 75005 ■ 01 44 32 18 00 ■ www. paris-pantheon.fr/en

Open Apr–Sep: 10am–6:30pm daily (Oct–Mar: to 6pm); closed 1 Jan, 1 May, 1 & 11 Nov, 25 Dec

Adm €11.50, concession €9 (under-18s & EU under-26s free)

■ Stop at La Crêperie *(12 Rue Soufflot; open 7am–midnight, from 8am Sun)* for crêpes or coffee.

■ Pre-booking a timed entry slot online is essential.

■ From April to October, visitors can visit the dome for an extra fee.

8 Pediment Relief

The bas-relief above the entrance shows a female figure, representing France, handing out laurels to the great men of the nation – the same way that Greeks and Romans honoured their heroes.

9 Tomb of Voltaire

A statue *(left)* of the great writer, wit and philosopher Voltaire (1694–1788) stands in front of his tomb.

10 Tomb of Victor Hugo

The body of the French author *(see p23)* was carried to the Panthéon in a pauper's hearse, at his own request.

TOP 10 ⭐ Sainte-Chapelle

This Gothic masterpiece is considered the most beautiful church in Paris, not least for its renovated 15 stained-glass windows soaring 15 m (50 ft) to a star-covered vaulted ceiling. It was built by Louis IX (1214–70) as a shrine for his holy relics of the Passion and completed in 1248. The church was damaged during the 1789 Revolution but restored in the mid-19th century.

1 Window of Christ's Passion

Located above the apse, this stained-glass depiction of the Crucifixion is the most beautiful window in the chapel.

2 Lower Chapel

Intended for use by the king's servants, and dedicated to the Virgin Mary, this chapel **(below)** is not as light and lofty as the Upper Chapel but is still a magnificent sight.

5 Upper Chapel Entrance

As you emerge, via a spiral staircase, into this airy space **(right)**, the effect of light and colour is utterly breath-taking. The 13th-century stained-glass windows, the oldest surviving in Paris, separated by stone columns, depict biblical scenes from Genesis right through to the Crucifixion. To "read" the windows, start in the lower left panel and follow each row left to right, from bottom to top.

6 The Spire

The open latticework and pencil-thin shape give the *flèche* (spire) a very delicate appearance. In fact, three earlier church spires burned down – this one was erected in 1853 and rises 75 m (245 ft) into the air.

3 Main Portal

Like the Upper Chapel, the main portal has two tiers. Its pinnacles are decorated with a crown of thorns as a symbol of the relics within.

4 Rose Window

The Flamboyant rose window **(right)**, depicting St John's vision of the Apocalypse in 86 panels, was a gift from Charles VIII in 1485. The green and yellow hues are brightest at sunset.

7 St Louis' Oratory
In the late 14th century Louis XI added an oratory where he could watch Mass through a small grille in the wall. The chapel originally adjoined the Conciergerie, the former royal palace on the Ile de la Cité *(see p79)*.

9 Seats of the Royal Family
During Mass, the royal family sat in niches located in the fourth bays on both sides of the chapel, away from the congregation.

RELICS OF THE PASSION

Louis IX, later St Louis, was the only French king to be canonized. While on his first Crusade in 1239, he purchased the alleged Crown of Thorns from the Emperor of Constantinople, and subsequently other relics, including pieces of the True Cross, nails from the Crucifixion and a few drops of Christ's blood, paying almost three times more for them than for the construction of Sainte-Chapelle itself. The relics resided in Notre-Dame and were rescued from the destructive fire in 2019.

8 Evening Concerts
Sainte-Chapelle has excellent acoustics. From March until November, classical concerts are held here several evenings a week.

10 Apostle Statues
Beautifully carved medieval statues of 12 apostles stand on the pillars along the walls. Badly damaged in the Revolution, most have been restored: the bearded apostle **(right)**, fifth on the left, is the only original statue.

NEED TO KNOW

MAP N3 ■ 6 Blvd du Palais, 75001 ■ 01 53 40 60 97 ■ www.sainte-chapelle.fr/en

Open Apr–Sep: 9am–7pm daily (Oct–Mar: to 5pm) (Opening hours can vary, check website for details)

Adm €11.50, concession €9; under-18s and 18–25s

(EU only) free; audio guides €3; €17, joint adm to Conciergerie *(see p79)*; temporary exhibits €1.50 extra; pre-booking a timed entry slot online is essential.

■ To experience a little 1920s-style elegance, try the old-fashioned Brasserie Les Deux Palais on the corner of the Boulevard du Palais and Rue de Lutèce for traditional Parisian fare.

■ A pair of binoculars comes in handy if you want to catch a glimpse of the church's uppermost glass panels.

🔟 ⭐ Hôtel des Invalides

The "*invalides*" for whom this imposing Hôtel was built were wounded soldiers of the late 17th century. Louis XIV had the building constructed between 1671 and 1678, and veterans are still housed here, although only a dozen or so compared to the original 4,000. They share their home with arguably the most famous French soldier of them all, Napoleon Bonaparte, whose body rests in a crypt directly below the golden dome of the Dôme Church. Other buildings accommodate military offices, the Musée de l'Armée and smaller military museums.

1 Invalides Gardens

The approach to the Hôtel is across public gardens and then through a gate into the Invalides Gardens themselves. Designed in 1704, their paths are lined by 17th- and 18th-century cannons.

3 Golden Dome

The second church at the hôtel was begun in 1677 and took 27 years to build. Its magnificent dome stands 107 m (351 ft) high and glistens as much now as it did when Louis XIV, the Sun King, had it first gilded in 1715.

4 Musée de l'Armée

The Army Museum *(see p119)* is one of the largest collections of militaria in the world **(left)**. Enthusiasts will be absorbed for hours, and even the casual visitor will be fascinated by the exhibits. The Département Moderne, which traces military history from Louis XIV to Napoleon III, is also worth a visit.

Dôme Church Ceiling **2**

The colourful, circular painting on the interior of the dome **(right)** above the crypt is the *Saint Louis in Glory* painted in 1692 by the French artist Charles de la Fosse. Near the centre is St Louis, who represents Louis XIV, presenting his sword to Christ in the presence of the Virgin Mary and angels.

7 Napoleon's Tomb

Napoleon's body was brought here from St Helena in 1840, some 19 years after he died. He rests in grandeur in a cocoon of six coffins **(left)**, almost "on the banks of the Seine", as was his last wish.

Hôtel des Invalides

5 Hôtel des Invalides

One of the loveliest sights in Paris, the Classical façade of the Hôtel **(below)** is four floors high and 196 m (645 ft) end to end. Features include the dormer windows with their variously shaped shield surrounds.

8 Church Tombs

Encircling the Dôme Church are the imposing tombs of great French military men, such as Marshal Foch and Marshal Vauban, who revolutionized military fortifications and siege tactics.

9 St-Louis-des-Invalides

Adjoining the Dôme Church is the Invalides complex's original church, worth seeing for its 17th-century organ, on which the first performance of Berlioz's *Requiem* was given.

10 Musée des Plans-Reliefs

Maps and models of French forts and fortified towns are displayed here. Some of them are beautifully detailed, such as the oldest model on display, of Perpignan, dating from 1686.

6 Musée de l'Ordre de la Libération

The Order of Libération, France's highest military honour, was created by Général de Gaulle in 1940 to acknowledge contributions during World War II. The museum details the history of the honour and the wartime Free French movement.

NEED TO KNOW

MAP D4 ■ 129 Rue de Grenelle, 75007 or 6 Blvd des Invalides, 75007 ■ 01 44 42 38 77 ■ www.musee-armee.fr

Open 10am–6pm daily (to 9pm Tue during temporary exhibitions); closed 1 Jan, 1 May, 25 Dec; pre-booking a timed entry slot online is recommended

Adm €14; under-18s free; under-26s (EU only) free; audio guides €5

■ Le Café du Musée, between the Varenne metro station and the Musée Rodin (see p120), is known for its various cocktails. It is a lovely spot for a drink.

Hôtel Guide

Approach from the Seine for the best view, and then walk around to the ticket office on the south side. You will need a ticket for the museums and to see Napoleon's Tomb. If time is short, concentrate on the Musée de l'Armée, before walking through to the cobbled courtyard in front of the Dôme Church.

The Top 10
of Everything

The elaborate interior of the Opéra National de Paris Garnier

🔟 Moments in History

1 Arrival of the Parisii

Although the remains of Neolithic settlements have been found dating back to 4500 BC, the first inhabitants are considered to be a Celtic tribe called the Parisii, who settled on the Ile de la Cité in the 3rd century BC. Hunters and fishermen, they named their village Lutetia, meaning "boatyard on a river". The tribe minted their own gold coins and a pagan altar has been found beneath Notre-Dame.

2 Roman Settlement

The Romans conquered the Parisii in 52 BC and rebuilt their city as an administrative centre on the Left Bank. The baths in the Musée National du Moyen Age (see p50) and the amphitheatre in Rue Monge are the only remains of the city's Roman incarnation as Lutetia. In AD 360 the Roman prefect was declared emperor and Lutetia was renamed Paris, after its original inhabitants.

3 Founding of France

Roman rule weakened under barbarian attacks. In 450 the prayers of a young nun, Geneviève, were credited with saving the city from invasion by Attila the Hun. She became the patron saint of Paris. But in 476 the Franks captured the city, Christianity became the official religion and Paris the capital of their new kingdom, France.

4 Charlemagne, Holy Roman Emperor

In 751 the Carolingian dynasty became rulers of France when Pepin the Short ascended the throne. His heir Charlemagne was crowned Holy Roman Emperor in 800 and moved the capital to Aix-la-Chapelle (now the city of Aachen). Paris fell into decline until Hugues Capet became king in 987, moving the capital back to his home city.

St Bartholomew's Day Massacre

5 St Bartholomew's Day Massacre

Catherine de Médicis, Henri II's queen, bore three French kings and one queen, Marguerite de Valois, who married the Protestant Henri of Navarre in August 1572. Catherine plotted to massacre the Protestant nobles who attended the wedding. The killings began on 24 August and thousands died. Henri of Navarre survived and later became Henri IV, the first Bourbon king.

6 French Revolution

Following decades of royal excess and the growing gulf between rich and poor, Paris erupted into Revolution with the storming of the Bastille prison in 1789.

Ste Geneviève, patron saint of Paris

7 Napoleon's Coronation

As Paris rose from the ashes of Revolution, a young general from Corsica, Napoleon Bonaparte *(see p22)*, saved the city from a royalist revolt, then led military victories in Italy and Egypt. He crowned himself Emperor of France in Notre-Dame in 1804.

8 The Second Empire

In 1851, Napoleon's nephew, Louis-Napoleon, seized power as Emperor Napoleon III. He appointed Baron Haussmann to oversee the massive building and public works projects that transformed Paris into the most glorious city in Europe. The wide boulevards, many public buildings, parks, the sewer system and the first department stores date from between 1852 and 1870.

9 The Paris Commune

Following France's defeat in the Franco-Prussian War *(see p27)* in 1871, many citizens rejected the harsh terms of the surrender and a left-wing group revolted, setting up the Paris Commune. But, after 72 days, government troops marched on the city. In a week of brutal street fighting (21–28 May), much of the city burned and thousands of rebellious citizens were killed.

10 Liberation of Paris

The occupation of France by Germany during World War II was a dark period for Paris. The city was the centre for the French Resistance. Allied forces liberated Paris on 25 August 1944; just two days earlier, the German commander Von Choltitz had ignored Adolf Hitler's order to burn the city to the ground.

The Liberation of Paris

TOP 10 EVENTS IN THE FRENCH REVOLUTION

Storming of the Bastille

1 14 July 1789
The storming of the Bastille prison, a symbol of repression, launches the Revolution.

2 4 August 1789
The abolition of feudalism, and the right of everyone to be a free citizen, is declared.

3 26 August 1789
Formal declaration of the Rights of Man and the Citizen, which incorporated the ideals of equality and dignity, later subsumed into the 1791 Constitution.

4 October 1789
Citizens march on Versailles and the royal family returns to Paris to be imprisoned in the Tuileries Palace.

5 20 June 1791
King Louis XVI and his family try to escape but are spotted in Varenne and return to Paris as captives.

6 10 August 1792
A mob storms the Tuileries and the royals are imprisoned in the Temple.

7 21 September 1792
The monarchy is formally abolished and the First Republic is proclaimed.

8 1792–4
"The Terror" reigns, under the radical Commune led by Robespierre, Danton and Marat. Thousands are executed by guillotine.

9 21 January 1793
Louis XVI is found guilty of treason and executed. His queen Marie-Antoinette follows him to the guillotine on 16 October.

10 28 July 1794
Robespierre is guillotined, marking the end of The Terror, and the Revolution draws to a close.

Historic Buildings

1 Hôtel des Invalides
See pp38–9.

2 Versailles
Louis XIV turned his father's old hunting lodge into the largest palace *(see p155)* in Europe and moved his court here in 1678. It was the royal residence for more than a century until Louis XVI and his queen Marie-Antoinette fled during the Revolution.

3 Conciergerie
Originally home to the keeper of the king's mansion and guards of the Palais de Justice, the Conciergerie *(see p79)* became a prison at the end of the 14th century. More than 4,000 citizens (including Marie-Antoinette) were held prisoner here during the Revolution, half of whom were guillotined. It remained a prison until 1914.

4 Hôtel de Ville
MAP P3 ■ 4 Pl de l'Hôtel de Ville, 75001 ■ 01 42 76 40 40 ■ Open for group tours and temporary exhibitions (booking essential: 01 42 76 54 04)

Paris's city hall sports an elaborate façade, with ornate stonework, statues and a turreted roof. It is a 19th-century reconstruction of the original town hall, which was burned down during the Paris Commune *(see p43)* of 1871. Though the square in front is pleasant now, it was once the site of executions: Ravaillac, assassin of Henri IV, was quartered alive here in 1610.

Central courtyard of the Hôtel Dieu

5 Hôtel Dieu
MAP N4 ■ 1 Parvis Notre-Dame–Pl Jean-Paul II, 75004

The Hôtel Dieu, now the hospital for central Paris, was built on the site of a foundling home in 1866–78; the original 12th-century building on the Ile de la Cité was demolished during the urban renewal schemes of the 19th century. Plans are underway to modernize and repurpose part of the historic building, while retaining current hospital services.

6 Palais de Justice
The enormous building that now houses the French law courts *(see p80)* and judiciary dates back to the Roman times and was the royal

Hôtel de Ville façade

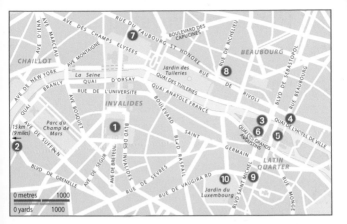

palace until the 14th century, when Charles V moved the court to the Marais. During the Revolution, thousands were sentenced to death in the Première Chambre Civile, allegedly the former bedroom of Louis IX.

7 Palais de l'Elysée

This imposing palace *(see p113)* has been the official residence of the President of the French Republic since 1873. It was built as a private mansion in 1718 and was owned by Madame de Pompadour, mistress of Louis XV, who extended the English-style gardens as far as the Champs-Elysées. After the Battle of Waterloo in 1815, Napoleon signed his second and final abdication here.

8 Palais-Royal

This former royal palace *(see p104)*, originally called the Palais-Cardinal, now houses State offices. It was built by Cardinal Richelieu in 1632, passing to the Crown on his death 10 years later, and was the childhood home of Louis XIV. The dukes of Orléans acquired it in the 18th century.

9 La Sorbonne

The city's great university *(see p125)* had humble beginnings in 1253 as a college for 16 poor students to study theology. France's first printing house was also established here in 1469. After suppression during the Revolution it became the University of Paris.

10 Palais du Luxembourg

MAP L6 ■ 15 Rue de Vaugirard, 75006 ■ 01 42 34 20 00 ■ Open for reserved group tours only (visites@senat.fr); gardens: open dawn–dusk daily

Marie de Médicis had architect Salomon de Brosse model this palace after her childhood home, the Pitti Palace in Florence. Shortly after its completion she was exiled by her son, Louis XIII. It was seized from the Crown during the Revolution to become a prison and it now houses the French Senate. Nearby is the Musée du Luxembourg.

Palais du Luxembourg

Places of Worship

1 **Notre-Dame**
See pp20–23.

2 **Sacré-Coeur**
See pp26–7.

3 **Sainte-Chapelle**
Although this lovely chapel *(see pp36–7)* is no longer used for worship, the soaring stained-glass windows encourage reverence.

4 **Eglise du Dôme**
The final resting place of Napoleon Bonaparte is the beautiful Dôme Church in the Hôtel des Invalides *(see pp38–9)* complex – an elaborate monument in French Classical style. Built as the chapel for the resident soldiers of the Invalides, its ornate high altar is in stark contrast to the solemn marble chapels surrounding the crypt, which hold the tombs of French military leaders. Its golden dome can be seen for miles around.

5 **St-Eustache**
For centuries, this Gothic edifice *(see p85)* was the market church serving the traders of Les Halles. Taking more than 100 years to build, it was finally completed

in 1637 and its cavernous interior displays the architectural style of the early Renaissance. Popular Sunday afternoon organ recitals and other classical concerts take place in this wonderfully atmospheric setting.

Façade of La Madeleine

6 **La Madeleine**
MAP D3 ■ Pl de la Madeleine, 75008 ■ Open 9:30am–7pm daily (services vary)
Designed in the style of a Greek temple in 1764, this prominent church in Paris's financial district, on the edge of the Opéra Quarter, is one of the city's most distinctive sights, spectacularly surrounded by 52 Corinthian columns. The church was consecrated to Mary Magdalene in 1845. The bronze doors, which include bas-reliefs of the Ten Commandments, and the Last Judgment on the south pediment, are exterior highlights, while the ornate marble and gold interior has many fine statues, including François Rude's *Baptism of Christ*. It is also a popular venue for classical concerts.

St-Eustache

7 **The Panthéon**
Modelled on the Pantheon in Rome, this domed late 18th-century church *(see pp34–5)* only served as a house of worship for two years, before becoming a monument and burial place for the great and the good of

the Revolution era. Later distinguished citizens are also buried here.

8 Grande Synagogue de la Victoire

MAP E2 ■ 44 Rue de la Victoire, 75009 ■ Open Mon–Fri mornings for group tours (call 01 45 26 95 36)

Built in the late 19th century, this elaborate synagogue is the second largest in Europe. The building is open only to those wishing to attend services and to groups who have arranged a visit in advance. Other smaller synagogues can be found in the Marais, which has long had a large Jewish community, including one at 10 rue Pavée, built in 1913 by Hector Guimard, the architect who designed the city's magnificent Art Nouveau metro stations.

9 Grande Mosquée de Paris

The city's Grand Mosque (see p136) was built during the 1920s as a tribute to North African Muslims who gave military support to France during World War I. Its beautiful Hispano-Moorish architecture, including a minaret, was executed by craftsmen brought over from North Africa. There is also a shaded interior courtyard where visitors can sit and sip a glass of mint tea.

10 St-Sulpice

Outstanding frescoes in the Chapel of the Angels by Eugène Delacroix are the highlight of this 17th-century church (see p125). With more than 6,500 pipes, its organ, designed by Jean-François Chalgrin in 1776, is one of the largest in the world. The novelist Victor Hugo married his childhood sweetheart Adèle Foucher here in 1822.

St-Sulpice church organ

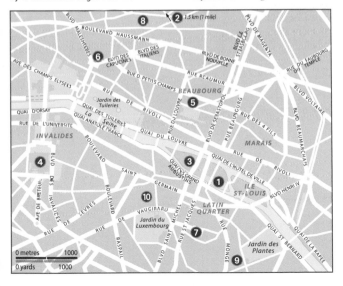

🔟 Novels Set in Paris

Performance of *Les Misérables*

1 Les Misérables
The 1862 novel by Victor Hugo (1802–85) is an all too vivid portrayal of the poor and the dispossessed in early 19th-century Paris. At its centre is the tale of nobleman Jean Valjean, unfairly victimized by an unjust system. The character of Marius, the young idealist, is based on Hugo's own experiences as an impoverished student.

2 The Hunchback of Notre-Dame
Better known by its English title, which inspired a film of the same name, Victor Hugo's Gothic novel was published in France in 1831 as *Notre-Dame de Paris (see p23)*. Set in the Middle Ages, it tells the strange and moving story of a hunchback bell-ringer, Quasimodo, and his love for Esmeralda.

3 A Tale of Two Cities
The finest chronicler of 19th-century London life, Charles Dickens (1812–70) chose to set his 1859 novel in London and Paris, against the background of the French Revolution *(see p43)*. His description of conditions in the Bastille prison makes for grim reading.

4 Le Père Goriot
Honoré de Balzac (1799–1850) chronicled Parisian life masterfully in his 80-volume *La comédie humaine* series, and this novel of 1835 is certainly among his finest. Balzac's former home *(see p142)* at 47 rue Raynouard in the 16th *arrondissement*, where he lived from 1840 to 1847, is open to the public.

5 Sentimental Education
Gustave Flaubert (1821–80) studied law in Paris but illness disrupted his chosen career and he devoted himself to literature. This work (*L'education sentimentale* in French), first published in 1870 in two volumes, stands alongside his greatest novel, *Madame Bovary* (1857), and marks the move away from Romanticism to Realism in French literature.

6 Bel-Ami
Guy de Maupassant (1850–93) published this, one of his best novels, in 1885, criticizing the get-rich-quick Parisian business world of the *belle époque*. Widely acknowledged as one of the world's greatest short-story writers, Maupassant is buried in the cemetery at Montparnasse *(see p156)* in Greater Paris.

Guy de Maupassant

7 A la Recherche du Temps Perdu
The master work of Marcel Proust (1871–1922) was written in 13 volumes, the first novel appearing in 1913. Proust lived on boulevard Haussmann, and his epic tale is the fictionalized story of his own life, and of Paris during the *belle époque*. Proust is buried in Père Lachaise Cemetery *(see p156)* in eastern Paris.

8 Suite Française
The German-occupied Paris of World War II is grippingly recounted in this 2004 bestseller by Ukranian-Jewish author Irène Nemirovsky (1903–42). She wrote her manuscript as the war raged; she was killed at Auschwitz. Her notebooks were rediscovered in the late 1990s, and the book was published to much acclaim.

9 A Certain Smile
Françoise Sagan (1935–2004) is perhaps best known for her scandalous 1954 novel, *Bonjour Tristesse*. Her 1955 novel *Un Certain Sourire*, which tells of a provincial Sorbonne student who has an affair with a married man, followed in a similar, deliciously wicked vein, its narrator another bold young woman who refused to subscribe to the morals and expectations of a patriarchal society.

10 Nana
Perhaps the greatest Parisian chronicler of them all, Emile Zola (1840–1902) was born, lived and died in the city, although he spent part of his youth in Aix-en-Provence in southern France. *Nana* was published in 1880 and tells a shocking tale of sexual decadence, through the eyes of the central character, a dancer and prostitute.

Painting of *Nana* by Edouard Manet

TOP 10 FOREIGN WRITERS WHO LIVED IN PARIS

Ernest Hemingway

1 Ernest Hemingway
The US author (1899–1961) wrote *A Moveable Feast* as an affectionate portrait of his time living in Paris from 1921 to 1926.

2 F. Scott Fitzgerald
Like Hemingway, US writer Fitzgerald (1896–1940) lived in Montparnasse and frequented La Coupole *(see p131)*.

3 George Orwell
The English novelist (1903–50) tells of his shocking experiences living in poverty in *Down and Out in Paris and London* (1933).

4 Samuel Beckett
The Irish-born playwright (1906–89) lived in Paris from 1928 until his death.

5 Anaïs Nin
US novelist Nin (1903–77) met her lover, fellow American Henry Miller, in Paris. Her *Diaries* tell of her time here.

6 Albert Camus
Algerian-born Camus (1913–60) moved to Paris in 1935 and lived here until his death.

7 Henry Miller
Miller (1891–1980) showed the seedier side of Paris in his novel *Tropic of Cancer* (1934).

8 Nancy Mitford
The author of *The Pursuit of Love* (1945) and other novels, Mitford (1904–73) lived in Paris from 1943 until her death.

9 James Joyce
Joyce (1882–1941) lived in Paris from 1920 to 1940. *Ulysses* was published here in 1922 by Shakespeare and Co.

10 Milan Kundera
Czech-born Kundera (b.1929) moved to Paris in 1978, writing *The Unbearable Lightness of Being* here.

🔟 Museums

The Lady and the Unicorn,
Musée National du Moyen Age

1 Musée National du Moyen Age

This splendid museum *(see p126)* dedicated to the art of the Middle Ages is known by several names. This includes the Musée de Cluny, after the beautiful mansion in which it is housed, and the Thermes de Cluny, after the Roman baths adjoining the museum. Highlights include the famous "Lady and the Unicorn" tapestries, medieval stained glass and exquisite gold crowns and jewellery.

2 Musée de l'Armée

Part of the Hôtel des Invalides complex relating to the military history of France, this museum *(see pp38–9)* has a huge number of military objects from the Middle Ages to World War II. The collection includes armour, artillery, weapons, uniforms and paintings. Admission includes entrance to the Dôme Church, containing the tomb of Napoleon Bonaparte.

3 Musée des Arts Décoratifs

Set over nine levels, adjoining the west end of the Louvre's Richelieu Wing, this arts museum *(see p104)* showcases furniture and tableware from the 12th century to the present. The breathtaking anthology of pieces ranges from Gothic panelling and Renaissance porcelain to 1970s carpets and chairs by Philippe Starck. Also part of the museum is the Musée de la Mode et du Textile, which mounts fashion exhibitions, and the Musée de la Publicité, which has exhibitions on advertising.

4 Musée du Louvre

French and Italian sculpture, Greek and Roman antiquities and paintings from the 12th to the 19th centuries are just some of the highlights of the world's largest museum *(see pp12–15)*.

5 Musée du Quai Branly – Jacques Chirac

In a city dominated by Western art, this fabulous museum *(see p120)* tips the balance in favour of arts from Africa, Asia, Oceania and the Americas. Must-sees include the African instruments. The striking Jean Nouvel-designed building is an attraction in itself.

6 Muséum National d'Histoire Naturelle

Paris's Natural History Museum *(see p135)* in the Jardin des Plantes contains a fascinating collection of animal skeletons, plant fossils, minerals and gemstones. Its highlight is the magnificent Grande Galerie de l'Evolution *(see p60)*, which depicts the changing interaction between man and nature during the evolution of life on Earth.

Muséum National d'Histoire Naturelle

Musée des Arts et Métiers

mansions – Carnavalet and Le Peletier de St-Fargeau – both decorated with gilded wood panelling, furniture and objets d'art, including paintings and sculptures of famous personalities, and engravings showing the creation of Paris.

9 Cité de l'Architecture et du Patrimoine

The Cité de l'Architecture *(see p141)* and the Musée des Monuments Français showcase French archi-tectural heritage and form one of the world's great architectural centres. The Galerie des Moulages houses models of great French cathedrals.

10 Musée Jacquemart-André

Set in a private mansion, this museum *(see p113)* was once the home of Edouard André and his artist wife Nélie Jacquemart. It houses their personal art collection, which fea-tures works by Boucher, Botticelli, Rembrandt and Fragonard, as well as excellent temporary exhibits.

7 Musée des Arts et Métiers

MAP G3 ■ 60 Rue Réaumur, 75003 ■ Open 10am–6pm Tue–Sun (to 9pm Fri) ■ Closed 1 Jan, 1 May, 25 Dec ■ Adm ■ www.arts-et-metiers.net

Housed in the Abbaye de St-Martin-des-Champs, this industrial design museum is a fascinating repository of printing machines, vintage cars, music boxes, early flying machines, automatons and other inventions.

8 Musée Carnavalet

The vast collection at this recently refurbished museum *(see p94)* charts the history of Paris. The museum occupies two adjoining

Musée Jacquemart-André

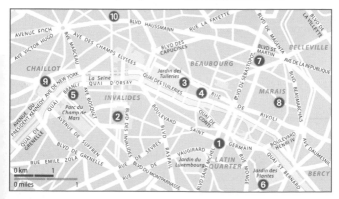

🔟 Art Galleries

1 Musée d'Orsay
See pp16–19.

2 Musée Rodin
On a sunny day, head straight for the gardens of the Musée Rodin (see p120), next to the Hôtel des Invalides complex, to enjoy some of the French sculptor's most famous works, including The Thinker and The Burghers of Calais, while strolling among the shady trees and rose bushes. Auguste Rodin (1840–1917) lived and worked for nine years in the beautiful 18th-century Hôtel Biron, where the rest of the collection is housed. The museum reopened

The Thinker, **Musée Rodin**

in autumn 2015 following a three-year renovation project and a complete reorganization of the collection.

3 Musée Picasso
The beautiful Hôtel Salé *(see p96)* showcases an extensive collection of paintings, sculptures, ceramics, etchings, drawings and other masterpieces by the famous Spanish-born artist Pablo Picasso (1881–1973) – covering all his creative periods. Large sculptures adorn the garden and courtyard while, inside the gorgeous 17th-century mansion *(see p93)*, twice as much as before of the collection is now on display. Be sure not to miss Picasso's own collection of paintings, including works by Cézanne, Renoir, Matisse and others of his contemporaries, located on the second floor.

4 Musée de l'Orangerie
MAP D3 ■ **Jardin des Tuileries, 75001** ■ **Open 9am–6pm Wed–Mon** ■ **Closed 1 May, 14 Jul (am), 25 Dec** ■ **Adm** ■ **www.musee-orangerie.fr**
The prime exhibits here are eight of Monet's waterlily canvases *(see p16)*, most of them painted between 1899 and 1921, and the gallery, located in a corner of the Tuileries. The Walter-Guillaume collection covers works by Matisse, Picasso, Modigliani and other modern masters from 1870 to 1930.

Fondation Louis Vuitton

⑦ Musée National d'Art Moderne

The revolutionary Pompidou Centre (see pp32–3) is the perfect home for France's Modern Art Museum. It features fascinating works across several levels. Level 5 retraces the history of modern art (between 1905 and 1965) before leading to the contemporary collection on level 4.

⑧ Musée Maillol

Works of the famous French artist Aristide Maillol, including his drawings, engravings, paintings, sculptures and plastercasts, are the focal point of this museum (see p127), which was created by his model, Dina Vierny (1919–2009). Other major artists feature in the temporary exhibitions.

⑤ Fondation Louis Vuitton

8 Ave du Mahatma Gandhi, Bois de Boulogne, 75116 ▪ Opening hours vary according to exhibitions and events ▪ Adm ▪ www.fondation louisvuitton.fr

Close to the Jardin d'Acclimatation in the Bois de Boulogne (see p159), Frank Gehry's dramatic glass structure contains a gallery and event space hosting contemporary arts exhibitions. A shuttle to the arts centre leaves Place Charles de Gaulle every 20 minutes (round-trip tickets €2).

⑨ Maison Européenne de la Photographie

If you're a photography fan, be sure not to miss this splendid gallery (see p95) located in the Marais. Its exhibitions range from portraits to documentary work, retrospectives to contemporary photographers.

⑥ Jeu de Paume

MAP D3 ▪ 1 Pl de la Concorde, 75008 ▪ Opening hours are subject to change, check website ▪ Closed 1 Jan, 1 May, 25 Dec ▪ Adm ▪ www.jeudepaume.org

This gallery is one of the finest exhibition spaces in the city, set within a 19th-century royal tennis court (jeu de paume). It has a strong reputation for showcasing outstanding photography, film and video installations.

⑩ Palais de Tokyo

MAP B4 ▪ 13 Ave du Président Wilson, 75116 ▪ Open noon–midnight Wed–Mon ▪ Adm ▪ www.palaisde tokyo.com

Dedicated to contemporary art, this lively museum in the Chaillot Quarter hosts regularly changing exhibitions and installations by international artists. It is one of the most cutting-edge art houses in Europe and has a bookshop as well as two restaurants.

ON AIR exhibition curated by Rebecca Lamarche-Vadel at Palais de Tokyo

TOP 10 Riverfront Sights

Eiffel Tower and the Seine, viewed from Pont Alexandre III

1 Eiffel Tower

Although the top of the Eiffel Tower *(see pp24–5)* can be seen above rooftops across the city, one of the best views of this Paris landmark is from the Seine. The Pont d'Iéna lies at the foot of the tower, bridging the river to link it to the Trocadéro Gardens. The tower, illuminated at night, is a highlight of a dinner cruise on the Seine.

2 Palais de Chaillot

The curved arms of the Palais de Chaillot *(see p141)* encircling the Trocadéro Gardens can be seen from the Seine. In the centre of the gardens magnificent fountains spout from the top of a long pool lined with statues, while two huge water cannons spray their charges back towards the river and the Eiffel Tower on the opposite bank.

3 Liberty Flame
MAP C3

A replica of the New York Statue of Liberty's torch was erected here in 1987 by the *International Herald Tribune* to mark their centenary and honour the freedom fighters of the French Resistance during World War II. It is located on the right bank of the Pont de l'Alma, the bridge over the tunnel where Diana, Princess of Wales, was fatally injured in an automobile crash in 1997. The Liberty Flame has now become her unofficial memorial and is often draped with notes and flowers laid in her honour.

Liberty Flame by Pont de l'Alma

4 Grand Palais and Petit Palais

Gracing either side of the magnificent Pont Alexandre III are these two splendid exhibition halls *(see p111)*, built for the Universal Exhibition of 1900. The iron Art Nouveau skeleton of the Grand Palais is topped by an enormous glass roof, which is most impressive when illuminated at night. The Petit Palais is smaller but similar in style, with a dome and many Classical features.

5 Pont Alexandre III

The most beautiful bridge *(see p112)* in Paris is the Pont Alexandre III, a riot of Art Nouveau decoration including

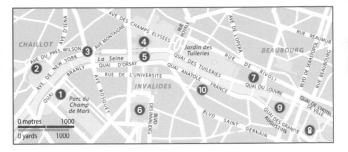

cherubs, wreaths, lamps and other elaborate statuary. Built for the Universal Exhibition of 1900, it leads to the Grand Palais and Petit Palais. There are wonderful views of the Invalides complex and the Champs-Elysées from the bridge.

6 Dôme Church
An impressive view of the Eglise de Dôme in the Hôtel des Invalides (see pp38–9) complex can be had from the Pont Alexandre III. The golden dome beckons visitors down the long parkway lined with streetlamps and statues.

7 Musée du Louvre
This grand museum (see pp12–15) stretches along the river from the Pont Royal to the Pont des Arts. The Denon Wing, which can be seen from the Seine, was largely built during the reigns of Henri IV and Louis XIII in the late 16th and early 17th centuries.

8 Notre-Dame
The great cathedral, although damaged (see pp20–23), is still majestic when viewed from the Left Bank of the Seine. It rises at the eastern end of the Ile de la Cité above the remains of the ancient tribes who first settled Paris in the 3rd century BC.

9 Conciergerie
This huge and imposing building (see p79), which served as a notorious prison during the French Revolution, commands the western end of the Ile de la Cité. The magnificent building retains some of the few

medieval features on the island, including a torture chamber, kitchens, a clock and the twin towers that rise above the Quai de l'Horloge.

10 Musée d'Orsay
The view of this stunning art gallery (see pp16–19) from the Right Bank of the Seine is one of its finest angles, showing off the arched terminals, great clock faces and grand façade of this former railway station, built in 1898–1900. Architect Victor Laloux designed it to harmonize with the Louvre and Tuileries Quarter across the river.

Sculptures at Musée d'Orsay

🔟 Parks and Gardens

Stately Palais du Luxembourg in the Jardin du Luxembourg

1 Jardin du Luxembourg

Parisians love this centrally located park *(see p125)*, set around the Palais du Luxembourg. The sweeping terrace is a great place for people-watching, while locals sunbathe around the octagonal Grand Bassin or sail toy boats in the water. Statues are dotted throughout the grounds, and there is a café.

2 Jardin des Tuileries

Now officially part of the Louvre, these gardens *(see p103)* were laid out in the 17th century as part of the old Palais de Tuileries. They stretch along the Seine between the Louvre and Place de la Concorde. The walkways are lined with lime and chestnut trees. Statues include bronze figures by Aristide Maillol.

3 Jardin des Plantes

Established as a medicinal herb garden for the king in 1635, these vast botanical gardens *(see p135)* are a wonderfully tranquil spot. Paths are lined with statuary and mature trees, including the oldest in Paris, grown from the stump of an *Acacia robinia* dating from 1636.

4 Bois de Boulogne

At the weekends, Parisians head for this vast park *(see p156)* on the western edge of the city, which has a boating lake and paths for cycling, jogging and strolling. There are three formal gardens, lakes and waterfalls, and even two horse-racing tracks. It's a good spot for a break from the city bustle.

5 Bois de Vincennes

Another great escape from the city, this vast park *(see p156)* is to the east of Paris what the Bois de Boulogne is to the west. A former royal hunting ground, it was landscaped in the 1860s. Now it features ornamental lakes and waterfalls, a zoo, a spring-time funfair and horse-racing tracks.

6 Parc Monceau

The most fashionable green space *(see p157)* in Paris, full of well-heeled residents of the nearby mansions and apartments. The lush landscaping dates from

Classical colonnade in Parc Monceau

the 18th century, and some architectural follies, such as the Classical colonnade, survive.

7 Jardin du Palais-Royal
MAP L1 ▪ Pl du Palais-Royal, 75001

These lovely gardens are enclosed by the 18th-century arcades of the Palais-Royal *(see p104)*. Modern sculptures include Daniel Buren's controversial striped columns.

8 Parc Clichy-Batignolles
147 Rue Cardinet, 75017 ▪ Metro Brochant

A relaxed, neighbourhood feel characterizes this park in the heart of the laid-back Batignolles district. It was developed with an eye to ecology and biodiversity. Locals come to skate, play *pétanque*, tend the community gardens and laze on the lawns, while wildlife and rare flora thrive in the wetlands-like environment.

9 Parc Montsouris
Blvd Jourdan, 75014 ▪ RER Cité Universitaire

Located south of Montparnasse, this large park in central Paris was laid out in the English style, atop an old granite quarry, by landscape architect Adolphe Alphand between 1865 and 1878. Hemingway *(see p49)* and other writers and artists frequented the park in the mid-20th century. It has a jogging path, lake and a bandstand.

10 Parc des Buttes-Chaumont
Rue Manin, 75019 ▪ Metro Buttes-Chaumont ▪ Open Sep–Apr: 7am–8pm daily; May–Aug: 7am–10pm Mon–Fri, 24 hours Sat & Sun

Baron Haussmann created this retreat *(see p61)* northeast of the city centre in 1867, from what was formerly a rubbish dump. His architects built artificial cliffs, waterfalls, streams and a lake complete with an island crowned by a Roman-style temple. There are fantastic views of the city from this hilly park. In the eastern part of the park is a trendy bar, Rosa Bonheur, which is open until late.

TOP 10 FOUNTAINS

Observatory Fountain

1 Observatory Fountain
MAP L6 ▪ Jardin du Luxembourg
Four bronze statues representing the continents hold aloft a globe.

2 Four Seasons Fountain
MAP C4 ▪ Rue de Grenelle
Paris in female form looks down on figures representing the Seine and Marne rivers, designed in 1739 by sculptor Edmé Bouchardon.

3 Fontaine des Innocents
Carved by Jean Goujon in 1547, this *(see p86)* is Paris's only Renaissance fountain.

4 Medici Fountain
MAP L6 ▪ Jardin du Luxembourg
This ornate 17th-century fountain with a pond was built for Marie de Médicis.

5 Molière Fountain
MAP E3 ▪ Rue de Richelieu
This 19th-century fountain honours the French playwright.

6 Agam Fountain
La Défense ▪ RER La Défense
Jewish architect Yaacov Agam designed this fountain of water and lights.

7 Châtelet Fountain
MAP N3 ▪ Pl du Châtelet
The two sphinxes of this 1808 fountain are appropriate to commemorate Napoleon's victory in Egypt.

8 Stravinsky Fountain
Birds squirt water from this colourful Pompidou Centre fountain *(see p32)*.

9 Trocadéro Fountains
Spouting towards the Eiffel Tower *(see pp24–5)*, these fountains are illuminated at night.

10 Versailles Fountains
The fountains at Versailles *(see p155)* flow to music at weekends in spring and in summer.

🔟 Off the Beaten Track

Wall of skulls and bones, Catacombs

1 Catacombs

1 Ave du Colonel Henri Rol-Tanguy, 75014 ▪ 01 43 22 47 63 ▪ Open 10am–8:30pm Tue–Sun ▪ Closed 1 Jan, 1 May, 25 Dec ▪ Adm ▪ www.catacombes.paris.fr

The catacombs are an underground warren of tunnels, filled with the bones of some six million Parisians, brought here from 1785 to 1865 as a solution to the problem of overflowing cemeteries. Aside from the macabre sight of walls lined with skulls and bones, it's a thrill to enter the tunnels, part of a vast quarry network that underlies the city. Limited numbers of visitors are allowed in at a time; pre-book a timed entry slot online.

2 Promenade Plantée

MAP H5

Starting near the Bastille Opera House (see p65) and ending at Bois de Vincennes, this 4-km (2.5-mile) walkway, much of it high above the streets on a former railway viaduct, is a wonderful way to see a little-visited part of the city. Planted all along with trees and flowers, the path runs past tall mansion blocks, whose decorative mouldings and balconies (not to mention smart interiors) are a treat to see close up.

3 Little-visited Louvre

While many flock to the *Mona Lisa* and *Venus de Milo*, canny visitors set out to discover other parts of the Louvre's collections (see pp12–15), such as the Islamic arts section. Opened in 2012, it includes beautiful Iznik tiles and exquisite glass, gold and ivory objects from Andalusia, Iraq and India – all under a stunning gold filigree roof.

4 Pavillon de l'Arsenal

MAP R5 ▪ 21 Blvd Morland, 75004 ▪ 01 42 76 33 97 ▪ Open 11am–7pm Tue–Sun ▪ www.pavillon-arsenal.com

A museum dedicated to urban planning and architecture, the Pavillon de l'Arsenal is home to a small but fascinating exhibition illustrating the architectural evolution of Paris. Using film, models and panoramic photographs, it explores how the city has developed over the centuries and what future plans hold.

5 Canal Barge Cruise

MAP J2 ▪ 12 Port de Solferino, 75007 ▪ Cruises dates vary, check website ▪ Adm ▪ www.pariscanal.com

A great way to see a different side of Paris is to take a barge along the Seine, the Marne river and Canal St-Martin. Some Paris Canal boats, for example, depart from the quay

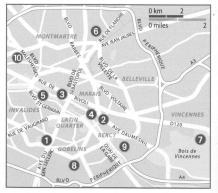

outside the Musée d'Orsay (see pp16–19) and make their way westwards to the island of Chatou, once frequented by Impressionist painters, or eastwards past Notre-Dame to Chennevières-sur-Marne, a favourite haunt of Pissaro.

Barge on Canal St-Martin

6 Le Centquatre-Paris
5 Rue Curial, 75019 ■ 01 53 35 50 00 ■ Metro Riquet ■ Open noon–7pm Tue–Fri, 11am–7pm Sat & Sun ■ www.104.fr

The "104" is a huge arts centre, housed in a converted 19th-century funeral parlour with a lofty glass roof. It contains numerous artists' studios and workshops, and puts on excellent exhibitions and installations, as well as music, dance, cinema and theatre.

7 Parc Floral de Paris
Route de la Pyramide, 75012 ■ Metro Chateau de Vincennes ■ Open 9:30am–8pm daily (winter: to dusk) ■ Adm Jun–Sep ■ www.parcfloraldeparis.com

Set within the Bois de Vincennes, this lovely park has wonderful displays of camellias, rhododendrons, ferns and irises. It hosts horticultural exhibitions and free jazz concerts in summer and has plenty to appeal to children, including an adventure park.

8 Buttes-aux-Cailles
Metro Corvisart

The Butte-aux-Cailles quarter, in the southeast of the city, is a bit like a mini-Montmartre, with its pretty cobbled streets and old-fashioned streetlamps. The main Rue de la Butte-aux-Cailles with its restaurants and bohemian bars buzzes well into the night.

9 Bercy Village
28 Rue François Truffaut, 75012 ■ Metro Cour St-Emilion ■ www.bercyvillage.com

The district of Bercy is where barges from all over France used to deliver wine to the capital. The former warehouses, a handsome ensemble of ochre-coloured stone buildings, have been converted into shops, restaurants and, fittingly, wine bars. It's well worth a wander, especially on Sundays when shops in most other parts of Paris are closed.

10 Musée Nissim de Camondo
MAP C2 ■ 63 Rue de Monceau, 75008 ■ 01 44 55 57 50 ■ Open 10am–5:30pm Wed–Sun ■ Adm

Wealthy art collector Count Moïse de Camondo had this grand mansion built to house his superb collection of 18th-century art. The rooms are full of tapestries, paintings, gilded furniture and Sèvres porcelain. As interesting as the artworks is the portrait that emerges of a well-to-do family, beset by tragedy (it is named for his son, killed in World War I) and ultimately victim to Auschwitz.

Musée Nissim de Camondo

🔟 Children's Attractions

Musée de la Magie et des Automates

1 Musée de la Magie et des Automates

MAP R4 ▪ 11 Rue St-Paul, 75004 ▪ 01 42 72 13 26 ▪ Open 2–7pm Wed, Sat, Sun (daily during school holidays, except Jul & Aug) ▪ Adm ▪ www.museedelamagie.com

Kids are enchanted by this museum of magic, located in the cellars of the former home of the Marquis de Sade. Magicians conjure up shows every half hour involving optical illusions, card tricks and lots of audience participation. Exhibits include working automata and memorabilia of magicians such as Houdini (1874–1926).

2 Parc Astérix

Plailly, 60128 ▪ RER B to Roissy CDG1, then shuttle from A3 ▪ Open Apr–Aug: 10am–6pm Mon–Thu (to 7pm Fri, Sat & Sun); Sep–Oct: 10am–6pm Sat & Sun; times vary during school holidays, check website ▪ Adm ▪ www.parcasterix.fr

There's not just the Gaul of Asterix and Obelix to discover here, but six worlds, including ancient Greece and Rome, and all with the charm of Goscinny and Uderzo's beloved comic books. Dozens of attractions include one of Europe's longest roller coasters.

3 Eiffel Tower

A trip to the top is one of the most memorable activities for children in Paris (see pp24–5).

4 Grande Galerie de l'Evolution

The most exciting and imaginatively designed section in the Muséum National d'Histoire Naturelle (see p135) is the Great Gallery of Evolution. Elephants, giraffes and other stuffed animals rise out of a recreated savannah, and a huge whale skeleton hangs from the ceiling, while special displays help tell the story of the development of life on Earth. Nature workshops are also held for children during school holidays.

5 Disneyland® Paris

The French offspring of America's favourite theme park (see p155) is a clone of its parent, and features two parks, including the Walt Disney Studios® complex. There are rides for children of all ages and most adults are equally enchanted.

6 Parc de la Villette

One of the city's top children's attractions (see p156), with activities for all ages. The huge Cité des Sciences et de l'Industrie, a high-tech hands-on science museum, gets star billing, while the Cité des Enfants is a science and nature attraction specifically for younger children. Kids also adore the Argonaute, a real 1950s submarine that voyaged around the world 10 times, the Géode with its IMAX screen and the futuristic outdoor playground.

Parc de la Villette

7 Jardin d'Acclimatation

MAP A2 ■ Bois de Boulogne, 75016 ■ Open 10am–8pm daily ■ Adm ■ www.jardindacclimatation.fr

This amusement park at the north end of the Bois de Boulogne (see p156) has roller coasters, pony rides and puppet shows. An electric train, "le Petit Train", runs to the park from Porte Maillot.

8 Musée des Arts Forains

Pavillons de Bercy, 53 Ave des Terroirs de France, 75012 ■ Metro Cour Saint-Emilion ■ 01 43 40 16 22 ■ See website for opening dates ■ Adm ■ www.arts-forains.com

A private museum in a former wine warehouse in Bercy Village (see p59). It is a secret wonderland filled with vintage fairground attractions, automata, theatre props, antique merry-go-rounds and a 1920s hall of mirrors. It is open by appointment for guided tours all year round, but visitors are welcome without prior reservations for 10 days over the Christmas and New Year period to try out the traditional fairground games and ride on the carousels.

9 Jardin du Luxembourg

A green oasis in the heart of the Left Bank, this (see p125) is one of the most popular parks in Paris. It has tennis courts, puppet shows, donkey rides and a modern playground (for a fee). But most fun of all is the traditional Parisian pastime of sailing model boats in the octagonal Grand Bassin and riding the 19th-century carousel.

10 Parc des Buttes-Chaumont

The highest in Paris, this park (see p57) is great for a family picnic. For many, this panoramic hilly site is the most pleasant and unexpected park in the city. Kids enjoy exploring the rugged terrain with its lake, grassy slopes, suspended bridges and waterfalls, as well as pony rides and puppet shows. Le Pavillon du Lac and Rosa Bonheur are perfect spots for drinks.

TOP 10 MERRY-GO-ROUNDS

Carousel by the Eiffel Tower

1 Eiffel Tower
The Parisian icon (see pp24–5) provides a dramatic backdrop to this solar-powered merry-go-round.

2 Jardin du Luxembourg
Children can play the traditional French game of rings on this historic 1879 merry-go-round.

3 Montmartre
At the foot of Sacré-Coeur (see pp26–7), this grand double-decker merry-go-round has gorgeous painted horses and carriages.

4 Parc de la Villette
An airplane, a hot-air balloon and a Tintin-style space rocket join the wooden horses on this two-storey merry-go-round.

5 Jardin d'Acclimatation
A traditional carousel with wooden horses is just one of the collection of merry-go-rounds here.

6 Jardins du Trocadéro
A wonderful hot-air balloon graces this dual platform merry-go-round (see p142).

7 Hôtel de Ville
Lucky riders jump on whenever this seasonal merry-go-round appears in the heart of the town (see p44).

8 Jardin des Plantes
The curious Dodo Manège (see p138) features extinct animals including horned, giraffe-like sivatherium.

9 Parc Monceau
This charming little carousel is much loved by the local children (see p157).

10 Jardin des Tuileries
Set among the trees, antique wooden horses spin round this enchanting merry-go-round (see p103).

Following pages *Interior of the Opéra National de Paris Garnier*

Entertainment Venues

1 Opéra National de Paris Garnier

Going to the opera here *(see p104)* is not just a night out, but a whole experience. The theatre went back to hosting opera after a spell as a dance-only venue. The building itself is an example of excessive opulence, complete with grand staircase, mirrors and marble – and even an artificial lake deep underground.

2 Folies-Bergère

MAP F2 ▪ 32 Rue Richer, 75009 ▪ 08 92 68 16 50 ▪ www.foliesbergere.com

The epitome of Parisian cabaret, the Folies were, for a time, little more than a troupe of high-kicking, bare-breasted dancers.

Poster for the Folies-Bergère

Today, the venue hosts everything from stand-up comedy to pop and rock concerts.

3 Le Lido

MAP C2 ▪ 116 bis, Ave des Champs-Elysées, 75008 ▪ 01 40 76 56 10 ▪ www.lido.fr

Home to the world-famous troupe of long-legged dancers, the Bluebell Girls, the Lido wows with fabulous special effects including aerial ballets and an on-stage skating rink. Many regard this dinner-cabaret as an essential Parisian experience.

4 Le Crazy Horse Paris

MAP C3 ▪ 12 Ave George V, 75008 ▪ 01 47 23 32 32 ▪ www.lecrazyhorseparis.com

More risqué than the other big-name cabaret shows, the Saloon has a reputation for putting on the most professional as well as the sexiest productions. Striptease features, along with glamorous dancing girls and other cabaret acts. The computer-controlled lighting effects are spectacular.

5 Le Cirque d'Hiver

MAP H3 ▪ 110 Rue Amelot, 75011 ▪ 01 47 00 28 81 ▪ www.cirquedhiver.com

Worth visiting for the façade alone, this whimsical, circular listed building, dating from 1852, plays host to the traditional Cirque Bouglione, complete with acts such as trapeze artists, clowns, jugglers and tame tigers.

6 Moulin Rouge

At the home of the Can-Can, Toulouse-Lautrec immortalized the theatre's dancers on canvas during the *belle époque* and the results are on display in the Musée d'Orsay *(see p17)*. The show *(see p148)* still has all the razzamatazz that has

The neon-lit exterior of the Moulin Rouge

been dazzling audiences since 1889. The pre-show dinner is optional.

7 Comédie-Française
MAP L1 ■ 1 Pl Colette, 75001 ■ 01 44 58 14 00 ■ www.comedie-francaise.fr

Paris's oldest theatre was founded in 1680 and is still the only one with its own repertory company, staging both classical and modern drama (in French). Commonly known as the Maison de Molière (House of Molière) – an homage to the 17th-century playwright said to be the patron of French actors – it has been based in the current building since 1799.

8 Opéra National de Paris Bastille
MAP H5 ■ Pl de la Bastille, 75012 ■ 08 92 89 90 90 (+33 1 71 25 24 23 from abroad) ■ www.operadeparis.fr

Opened in 1992, this large modern building was heavily criticized, not least for its acoustics and poor facilities. However, this is still the best place to see opera in Paris.

9 Théâtre du Châtelet
MAP N3 ■ 2 Rue Edouard Colonne, 75001 ■ 01 40 28 28 40 ■ www.chatelet.com

Inaugurated in 1862 along with the Théâtre de la Ville opposite it, this was at the time the city's largest concert hall. Many years of renovations saw it refreshed in 2019. Its outreach programme draws new audiences to its varied repertoire of music, dance, theatre and Broadway shows.

10 Théâtre de la Ville
MAP N3 ■ 2 Pl du Châtelet, 75004 ■ 01 42 74 22 77 ■ Closed for renovations until 2021 ■ www.theatredelaville-paris.com

Once known as the Sarah Bernhardt Theatre, after the great Parisian actress *(see p160)* who performed here and managed the theatre in the 19th century, today it puts on a range of theatre, dance, and classical and world music shows. Check website for temporary venues.

TOP 10 JAZZ CLUBS

Performance at New Morning

1 New Morning
MAP F2 ■ 7–9 Rue des Petites Ecuries
An eclectic mix of music, with jam sessions and impromptu performances.

2 Au Duc des Lombards
MAP N2 ■ 42 Rue des Lombards
The best overseas jazz artists come here to play with home-grown talent.

3 Baiser Salé
MAP N2 ■ 58 Rue des Lombards
Jazz, blues and World Music are the mainstays at this tiny cellar club.

4 Caveau des Oubliettes
MAP F5 ■ 52 Rue Garlande
Jazz in an ex-dungeon, with free jam sessions on Tuesday–Thursday & Sunday.

5 La Bellevilloise
MAP F1 ■ 19–21 Rue Boyer
An alternative music venue in Belleville, which is a local favourite for live music.

6 Jazz Club Etoile
MAP A2 ■ 81 Blvd Gouvlon-St-Cyr
Features visiting African-American musicians. Jazzy Brunch on Sunday.

7 Sunset-Sunside
MAP N2 ■ 60 Rue des Lombards
A double serving of late-night jazz: acoustic and modern at street level; electric, fusion and groove in the cellar.

8 Jazz Café Montparnasse
MAP D6 ■ 13 Rue du Commandant Mouchotte
Doors close at 2am, but open again six hours later on weekdays. Great place to wine and dine with eclectic music.

9 Le Petit Journal St-Michel
MAP M5 ■ 71 Blvd St-Michel
New Orleans-style swinging jazz in a lively Latin Quarter cellar.

10 Caveau de la Huchette
MAP N4 ■ 5 Rue de la Huchette
Worth every penny of the entrance fee.

Fine Dining

Elegant interior of Taillevent

1 Astrance

There is probably no table in Paris that is more coveted than one in the dining room of culinary genius Pascal Barbot (see p145). His imaginative tasting menus are a culinary journey; the wine cellar is superb. You'll need to book a month ahead for lunch, two months for dinner.

2 Jean-François Piège – Le Grand Restaurant

One the most exciting restaurants (see p107) in Paris, mostly thanks to Piège's masterful cooking, which may include dishes such as a tower of spaghetti with belly pork and truffles, and blue lobster cooked in fig leaves. Everything is spot on here, from the meticulously prepared cuisine to the striking decor.

3 Le Jules Verne

Now in the hands of Meilleur Ouvrier de France award-winner Frédéric Anton, this restaurant (see p123) on the second floor of the Eiffel Tower has entered the 21st century. It has been revamped with a pared-back decor and there is a suitably luxurious menu, replete with truffles in winter. Service is excellent and the panoramic views are simply breathtaking, but you will need to book in advance.

4 Taillevent

Exquisite haute cuisine in a 19th-century mansion, Taillevent's (see p117) atmospheric oak-panelled dining room is frequented by a mix of businessmen and romantic couples. Dishes such as rex rabbit with Cremona mustard and black radish feature on the seasonal menu and there's an extensive and exceptional wine list. You need to book well ahead to dine here.

5 Septime

Chef Bertrand Grébaut trained with Passard before setting up this Michelin-starred bistro (see p101) serving excellent seasonal dishes. The elegant, minimalistic decor and an open kitchen complement Grébaut's avant-garde cooking. There are set menus at both lunch and dinner.

Stylish bistro Septime

6 Alain Ducasse au Plaza Athénée

The star chef's interpretation of modern haute cuisine – based on fish, vegetables and grains – is served in this glamorous restaurant (see p117), along with a selection of fine wines.

7 David Toutain

Having worked with some of the best chefs in Paris, David Toutain has set the bar high, as proved by his restaurant's (see p123) two Michelin stars. On offer are surprising tasting menus which include signature dishes such as white chocolate salsifies and other original touches.

8 Pierre Gagnaire

Famous French chef Pierre Gagnaire, an advocate of molecular gastronomy, grows his own produce and creates culinary magic at this modern French diner (see p117). Try the foie gras roasted with anchovies which is served with red tuna tartare and tamarillo.

9 Arpege

Alain Passard's three-Michelin-star restaurant (see p122) is highly regarded in Paris. Dishes using produce from the biodynamic garden, might include beetroot in a hibiscus-salt crust with bitter orange. Try his superb signature apple tart.

L'Atelier de Joël Robuchon

10 L'Atelier de Joël Robuchon

Take a seat at the lacquered bar of this two-Michelin-starred restaurant (see p133) to experience France's top chef Joël Robuchon's take on contemporary cuisine. An open kitchen surrounded by 40 seats allows diners to observe while the meticulously crafted dishes are prepared. Signature dishes are the merlan Colbert (fried whiting), and carbonara with Alsatian cream and bacon.

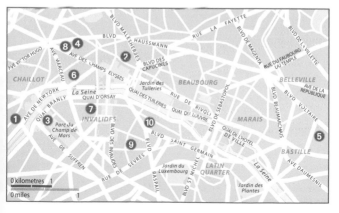

🔟 Cafés and Bars

① Café de Flore

A hang-out for artists and intellectuals since the 1920s, Café de Flore (see p131) attracted regulars including Salvador Dalí and Albert Camus. During World War II Jean-Paul Sartre and Simone de Beauvoir more or less lived at the Flore. Although its prices have skyrocketed since then, its charming

Café de Flore

Art Deco decor hasn't changed and it's still a perennial favourite with French filmmakers and literati. Reliable coffee, best enjoyed outside.

② Le Progrès

Don't be fooled by the fairly unremarkable exterior of this Parisian bar and café (see p100). Inside, an eclectic mix of locals are always congregating to catch up with friends and people-watch, a drink in hand the meanwhile. Wood panelling and chalkboards give the café a truly authentic, old-world feel.

③ Café Marly

Overlooking the courtyard of the Louvre, this café (see p107) is as sleek as the former palace is royal. From morning coffee to evening wine, Café Marly is the place to rest in between visits to the museum. While it is a far cry from the usual corner café, the experience is justifiably regal thanks to its plush interior and velvet armchairs.

④ Carette

This pavement café (see p101), situated just around the corner from the Jardins du Trocadéro, is the perfect setting for lunch. French staples line the menu, and they serve an excellent Sunday brunch. Find a table on the terrace for an exemplary *croque monsieur* or one of the picture-perfect pastries.

⑤ Café de la Paix

Café de la Paix (see p107) can be found along one of Haussmann's grand boulevards, and has views of the opulent Opéra Garnier. This setting makes it hard to contest the pricier coffee served inside. The café is decked floor to ceiling with decor typical of the Napoleon III style, making it a historic monument. Sip drinks and discuss current affairs like Maupassant or Zola would have in the 19th century.

⑥ La Closerie des Lilas

The main restaurant here (see p161) is expensive, but the bar is a good spot to soak up the atmosphere of this historic site, where artists and writers such as Georges Braque and Gertrude Stein came to mingle since its founding in 1847. Look out for the famous names of visitors etched on the tables in the bar. The outdoor seating makes for a lovely, leafy setting in summer. The busy brasserie also has live piano music in the evenings and attracts a chic crowd.

⑦ Les Deux Magots

This café (see p131) was a rival to the neighbouring Flore as a rendezvous for the 20th-century

Pavement tables at Les Deux Magots

intellectual élite. Hemingway, Oscar Wilde, Djuna Barnes, André Breton and Paul Verlaine were all regulars, and Picasso met his muse Dora Maar here in 1937. Like many iconic Parisian cafés, Les Deux Magots is pricey, but the outside tables facing the boulevard and square – ideally experienced with a glass of fizz – are definitely worth the cost.

8 Café de la Mairie

Looking onto the breathtaking St-Sulpice, this classic café *(see p130)* has a fabulous setting reminiscent of a scene from a Parisian film. It is always thrumming with local patrons sipping coffee while they watch the world go by, particularly in summer when additional tables and chairs are set up on the street outside. It's an ideal option for a quick lunch or glass of wine between shopping and sightseeing.

9 La Fontaine de Belleville

The city's best-known roaster *(see p161)* brings artisan drinks to a classic café setting, meaning coffee aficionados can finally revel in a venue with a true Parisian feel. Light breakfasts, delicious desserts and evening cocktails make this place a perfect stop at any time of the day – and lunchtime is the ideal moment for a classic *croque monsieur*. Just up the street from the canal, La Fontaine de Belleville offers a welcome break from the crowds bustling for a waterfront table.

10 Le Relais de la Butte

The terrace in front of this unassuming café *(see p153)*, located high up in Montmartre, is one of Paris's best outdoor theatres. Locals pass the evening watching the sun set over the city as the lights begin to sparkle. The food and drink play second fiddle to the experience of sitting in this little leafy enclave, which in the summer is always busy. Montmartre is laden with watering holes of varying quality, but Le Relais de la Butte is always a sure bet, as long as the weather cooperates.

TOP 10 WINE BARS

La Belle Hortense exterior

1 La Belle Hortense
MAP G4 ▪ 31 Rue Vieille du Temple
▪ 01 48 04 74 60
A wine bar that doubles as a bookshop.

2 L'Avant Comptoir
MAP M5 ▪ 3 Carrefour de l'Odéon
▪ 01 44 27 07 97
Jostle around the zinc bar for delicious little bites, and glasses of natural wine.

3 Frenchie Bar à Vins
MAP F3 ▪ 6 Rue du Nil ▪ 01 40 39 96 19
A superb international wine list.

4 Le Barav
MAP R1 ▪ 6 Rue Charles-François Dupuis ▪ 01 48 04 57 59
Well-priced wines in the upper Marais.

5 Le Garde Robe
MAP M2 ▪ 41 Rue de l'Arbre Sec
▪ 01 49 26 90 60
Cheeses, oysters and charcuterie round out the menu of natural wines here.

6 Septime La Cave
3 Rue Basfroi ▪ 01 43 67 14 87
Quaint wine store of Septime *(see p66)*.

7 Verjus Bar à Vins
MAP E3 ▪ 47 Rue Montpensier
▪ 01 42 97 54 40
This cosy wine bar specializes in independent French winemakers.

8 Déviant
MAP F2 ▪ 39 Rue des Petites Ecuries
▪ 01 48 24 66 79
Natural wines pair with small plates here.

9 Le Baron Rouge
An unpretentious, long-time favourite *(see p101)* near the Aligre market that serves fresh oysters when in season.

10 Quedubon
MAP H2 ▪ 22 Rue du Plateau
▪ 01 42 38 18 65
A list of over 200 natural wines.

Shops and Markets

Galeries Lafayette

1 Galeries Lafayette
MAP E2 ■ 40 Blvd Haussmann, 75009

This expansive store opened in 1894 as a monument to Parisian style, topped by a glorious steel-and-glass dome. Along with designer clothes, there's a fabulous food hall. The seventh floor has great views.

2 Flower and Bird Markets
MAP P4 ■ Pl Louis-Lépine, 75004

Dating from 1808, the colourful Marché aux Fleurs – Reine Elisabeth II (flower market) on the Ile de la Cité is the oldest and one of the largest flower markets in Paris. Its blooms brighten up the area between the stark walls of the Conciergerie and Hôtel Dieu from Monday to Saturday – everything from orchids to orange trees. On Sundays it is joined by the Marché aux Oiseaux (bird market).

3 Printemps
MAP E2 ■ 64 Blvd Haussmann, 75009

One of Paris's top department stores, the iconic Printemps opened in 1864. Its goods range from designer clothing and accessories to mid-range labels and funky fashions, home decor and furniture. The sixth-floor brasserie is crowned with a lovely Art Nouveau stained-glass cupola.

4 Bastille Market
MAP H5 ■ Blvd Richard-Lenoir, 75011

Every Thursday and Sunday morning, this market stretches along the tree-lined boulevard that separates the Marais from the Bastille. Sunday is the best day, when locals come to socialize as well as shop for fish, meat, bread and cheese. Some stalls sell North African and other international food.

5 Place de la Madeleine
This is a gourmand's delight (see p104). Some of the most delectable speciality food shops in Paris are dotted around the edges of this square, including the famous

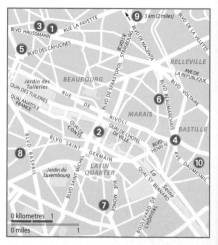

Fauchon food hall. There's Maille for mustard, Kaspia for caviar, Marquise de Sévigné for chocolates and La Maison de la Truffe *(see p106)* for truffles. Several elegant *salons de thé* offer a spot to sit and sip too.

its own line of menswear as well as the enormous La Grande Epicerie food hall.

Merci

Featuring homeware, clothing, furniture and a range of curated design products, Merci *(see p98)* is a playful alternative to traditional department stores. After a spot of shopping, visit the canteen on the kitchen level or grab a coffee at the charming ground-floor café. It's the place to shop and be seen just north of the Marais.

(7) Rue Mouffetard

One of the oldest market streets *(see p136)* in Paris winds downhill through the Latin Quarter every morning Tuesday to Sunday. Although this formerly cheap and bohemian market has been discovered as a tourist spot, it retains its charm, the narrow streets lined with speciality shops. There are also some good restaurants in the quieter side streets.

(8) Le Bon Marché

MAP D5 ▪ 22 Rue de Sèvres, 75007

Paris's first department store was founded on the Left Bank in 1852, its structure partially designed by Gustave Eiffel *(see p25)*. Today it's even more hip than its competitors, with an in-store boutique featuring avant-garde fashions. It also has designer clothes,

Le Bon Marché

Stall at Marché aux Puces de St-Ouen

(9) Marché aux Puces de St-Ouen

Porte de Clignancourt, 75018
▪ **Metro Porte de Clignancourt**

Every Saturday to Monday the largest antiques market in the world is held here. There are actually several markets here: the oldest, Marché Vernaison, is the most charming. Marché Biron offers a wide range of art, fine furniture, interesting jewellery and paintings.

(10) Marché d'Aligre

MAP H5 ▪ Pl d'Aligre, 75012

Away from the tourist bustle, this market retains its authentic Parisian atmosphere. An indoor hall houses vendors selling cheese, artisan beer, olive oil and charcuterie among other high-quality goods. Outside, inexpensive fruit, vegetables and flowers fill the street-side stands each morning from Tuesday to Sunday.

🔟 Paris for Free

Picturesque Place des Vosges

fine Art Nouveau pieces. There's a charming inner garden with a café too. Check the website for details about occasional free lunchtime concerts held in the auditorium.

1 Place des Vosges
Originally named Place Royale, this exceptionally beautiful arcaded square (see p93) dating to 1605 is a peaceful area to stroll and sit. The Classical arcades contain many art galleries. At No. 6, the Maison de Victor Hugo is the former dwelling of the famous writer and contains a museum dedicated to his life. The permanent collections are free.

2 Festival de Cinéma en Plein Air
229 Ave Jean Jaurès, 75019 ■ Metro Porte de Pantin ■ www.lavillette.com
Each summer a giant screen is placed in Parc de la Villette (see p156), showing movies (in the original language, with French subtitles) in the open air every evening for a month. The films, which range from classics to the less well-known, are all free. Deckchairs and blankets are available for hire, and many people bring their own picnic to make an evening of it.

3 Musée des Beaux Arts de la Ville de Paris
The grand Neo-Classical Petit Palais (see p112) is anything but "little", and is home to this fascinating collection of art and artifacts, including some

4 Free Visits to Museums
On the first Sunday of every month, admission to the permanent collections of most Paris museums, including the Louvre (Oct–Mar), Pompidou Centre, Musée Rodin and Musée d'Orsay, is free to everyone.

5 Hôtel de Ville
Paris's grand city hall (see p44) hosts regular excellent, free exhibitions, usually on a Parisian theme; a recent show focused on the Liberation of Paris. Free events often take place on the forecourt, but the wide square is just as fine a place to people-watch on any regular day.

6 Berges de Seine
MAP B4–E4 ■ www.lesberges. paris.fr
The Berges de Seine, the stretch of river between the Musée du Quai Branly – Jacques Chirac and Musée d'Orsay, is an attractive, lively promenade with loads of free activities, such as concerts and workshops, board games, a climbing wall and play spaces for children. There's a riverfront walkway on the Right Bank too.

Berges de Seine

7 Les Journées du Patrimoine

www.journeesdupatrimoine.
culture.fr

On the third weekend of September, many buildings that are normally off-limits, such as the Elysée Palace, are opened up to the public for free.

8 Musée d'Art Moderne de la Ville de Paris

This museum of modern art *(see p142)*, with a forecourt giving onto the Seine, may not rival the Pompidou's collection, but it's free and one often offers a calmer atmosphere. Almost all of the major 20th-century artists who worked in France are represented, including Picasso, Braque, Chagall and Modigliani, along with some new modern artists.

9 Cimetière du Père Lachaise

It is easy to while away an entire afternoon at Père Lachaise cemetery *(see p156)*, tracking down celebrity graves including those of Oscar Wilde, Colette, Balzac, Edith Piaf, Chopin and Jim Morrison. With its moss-grown tombs and ancient trees, it's also an atmospheric and romantic place for a long stroll.

Grave of Frédéric Chopin, Père Lachaise

10 Organ and Choir Recitals

Free organ recitals are given at 5pm on Sundays in the beautiful church of St-Eustache *(see p85)*, which has one of the finest organs in France. La Madeleine *(see p46)* and Saint-Roch also host free classical music concerts.

TOP 10 BUDGET TIPS

A classic French breakfast

1 Out for breakfast
Having breakfast at a café will cost considerably less than at a hotel.

2 Youth savings
State-run museums, including the Louvre, are free for anyone under 18 and EU citizens under 26.

3 Set-price lunch
Fixed price *(prix fixe)* lunches are usually good value and almost always cost less than evening meals. They can be a great way of dining at a top restaurant without breaking the bank.

4 Cutting transport costs
Buying a *carnet* of tickets, a *Mobilis* or *Paris Visite* card will save on transport costs *(see p165)*.

5 Lodgings for less
It's almost always cheaper to stay in an apartment, B&B or hostel than at a hotel *(see p171)*.

6 Cut-price entertainment
Half-price same-day theatre and concert tickets are sold at kiosks on Place de la Madeleine.

7 Order a carafe
A carafe of wine is better value than a bottle, and the house wine is generally very good.

8 Museum pass
With so many museums to visit, the *Paris Museum Pass* offers savings (www.parismuseumpass.com).

9 Sightseeing by bus
The bus is a great way of sightseeing cheaply – for example, number 24 takes a scenic route along the Seine.

10 Cheaper movies
Cinemas in the 5th *arrondissement* (around the Panthéon) are cheaper than those elsewhere.

⟦TOP 10⟧ Festivals and Events

Fête de la Musique street performers

① Street Music
www.fetedelamusique.culture.gouv.fr

Parisians love to celebrate music. The Fête de la Musique, held on the summer equinox, is Paris's largest music festival, when amateur and professional musicians take to the streets. There are performances in Place de la République and concert venues, but the most fun is to be had wandering through neighbourhoods.

② Garden Magic
www.chateauversailles-spectacles.fr

During summer weekend evenings the gardens of Versailles are home to the Grandes Eaux Nocturnes. Superb illuminations and install-ations, plus a dazzling firework display over the Grand Canal, make this a midsummer night's dream.

③ All That Jazz
www.parisjazzfestival.fr
▪ www.jazzalavillette.com

Paris has a long tradition of jazz, which was introduced to the city in World War I. A summer highlight is the Paris Jazz Festival. The Parc Floral in the Bois de Vincennes *(see p156)* is the main setting, blending a verdant backdrop with jazz melodies. Jazz à la Villette in September takes place in the Cité de la Musique.

④ Film Screenings
www.feteducinema.com

Cinema is embedded in Paris's culture. The four-day Fête du Cinema, held in early summer, allows film buffs to watch films at cinemas across Paris for just €4. The focus is on niche, independent movies.

⑤ Cycling Mania
www.letour.fr

Don't miss the Tour de France if you want to understand the French passion for cycling. Held annually since 1903, the world's greatest and most gruelling cycle race approaches Paris after 23 days. On the final laps the riders pass the Louvre, race along the banks of the Seine, hurtle down the Rue de Rivoli and cross the finish line on the Champs-Elysées.

The Tour de France event in Paris

6 City Beach
www.paris.fr

This popular summer event transforms a stretch of the Seine quais and the Canal du l'Ourcq into a mini Cannes, with tons of soft sand, deck chairs, parasols and palm trees.

7 Performing Arts
www.festival-automne.com

From plays and cabarets to music and dance, Paris stages a huge range of shows. For contemporary performing arts, head to the Festival d'Automne à Paris. Founded in 1972, this festival encourages people from all walks of life to performances of dance, music, film and drama.

8 Avant-Garde Art
www.parisinfo.com

A leader in avant-garde art in the early 20th century, Paris continues its cutting-edge artistic legacy with the Nuit Blanche, first held here in 2002. This free all-night contemporary art event in early October gives a fresh perspective on the city, with installations and illuminations of famous landmarks.

9 Grape Harvest Celebrations
www.fetesdesvendangesde montmartre.com

Paris was once a major wine producer but these days only the vineyards at Montmartre produce wine *(see p149)*, yielding just under a thousand bottles of Clos de Montmartre every year. To celebrate the grape harvest in early October, the Fêtes des Vendanges is held over five days on the Butte Montmartre and neighbouring districts with wine, food stalls, music and street theatre.

10 Foodie Festivals
www.omnivore.com
■ www.paristastefestivals.com

Legendary for its cuisine, Paris is a foodie heaven. Try modern cuisine at Omnivore, a festival in March dedicated to culinary innovation, or savour dishes from leading chefs at Taste of Paris in May.

TOP 10 SPORTS EVENTS

Paris Marathon runners

1 Six Nations Rugby
www.stadefrance.com
The French team plays England, Scotland, Ireland, Wales and Italy.

2 La Verticale de la Tour Eiffel
www.verticaletoureiffel.fr
Race to the top of this iconic monument.

3 Paris Marathon
www.schneiderelectricparis marathon.com
Runners start at the Champs-Elysées and end at Avenue Foch.

4 Football Cup Final
www.stadefrance.com
The biggest event in French football.

5 French Tennis Open
www.rolandgarros.com
This legendary clay-court tournament is part of the prestigious Grand Slam.

6 Top 14 Rugby Final
www.stadefrance.com
Some of the world's finest rugby players take part in the final of the French Rugby league.

7 Prix de Diane Longines
www.evenements.france-galop.com
This upmarket horse race in Chantilly, north of Paris, is named after the mythological goddess Diana.

8 La Parisienne
www.la-parisienne.net
Europe's largest women-only race in aid of breast cancer research.

9 Qatar Prix de l'Arc de Triomphe
www.parislongchamp.com
This world-renowned horse race was first held in 1920

10 Rolex Paris Masters
www.rolexparismasters.com
After the French Open, this is regarded as the country's next major tennis championship.

Paris
Area by Area

A Gothic gargoyle stares out over Paris
from Notre-Dame's western façade

🔟 Ile de la Cité and Ile St-Louis

Paris was born on the Ile de la Cité. The first settlers came to this island on the Seine in 300 BC and it has been a focus of church and state power over many centuries, home to the great cathedral of Notre-Dame and the Palais de Justice. This tiny land mass is also the geographical heart of the city – all distances from Paris are measured from Point Zéro, just outside Notre-Dame. While the Ile de la Cité bustles with tourists, the smaller Ile St-Louis, linked to its neighbour by a footbridge, has been an exclusive residential enclave since the 17th century. Its main street is lined with shops, galleries and restaurants and is a lovely place for a stroll.

Notre-Dame chimera

ILE DE LA CITÉ AND ILE ST-LOUIS

1 **Top 10 Sights**
see pp79–81

1 **Places to Eat**
see p83

1 **Shopping**
see p82

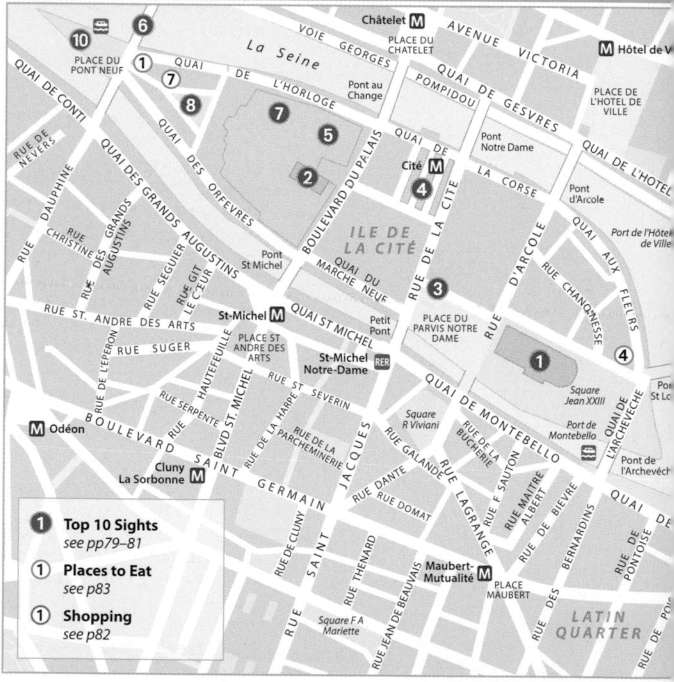

Notre-Dame
See pp20–23.

Sainte-Chapelle
See pp36–7.

3 Crypte Archéologique
MAP P4 ■ 7 Parvis Notre-
Dame – Pl Jean-Paul II, 75004 ■ Open
10am–6pm Tue–Sun ■ Adm

Fascinating remnants of early
Paris dating back to Gallo-Roman
times were discovered in 1965,
during an excavation of the square
in front of Notre-Dame in order to
build an underground car park. The
archaeological crypt displays parts
of 3rd-century Roman walls, rooms
heated by hypocaust, as well as
remains of medieval streets and
foundations. The scale models
showing the evolution of the city
from its origins as a Celtic settlement are interesting.

Marché aux Fleurs, Ile de la Cité

**4 Marché aux Fleurs –
Reine Elizabeth II**
MAP N3

One of the last remaining flower
markets in the city centre, the
beautiful Marché aux Fleurs *(see
p70)* is also the oldest, dating from
the early 19th century. It is held year-
round, Monday to Saturday, in place
Louis-Lépine, filling the north side of
the Ile de la Cité with dazzling blooms
from 8am to 7:30pm. There is also a
bird market here on Sundays, which
sells some rare species.

5 Conciergerie
MAP N3 ■ 2 Blvd du Palais,
75001 ■ Open 9:30am–6pm daily
■ Adm

This imposing Gothic palace, built by
Philippe le Bel (the Fair) in 1301–15,
has a rich history. Parts of it were
turned into a prison, controlled by
the concierge, or keeper of the king's
mansion, hence the name. Ravaillac,
assassin of Henri IV, was tortured
here, but it was during the Revolution
that the prison became a place of
terror, when thousands were held
here awaiting execution by guillotine.
Today you can see the Salle des
Gardes and the magnificent vaulted
Salle des Gens d'Armes (Hall of the
Men-at-Arms), a torture chamber,
the Bonbec tower and the prison.
The cell where Marie-Antoinette was
held, and the history of other famous
Revolution prisoners, is on display.
Outside, look for the square Tour
de l'Horloge, erected in 1370, which
houses the city's first public clock,
still ticking.

Pont Neuf, Paris's oldest bridge, spanning the Seine

6 Pont Neuf
MAP M3

The name – New Bridge – is somewhat incongruous for the oldest surviving bridge in Paris. Following its completion in 1607, Henri IV christened it by charging across on his steed; the bronze equestrian statue of the king was melted down during the Revolution but replaced in 1818. Decorated with striking carved heads, the bridge was unique for its time in that it had no houses built upon it. It has 12 arches and a span of 275 m (912 ft) extending to both sides of the island.

7 Palais de Justice
MAP M3 ■ 10 Blvd du Palais, 75001 ■ Open 9am–6pm Mon–Fri (ID required)

Stretching across the west end of the Ile de la Cité from north to south, the Palais de Justice, along with the Conciergerie, was once part of the Palais de la Cité, seat of Roman rule and the home of the French kings until 1358. It took its present name during the Revolution – prisoners passed through the Cour du Mai (May Courtyard) on their way to execution during this time – though the Revolutionary Tribunal eventually degenerated during Robespierre's Reign of Terror. In 2018, most of the central law courts that had been housed here moved into new premises in the 17th *arrondissement*.

8 Place Dauphine
MAP M3

In 1607, Henri IV transformed this former royal garden into a triangular square and named it after his son, the Dauphin and future King Louis XIII. Surrounding the square were uniformly built houses of brick and white stone; No. 14 is one of the few

Palais de Justice

THE GUILLOTINE

Dr Joseph Guillotine invented his "humane" beheading machine at his home near the Odéon and it was first used in April 1792. During the Revolution some 2,600 prisoners were executed on the places du Carrousel, de la Concorde, de la Bastille and de la Nation, after awaiting their fate in the Conciergerie prison.

that retains its original features. One side was destroyed to make way for the expansion of the Palais de Justice. Today this quiet spot is a good place to relax over a drink or meal (see p83).

⑨ St-Louis-en-l'Ile
MAP Q5 ▪ 19 Rue St-Louis-en-l'Ile, 75004 ▪ Open 10am–1pm & 2–7:30pm Tue–Fri, 9:30am–1pm & 2–7:30pm Sat, 9am–1pm & 2–7pm Sun

This Baroque church was designed between 1664 and 1726 by the royal architect Louis Le Vau. The exterior features an iron clock (1741) at the entrance and an iron spire, while the interior, richly decorated with gilding and marble, has a statue of St Louis holding his Crusader's sword.

Square du Vert-Galant

⑩ Square du Vert-Galant
MAP M3

The tranquil western tip of the Ile de la Cité, with its verdant chestnut trees, lies beneath the Pont Neuf – take the steps behind Henri IV's statue. The king had a notoriously amorous nature and the name of this peaceful square recalls his nickname, meaning "old flirt". From here there is a wonderful view of the Louvre (see pp12–15) and the Right Bank. It is also the departure point for cruises on the Seine on Les Vedettes du Pont Neuf (see p171).

A DAY ON THE ISLANDS

[Map showing: Pont Neuf, La Rose de France, Conciergerie, Place Dauphine, Marché aux Fleurs, Sainte-Chapelle, Ile St-Louis, Crypte Archéologique, Notre-Dame, Le Flore en l'Ile, Berthillon]

▶ MORNING

View the exterior of the famous **Notre-Dame** (see pp20–23). This 850-year old cathedral suffered extensive damage in a major fire in 2019. It is now closed for renovations. From here head for the fragrant **Marché aux Fleurs** (see p79). You can buy all kinds of garden accessories, flowers and seeds. Take a coffee break at **Le Flore en l'Ile** (see p83), with its views of the cathedral and the Seine.

The **Crypte Archéologique** (see p79) is worth a half-hour visit, before strolling towards **Place Dauphine**. This historic square is the perfect place to relax.

There are plenty of places for lunch, but on a sunny day try **La Rose de France** (see p83), which has terrace seating.

AFTERNOON

Soak up the views of the city from **Pont Neuf** before heading towards the **Conciergerie** (see p79). See Marie-Antoinette's prison cell in this Gothic palace-turned-prison. Next, spend the rest of the afternoon at the ethereal **Sainte-Chapelle** (see pp36–7) when the sun beams through the lovely stained-glass windows. From here, start strolling the narrow streets of the beautiful **Ile St-Louis**, which are filled with shops and galleries (see p82) selling a wide range of Parisian products.

Wind up with an afternoon treat by visiting **Berthillon** (see p83), considered the best ice-cream purveyor in all of France.

See map on pp78–9 ◀

Shopping

1 Lafitte
MAP P4 ▪ 8 Rue Jean du Bellay, 75004 ▪ Closed Sun, Mon

Foie gras and other regional products from the southwest await those looking to indulge in French gastronomy.

2 Oliviers & Co
MAP Q5 ▪ 81 Rue St-Louis-en-l'Ile, 75004 ▪ Closed Sun

This speciality food shop stocks high-quality olive oils from Provence and the Mediterranean basin. Check out the flavoured vinegars and truffled condiments too.

3 Librairie Ulysse
MAP Q5 ▪ 26 Rue St-Louis-en-l'Ile, 75004 ▪ Closed am & Sun–Mon

Today Paris, tomorrow the world. This eccentric travel bookshop will take you anywhere you want with thousands of titles, antiquarian and new, in French and English – including many on Paris itself.

4 Clair de Rêve
MAP Q5 ▪ 35 Rue St-Louis-en-l'Ile, 75004 ▪ Closed Sun

This boutique sells original puppets, robots and miniature theatres, making it an ideal shop if you're looking for a present with a difference.

5 Laguiole
MAP Q4 ▪ 35 Rue des Deux Ponts, 75004 ▪ Closed Sun (am)

Browse an array of knives and cutlery sets from this iconic cutlery brand, which hails from the Aveyron region of southern France. Look for the famous bee motif on the handles.

6 Pylones
MAP Q5 ▪ 57 Rue St-Louis-en-l'Ile, 75004 ▪ Closed Mon

Rubber and painted metal are used to create the whimsical jewellery and accessories sold here, along with a selection of novelty gifts.

7 Boulangerie Saint Louis
MAP Q5 ▪ 80 Rue St-Louis -en-l'Ile, 75004

One of the few bakeries on the island, this tiny boulangerie has everything classic, ranging from hearty baguette sandwiches to buttery croissants.

8 Maison Moinet
MAP Q5 ▪ 45 Rue St-Louis-en-l'Ile, 75004 ▪ Closed Mon

A family-run confectioner from Vichy, this cute shop sells traditional French sweets and chocolates. It is an enticing treat for all ages.

9 La Ferme Saint-Aubin
MAP Q5 ▪ 76 Rue St-Louis-en-l'Ile, 75004 ▪ Closed Mon (am)

Cheese in all shapes and sizes from across France are sold at this *fromagerie*. An aromatic delight.

10 Carion Minéraux
MAP Q5 ▪ 92 Rue St-Louis-en-l'Ile, 75004 ▪ Closed Sun, Mon

A wealth of meteorites, fossils and minerals. Some are made into imaginative jewellery.

Clair de Rêve boutique

Places to Eat

 Taverne Henri IV
MAP M3 ■ 13 Pl du Pont-Neuf,
75001 ■ 01 43 54 27 90 ■ Closed Sun,
Aug ■ €

A cosy wine bar with an extensive
wine list and simple plates of
charcuterie, cheese and snails.

 Le Sergent Recruteur
MAP Q4 ■ 41 Rue St-Louis-
en-l'Ile, 75004 ■ 01 85 15 26 80
■ Closed Sun, Mon ■ €€€

Served in a stylishly refurbished
space, the Michelin-starred tasting
menus include imaginative modern
interpretations of traditional dishes.

Les Fous de L'Ile
MAP Q4 ■ 33 Rue des
Deux Ponts, 75004 ■ 01 43 25 76
67 ■ €€

This modern Parisian bistro
serves typical dishes such as
entrecôte or steak tartare. It also
hosts exhibitions and live music.

Le Petit Plateau
MAP G5 ■ 1 Quai aux Fleurs,
75004 ■ 01 44 07 61 86 ■ €

This tearoom is a great lunch
spot, serving delicious homemade salads, quiches and cakes.

**Brasserie de
l'Isle St-Louis**
MAP P4 ■ 55 Quai de Bourbon,
75004 ■ 01 43 54 02 59 ■ Closed
Wed, Aug ■ €€

Wooden tables and a rustic look
complement hearty Alsace fare,
such as tripe in Riesling wine.
The terrace welcomes alfresco
diners in summer.

 Isami
MAP P5 ■ 4 Quai d'Orléans,
75004 ■ 01 40 46 06 97 ■ Closed Sun,
Mon, Aug ■ €€€

This is consistently voted one of
the best Japanese restaurants in the
city. The sushi and sashimi platters
are a work of art but space is limited
so be sure to book ahead.

PRICE CATEGORIES
For a three-course meal for one with half
a bottle of wine (or equivalent meal),
taxes and extra charges

€ under €30 €€ €30–€50 €€€ over €50

La Rose de France
MAP M3 ■ 24 Pl Dauphine,
75001 ■ 01 43 54 10 12 ■ €€

Dine on French classics on the lovely
terrace or in the cosy dining room.

La Rose de France

 L'Ilot Vache
MAP Q5 ■ 35 Rue St Louis
en l'Ile, 75004 ■ 01 46 33 55 16 ■ €€

French classics still have some
surprises – duck confit with
raspberries, for example – at this
tiny, unpretentious eatery. The table
displays of flowers are spectacular.

Le Flore en l'Ile
MAP P5 ■ 42 Quai d'Orléans,
75004 ■ 01 43 29 88 27 ■ €€

Go for the views as well as the food
at this bistro-cum-tearoom, open
from breakfast until 2am.

Berthillon
MAP G5 ■ 31 Rue St-Louis-
en-l'Ile, 75004 ■ 01 43 54 31 61
■ Closed Mon, Tue, 1 week Feb,
1 week Easter, Aug, late Oct ■ No
credit cards ■ €

There is always a queue outside
this legendary ice cream and
sorbet shop and tearoom but it
is worth the wait.

See map on pp78–9

Beaubourg and Les Halles

The small but lively Beaubourg Quarter, brimming with art galleries and cafés, has become a major tourist attraction since the Centre Georges Pompidou

Fontaine des Innocents

opened in 1977. Les Halles was the city's marketplace for 800 years – novelist Emile Zola called it "the belly of Paris". Its glass-roofed pavilions were demolished in 1969 but many of the surrounding bistros and speciality shops are still here.

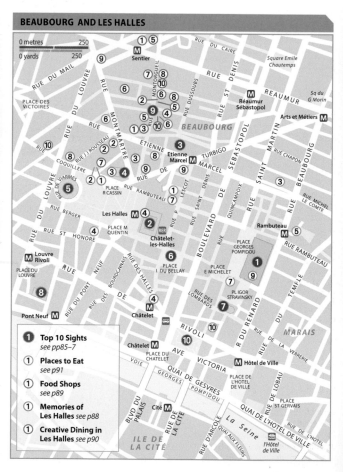

BEAUBOURG AND LES HALLES

1 Top 10 Sights
see pp85–7

1 Places to Eat
see p91

1 Food Shops
see p89

1 Memories of
Les Halles *see p88*

1 Creative Dining in
Les Halles *see p90*

Centre Georges Pompidou

See pp32–3.

 **Forum des Halles**
MAP N2

Ten years after the original market was demolished, the so-called "largest urban hole in Europe" was filled with this controversial shopping complex. This largely underground maze caters mainly to the young with designer-name boutiques. Outside, buskers, young people and tourists throng the steps and gardens. Part of a continuing project to revitalize the neighbourhood under the leadership of French architect David Mangin, the revamped shopping centre now has a huge undulating glass-and-steel roof, known as "the Canopy".

 **Tour Jean Sans Peur**
MAP N1 ▪ 20 Rue Etienne Marcel, 75002 ▪ 01 40 26 20 28 ▪ Open 1:30–6pm Wed–Sun ▪ Adm

After the Duke of Orléans was assassinated on his orders in 1407, the Duke of Burgundy feared reprisals. To protect himself, he built this 27-m- (88-ft-) tall tower onto his home, the Hôtel de Bourgogne, and moved his bedroom up to the fourth floor (reached by a flight of 140 steps). A remnant of the 15th-century residence, the tower later became a theatre in the 17th to 18th centuries. Today it hosts exhibitions on life in the Middle Ages.

St-Eustache
MAP M1 ▪ 2 Impasse St-Eustache, 75001 ▪ Open 10am–6pm Mon–Fri, 10am–7pm Sat & Sun

With its majestic arches and pillars, St-Eustache is one of the most beautiful churches in Paris. Although Gothic in design, it took 105 years to build (1532–1637) and its interior decoration reflects the Renaissance style of this time. The church was modelled on Notre-Dame *(see pp20–23)*, with double side aisles and a ring of side chapels. The stained-glass windows made from sketches by

Chapelle de la Vierge, St-Eustache

Philippe de Champaigne (1631) and the tomb of politician Jean-Baptiste Colbert (1619–83) are the highlights. Don't miss the naïve sculpture in the Chapelle des Pélerins d'Emmaüs, which recalls Les Halles' market days, or the Keith Haring triptych in the Chapelle St-Vincent-de-Paul.

Bourse de Commerce – Collection Pinault
MAP M1 ▪ 2 Rue de Viarmes, 75001 ▪ www.boursedecommerce.fr

The circular building that houses the Commodities Exchange was erected as a grain market in 1767 and remodelled in the 19th century. The building is undergoing extensive renovations to transform it into Paris's newest contemporary cultural centre and is scheduled to reopen in spring 2021. The centre will feature billionaire businessman François Pinault's art collection as well as host concerts, screenings and conferences.

Façade of the Bourse de Commerce

6 Fontaine des Innocents
MAP N2 ■ Rue St-Denis & Rue Berger, 75001

The Square des Innocents is a Les Halles crossroads and a hang-out for street performers and young people. It was built atop a cemetery in the 18th century, from which two million human remains were transferred to the Catacombs (see p58) at Denfert-Rochereau. The Renaissance fountain, the last of its era built in the city, was designed by Pierre Lescot and carved by sculptor Jean Goujon in 1547. It originally stood against a wall on rue St-Denis, and was moved to the new square, when the fourth side was added.

7 Eglise St-Merry
MAP P2 ■ 76 Rue de la Verrerie, 75004 ■ Open 3–7pm Mon–Sat (Nov– Mar: 2–6pm)

Formerly the parish church of the Lombard moneylenders, St-Merry was built between 1520 and 1612, and reflects the Flamboyant Gothic style. Its name is a corruption of St-Médéric, who was buried on this site in the early 8th century. The bell in the church's northwest turret, thought to be the oldest in Paris, dates from 1331. Other high-lights include the decorative west front, the 17th-century organ loft, beautiful stained glass and carved wood panelling. There are free concerts at the weekends. Check www.accueilmusical.fr for timings.

Stained glass in Eglise St-Merry

GEORGES POMPIDOU

Georges Pompidou (1911–74) had the unenviable task of following Général de Gaulle as President of France, from 1969 until his death. During his tenure he initiated many architectural developments in Paris, including the controversial but ultimately successful Pompidou Centre, and the less popular scheme to demolish the Les Halles market.

8 St-Germain l'Auxerrois
MAP M2 ■ 2 Pl du Louvre, 75001 ■ Open 9am–7pm daily ■ www.saintgermainauxerrois.fr

When the Valois kings moved to the Louvre (see p12) palace in the 14th century, this became the church of the royal family. On 24 August 1572, the tolling of its bell was used as the signal for the St Bartholomew's Day Massacre, when thousands of Huguenots who had come to Paris for the wedding of Henri of Navarre to Marguerite of Valois (see p22) were murdered. The church fea-tures a range of architectural styles, from its Flamboyant Gothic façade to its Renaissance choir. Check the website for details about the monthly guided tours.

9 Rue Montorgueil
MAP N1

This bustling market street was once part of the oldest marketplace of Paris, the historic Les Halles. Today, the centrally located and picturesque street has countless wine shops, bistros, boutiques, restaurants and gourmet cheese and pastry shops, all of which are a visitor's delight. Many Parisian chefs frequent the shops along Rue Montorgueil along with locals and tourists alike. Its charming and lively cafés are perfect for people-watching after indulging in delicious goods from any of its excellent bakeries.

⑩ Tour St-Jacques
MAP N3 ■ **Sq de la Tour St-Jacques, 75004**

The late Gothic tower, dating from 1523, is all that remains of the church of St-Jacques-la-Boucherie, once the largest medieval church in Paris and a starting point for pilgrims on their journey to Santiago de Compostela in Spain. In the 17th century the mathematician and physicist Blaise Pascal used the tower for barometrical experiments. The church was pulled down after the Revolution. Visitors can take a tour to the top of the tower and visit the gardens (book online at www.desmotsetdesarts.com).

Tour St-Jacques

A DAY IN LES HALLES

▶ MORNING

Start your day with breakfast at Le Zimmer Café *(1 Pl du Châtelet; 01 42 36 74 03; open 7:30am–1am daily)* before exploring the permanent collection of the Musée National d'Art Moderne at the **Centre Georges Pompidou** *(see pp32–3)*. Stop for refreshments at **Le Georges** *(see p91)*, a chic brasserie at the top of the Centre Pompidou, which offers great views along with drinks, snacks or main meals.

On leaving the Centre, turn left into Place Igor Stravinsky to admire the colourful **Stravinsky Fountain** *(see p32)*.

If you have booked ahead, take your seat at Michelin-starred bistro **Benoit** *(see p91)*, whose lunchtime menu is far cheaper than in the evening.

AFTERNOON

Pass the **Fontaine des Innocents** as you head for Les Halles, but first pay a visit to the church of **St-Eustache** *(see p85)*, where the workers of the old Les Halles market worshipped.

Walk under the green canopy over the **Forum des Halles** *(see p85)* and head for charming **Rue Montorgueil** and the little streets surrounding it – there are plenty of food shops and cafés to explore.

Finish the day at the classic brasserie **Au Pied de Cochon** *(see p91)*, which has a smart burgundy-and-cream terrace. It is a great spot for comfort foods such as pork terrine and onion soup *au gratin*.

See map on p84 ←

Memories of Les Halles

Sumptuous interior of Au Pied de Cochon

1 Au Pied de Cochon
This 24-hour brasserie (see p91) still serves dishes that used to appeal to the earthy tastes of market workers, including the eponymous pigs' trotters.

2 Le Cochon à l'Oreille
MAP F3 ■ 15 Rue Montmartre, 75001

Dating back to the early 20th century, this ornate former working men's café/bar, decorated with historic tiles and murals, has only a small dining room, so book in advance.

3 St-Eustache Sculpture
The lively naïve sculpture by Raymond Mason in the church's Chapelle des Pélerins d'Emmaüs is a tribute to the beloved market. Its colourful figures depict *The Departure of Fruit and Vegetables from the Heart of Paris, 28 February 1969.*

4 Aurouze
MAP F4 ■ 8 Rue des Halles, 75001

This shop is credited with getting rid of Les Halles' most unwelcome inhabitants – rats. The window display is a taxidermy tribute to the once-common vermin.

5 Stöhrer
MAP N1 ■ 51 Rue Montorgueil, 75002

One of Paris's loveliest, old-fashioned patisseries, founded in 1730 by a chef who had worked for Louis XV.

6 Au Rocher de Cancale
MAP N1 ■ 78 Rue Montorgueil, 75002

Once a gathering space for artists and writers during the early 19th century, this place is known for its oysters.

7 La Fresque
MAP N1 ■ 100 Rue Rambuteau, 75001

This wonderful restaurant used to be a fishmonger. Original tiles and a fresco of a fishing scene still decorate the back room.

8 Dehillerin
MAP M1 ■ 18 Rue Coquillière, 75001

Since 1820, everyone from army cooks to gourmet chefs has come here for copper pots, cast-iron pans and cooking utensils.

9 Duthilleul et Minart
MAP P1 ■ 14 Rue de Turbigo, 75001

For more than 100 years this shop has sold French work clothes and uniforms, such as chef's hats and watchmaker's smocks.

10 A la Cloche des Halles
MAP M1 ■ 28 Rue Coquillière, 75001

This wine bar and restaurant practically chimes with history. The "cloche" is the bronze bell whose peal once signalled the start and end of the market day.

Food Shops

 G. Detou
MAP N1 ■ 58 Rue Tiquetonne, 75002

The shelves at this chef's paradise are laden with chocolates, teas, artisanal mustards and more.

 Mariage Frères
MAP N1 ■ 190 Rue Montorgueil, 75002

This elegant and fragrant tea boutique has a dizzying array of teas and teapots.

 Charles Chocolatier
MAP N1 ■ 15 Rue Montorgueil, 75002

On a cold day, stop in at this family-run chocolate shop for a take-out cup of their luscious hot chocolate; the ice creams in summer are delectable, too.

 A la Mère de Famille
MAP N1 ■ 82 Rue Montorgueil, 75002

This branch of the oldest confectionary shop in Paris stocks regional French sweets, all in the brand's vintage-inspired packaging.

 **La Fermette**
MAP N1 ■ 86 Rue Montorgueil, 75002

The enthusiastic cheesemongers here are ready with tips and tastings to help visitors make the perfect choice from the piles of cheese on display.

Boulangerie Collet
MAP N1 ■ 100 Rue Montorgueil, 75002

Run by the same family for two generations, this traditional boulangerie is particularly known for its viennoiseries and light-as-air meringues.

 Delitaly
MAP F3 ■ 5 Rue des Petits Carreaux, 75002

You'll find fresh and dried pastas, gourmet olive oils, tubs of antipasti and a mouthwatering selection of salami and other cured meats at this Italian deli.

 Eric Kayser
MAP F3 ■ 16 Rue des Petits Carreaux, 75002

Beyond excellent baguettes, choose from all manner of delicious pastries and other baked goods to stock up on for tea.

 Librairie Gourmande
MAP F3 ■ 92–96 Rue Montmartre, 75002

This fabulous bookshop has an extensive collection of books on wine and cooking, some in English.

Boucherie Roger
MAP N1 ■ 62 Rue Montorgueil, 75002

From roasted chicken to meat pâté, this place has it all for you. They even prepare their own cuts in-house.

Visitors at Boucherie Roger

See map on p84 ←

Creative Dining in Les Halles

Cosy interior of Lockwood

1 Lockwood
MAP F3 ■ 73 Rue d'Aboukir, 75002

Enjoy artisan coffee and brunch at the weekend, or spend an evening in Lockwood's underground bar with light bites and great cocktails.

2 O Château
MAP M1 ■ 68 Rue J J Rousseau, 75001

Get tips for buying wine at O Château. This wine bar runs very popular sessions with English-speaking sommeliers. Consider a tasting dinner in one of their vaulted cellars.

3 Fou de Patisserie
MAP N1 ■ 45 Rue Montorgueil, 75002

This retailer excels in bringing the best pastries from around the city to Les Halles. Sample pastries from some of the most popular chefs such as Pierre Hermé and Cyril Lignac. Here, shoppers can find cakes and other creative products by Paris's biggest names.

4 Champeaux
MAP N1 ■ La Canopée, Forum des Halles, Porte Rambuteau, 75001

Chef Alain Ducasse specializes in French classics and creative cocktails at this ultra-contemporary diner. Good service makes it a perfect stop at any time of the day.

5 Boneshaker Donuts
MAP F3 ■ 77 Rue d'Aboukir, 75002

Away from the traditional pastry shops of Les Halles, Boneshaker produces delicious gourmet, small batch doughnuts.

6 La Cevicheria
MAP F3 ■ 14 Rue Bachaumont, 75002

Try some fresh ceviche – a speciality of raw fish from various Latin American countries. At La Cevicheria it is inspired by its Peruvian version.

7 Lai'Tcha
MAP M1 ■ 7 Rue du Jour, 75002

Michelin-starred chef Adeline Grattard's casual eatery, housed in a handsome modern space, is a dumpling bar in the daytime and a Chinese bistro in the evening – think scallop sticky rice and king crab rolls.

8 Experimental Cocktail Club
MAP F3 ■ 37 Rue St Sauveur, 75002

Although French wine will always reign supreme, the cocktails at this speakeasy-style bar are a welcome addition to the drink options in Les Halles. Dress to impress and prepare to elbow your way to the busy bar.

9 Chacun Ses Gouts
MAP N1 ■ 20 Rue Montorgueil, 75001

With fresh, rich milk from Normandy, and French sweets and fruits for garnishing, this elegant frozen yoghurt shop shouldn't be missed.

10 Grillé
MAP N1 ■ 6 Rue des Petits Carreaux, 75002

A new-generation gourmet kebab spot, Grillé serves delicious high-quality meats and baked-to-order flatbreads.

Places to Eat

1 AG Les Halles
MAP N1 = 14 Rue Mondétour,
75001 = 01 42 61 37 17 = €€€

Liberian-born chef Alan Geaam has
three bistros in Paris, but the Les
Halles spot is the prettiest thanks to
its Art Deco glass ceiling. The food is
excellent and creatively presented.

2 Au Pied de Cochon
MAP M1 = 6 Rue Coquillière,
75001 = 01 40 13 77 00 = €€

A Les Halles favourite, this specializes
in pig dishes. There are traditional
brasserie options too, such as oysters
and steak. Open 24 hours a day.

3 L'Ambassade d'Auvergne
MAP P1 = 22 Rue du Grenier
St-Lazare, 75003 = 01 42 72 31 22
= Closed 2 weeks in Aug = €€

With the ambience of a rustic inn,
this restaurant transports you to
rural Auvergne. Plenty of pork and
cabbage dishes are served here.
Shared tables; good for solo diners.

4 Tour de Montlhéry, Chez Denise
MAP M2 = 5 Rue des Prouvaires,
75001 = 01 42 36 21 82 = Closed Sat,
Sun mid-Jul–mid-Aug = €€

A Les Halles legend for its huge
portions and convivial atmosphere.
Book in advance.

5 Le Hangar
MAP G4 = 12 Impasse
Berthaud, 75003 = 01 42 74 55 44
= Closed Sun & Mon = €€

This small, friendly bistro is no
secret to the locals, who keep
returning for the fabulous food,
including the steak tartare and
great desserts such as moelleux
au chocolat.

6 Le Tambour
MAP N1 = 41 Rue Montmartre,
75002 = 01 42 33 06 90 = €€

This 24-hour bistro draws a lively
crowd with its friendly service and
hearty French fare.

PRICE CATEGORIES
For a three-course meal for one with half
a bottle of wine (or equivalent meal),
taxes and extra charges
....
€ under €30   €€ €30–€50   €€€ over €50

7 Café Beaubourg
MAP P2 = 43 Rue St-Merri,
75001 = 01 48 87 63 96 = €€€

The terrace here overlooks the
Pompidou Centre. Steak tartare
is a house special.

8 L'Escargot Montorgueil
MAP N1 = 38 Rue Montorgueil,
75001 = 01 42 36 83 51 = €€€

At the heart of Rue Montorgueil, this
Parisian institution is known for its
signature French dish of snails, after
which it is named. Enjoy the view
from the terrace.

9 Le Georges
MAP G4 = Centre Georges
Pompidou, 19 Rue Beaubourg,
75004 = 01 44 78 47 99 = Closed
Tue = €€€

Sleek design and a great view make
this museum restaurant a superb
choice for a glamorous night out.

Interior of Benoit bistro

10 Benoit
MAP P1 = 20 Rue St-Martin,
75004 = 01 42 72 25 76 = Closed Aug
= €€€

Opened in 1912, this Michelin-starred
location is, justifiably, the most expensive bistro in Paris. Try the lunchtime
menu to keep the cost down.

See map on p84

TOP 10 Marais and the Bastille

For many, the Marais is one of the most enjoyable quarters of Paris, with chic shops, galleries and dining, as well as fine museums and atmospheric medieval lanes, but the district was little more than a muddy swamp until Henri IV built the Place Royale (now Place des Vosges) in 1605. Following its notoriety as the birthplace of the Revolution, the Bastille district sank into oblivion, until artists and designers arrived in the 1990s. Its streets are now home to the city's liveliest nightspots.

Statue, Musée Carnavalet

MARAIS AND THE BASTILLE

① Musée Cognacq-Jay
MAP Q3 ■ 8 Rue Elzévir, 75003
■ Open 10am–6pm Tue–Sun
■ www.museecognacqjay.paris.fr

This small but excellent museum illustrates the sophisticated French lifestyle in the so-called Age of Enlightenment, which centred on Paris. The beautiful 18th-century art and furniture on display were once the private collection of Ernest Cognacq and his wife, Marie-Louise Jay, founders of the former Samaritaine department store by Pont Neuf. It is superbly displayed in the Hôtel Donon, an elegant late-16th-century town mansion.

Elegant Place des Vosges

② Place des Vosges
MAP R3

Paris's oldest square – one of the world's most beautiful – was commissioned by Henri IV. Its 36 houses with red-gold brick and stone façades, slate roofs and dormer windows were laid out with striking symmetry in 1612. While the buildings were originally meant to house silk weavers, the likes of Cardinal Richelieu (1585–1642) and playwright Molière (1622–73) quickly moved in; this remains an upper-class residential address. However, everyone can enjoy a stroll around the area and visit the art galleries under the arcades.

③ Musée Picasso
MAP R2 ■ 5 Rue de Thorigny, 75003 ■ Open 10:30am–6pm Tue–Fri, 9:30am–6pm Sat & Sun ■ Closed 1 Jan, 1 May, 25 Dec ■ Adm (free first Sun of month) ■ www.museepicasso paris.fr

When the Spanish-born artist Pablo Picasso died in 1973, his family donated thousands of his works to the French state in lieu of estate taxes. Thus Paris enjoys the largest collection of Picassos in the world. Housed in the grand Hôtel Salé (see p96), which emerged from extensive renovations in late 2014, the collection (see p52) displays the range of his artistic development, from his Blue and Pink periods to Cubism, and reveals his mastery in a wide range of techniques and materials. Larger sculptures are housed in the garden and courtyard of the museum.

Parmentier
REPUBLIQUE
PARMENTIER
mbroise
BOULEVARD VOLTAIRE
N VERT
SEDAINE
Voltaire Ⓜ
ROQUETTE
RUE CODEROY CAVAIGNAC
VOLTAIRE
Charonne Ⓜ
②
CHARONNE
⑥
⑨
⑦
AVE LEDRU ROLLIN
RUE TROUSSEAU DE
RUE FAIDHERBE
Ledru Rollin Ⓜ
⑥
Faidherbe-Chaligny Ⓜ
UE DU FAUBOURG ST ANTOINE
⑨
RUE CROZATIER
RUE DE PRAGUE
RUE BAUDELAIRE
⑦
PLACE D'ALIGRE

0 metres 300
0 yards 300

4 Musée Carnavalet

MAP R3 ▪ 16 Rue des Francs Bourgeois, 75003 ▪ Opening hours are subject to change, check website ▪ Adm ▪ www.carnavalet.paris.fr

Devoted to the history of Paris, this renovated museum sprawls through two mansions, the 16th-century Carnavalet and 17th-century Le Peletier de Saint-Fargeau. The former was the home of Madame de Sévigné, the famous letter-writer, from 1677 to 1696 and a gallery here is devoted to her life. The extensive museum contains period rooms filled with art and portraits, plus Revolutionary artifacts and memorabilia of 18th-century philosophers Rousseau and Voltaire.

5 Place de la Bastille

MAP H5

Originally, the Bastille was a fortress built by Charles V to defend the eastern edge of the city, but it soon became a jail for political prisoners. Angry citizens, rising up against the excesses of the monarchy, stormed the Bastille on 14 July 1789 *(see p43)* and destroyed this hated symbol of oppression, sparking the French Revolution. In its place is the bronze 52-m- (171-ft-) high Colonne de Juillet (July Column), crowned by the Angel of Liberty, which commemorates those who died in the 1830 and 1848 revolutions. Behind it is the Opéra Bastille, once the largest opera house in the world, which opened on the bicentennial of the Revolution in 1989. In order to divert traffic, certain sections of this busy square have now been pedestrianized.

THE JEWISH QUARTER

The Jewish Quarter, centred on rues des Rosiers and des Écouffes, was established in the 13th century and has attracted immigrants since the Revolution. Many Jews fled here to escape persecution in Eastern Europe, but were arrested during the Nazi Occupation. Since World War II, Sephardic Jews from North Africa have found new homes here.

Passage Lhomme

6 The Passages

MAP H5

The Bastille has been the quarter of working-class artisans and craft guilds since the 17th century and many furniture makers are still located in these small alleyways, called *passages*. Rue du Faubourg St-Antoine is lined with shops selling a striking array of traditional period furniture and modern designs, but don't miss the narrow *passages*, such as Passage Lhomme, that run off this and other streets in the Bastille. Many artists and craftspeople have their *ateliers* (workshops) in these atmospheric alleys.

7 Musée de la Chasse et de la Nature

MAP Q2 ▪ 62 Rue des Archives, 75003 ▪ Opening hours are subject to change, check website ▪ Closed public hols ▪ Adm (free first Sun of month) ▪ www.chassenature.org

Occupying two well-preserved 17th- and 18th-century mansions, this refurbished museum explores the history of hunting, and humanity's relationship with the natural world. Curated to resemble the home of a rich collector, the museum displays tapestries and gilt-framed period paintings alongside taxidermy animals, and fascinating curiosity cabinets. There are surprises in each elegantly organized room, from the astonishing Jan Fabre-designed ceiling of owl feathers to the sleepy fox curled up on a chair.

(8) Rue de Lappe
MAP H5

Once famous for its 1930s dance halls (bals musettes), rue de Lappe is still the Bastille's after-dark hotspot. This short, narrow street is filled with bars, clubs, restaurants and cafés, and positively throbs with music. Crowds of night-owls trawl the cobblestones looking for action, and spill into the adjoining rue de la Roquette and rue de Charonne, where there are even more trendy bars and restaurants.

(9) Maison Européenne de la Photographie
MAP Q3 ▪ 5–7 Rue de Fourcy, 75004 ▪ Open 11am–8pm Wed–Fri, 10am–8pm Sat & Sun ▪ Adm ▪ www.mep-fr.org

This excellent gallery showcases contemporary European photography. It is housed in an early-18th-century mansion, Hôtel Hénault de Cantorbre, where a mix of historic features and modern spaces shows off the gallery's permanent collection and changing exhibitions of items from its archives.

(10) Maison de Victor Hugo
MAP R4 ▪ 6 Pl des Vosges, 75004 ▪ Open 10am–6pm Tue–Sun ▪ Closed public hols ▪ Adm for exhibitions ▪ www.maisons victorhugo.paris.fr

French author Victor Hugo (1802–85) lived on the second floor of the Hôtel de Rohan-Guéménée, the largest house on the place des Vosges, from 1832 to 1848. He wrote most of *Les Misérables* here (see p48), among other works. In 1903, the house became a museum covering his life.

Busts, Maison de Victor Hugo

A DAY IN THE MARAIS

MORNING

Begin at the **Musée Carnavalet** with its impressive 18th-century memorabilia. Afterwards, walk to the **Place des Vosges** (see p93): take in the whole square from the fountains in the centre.

Have a coffee at **Ma Bourgogne** (19 Pl des Vosges; 01 42 78 44 64; open 8am–1am daily), right on the square. Head towards **Maison de Victor Hugo**, then go to the south-west corner of the square, through a wooden door to the garden of the **Hôtel de Béthune-Sully** (see p96).

AFTERNOON

If the weather is nice, join the queue at **L'As du Fallafel** (see p101) for a hearty falafel wrap to eat in the nearby square Charles Victor Langlois. Otherwise, for shelter and a greater choice, head for the lively **Marché des Enfants Rouges** (see p101) and its international food stalls.

Spend a leisurely afternoon exploring the Marais, with its narrow, picturesque streets lined with shops and cafés. Pop into the fashionable boutiques along the **Rue des Francs Bourgeois** and **Rue Vieille du Temple**; bite into a slice of *babka* in the Jewish Quarter on **Rue des Rosiers**; then explore the ultra-hip Upper Marais, where concept store **Merci** (see p98) holds court.

Walk through **Place de la Bastille** – once the site of the city's dreaded prison – on the way to dinner in style beneath the chandeliers of **Le Train Bleu** (20 Blvd Diderot; 01 43 43 09 06), set inside the Gare de Lyon train station.

See map on pp92–3

Mansions

The beautiful Hôtel de Soubise

1 Hôtel de Soubise
MAP Q2 ■ 60 Rue des Francs Bourgeois, 75003 ■ Open 10am–5:30pm Mon, Wed–Fri, 2–5:30pm Sat & Sun

Along with the adjacent Hôtel de Rohan, this mansion contains the national archives.

2 Hôtel Salé
Built in 1656–9 for Aubert de Fontenay, a salt-tax collector, this mansion is now the home of the Musée Picasso *(see p93)*.

3 Hôtel Guénégaud
MAP P3 ■ 60 Rue des Archives, 75003 ■ Adm

Designed by the architect François Mansart in the mid-17th century, this splendid mansion houses the Musée de la Chasse et de la Nature *(see p94)*.

4 Hôtel de Beauvais
MAP P3 ■ 68 Rue François Miron, 75004 ■ Closed to the public

The young Mozart performed at this 17th-century mansion. Notice the balcony decorated with goats' heads.

5 Hôtel de St-Aignan
MAP P2 ■ 71 Rue du Temple, 75003 ■ Open 11am–6pm Tue–Fri, 10am–7pm Sat & Sun (for permanent exhibits) ■ Adm ■ www.mahj.org

The plain exterior hides an enormous mansion within. It is now the Museum of Jewish Art and History.

Medieval façade of Hôtel de Sens

6 Hôtel de Coulanges
MAP Q2 ■ 35 Rue des Francs Bourgeois, 75004

This 17th-century mansion was given a fresh makeover by new tenant Collectif Coulanges and is now a concept store and cultural space.

7 Hôtel de Béthune-Sully
MAP R4 ■ 62 Rue St-Antoine, 75004 ■ Closed to the public, except the bookshop (open 1–7pm Tue–Sun) & the gardens

Headquarters of the Centre des Monuments Nationaux, this 17th-century mansion houses a bookshop specializing in French culture and heritage.

8 Hôtel de Lamoignon
MAP Q3 ■ 24 Rue Pavée, 75004 ■ Closed to the public

This mansion was built in 1584 for the daughter of Henri II.

9 Hôtel de Marle
MAP G4 ■ 11 Rue Payenne, 75003 ■ Open 12–6pm Wed–Sun; café: 12–6pm Tue–Sun

The Swedish Institute and its pretty courtyard café are located here.

10 Hôtel de Sens
MAP Q4 ■ 1 Rue Figuier, 75004 ■ Closed to the public, except the library

One of Paris's few medieval mansions. Henri IV's wife Marguerite de Valois *(see p22)* lived here after their divorce. It is now home to a fine arts library.

Galleries

 Galerie Marian Goodman
MAP P2 ▪ 79 Rue du Temple, 75003 ▪ Open 11am–7pm Tue–Sat ▪ mariangoodman.com

Housed in a 17th-century mansion, this gallery is a slice of New York style. Artists include Jeff Wall and video-maker Steve McQueen.

 Galerie Akié Arichi
MAP H5 ▪ 26 Rue Keller, 75011 ▪ Open 2–7pm Tue–Sat ▪ www.akiearichi.com

Exhibitions here cover photography, sculpture and painting, often with an Asian influence.

3 Galerie Alain Gutharc
MAP H4 ▪ 7 Rue St-Claude, 75003 ▪ Open 11am–7pm Tue–Sat ▪ www.alaingutharc.com

Alain Gutharc devotes his space to the work of contemporary French artists.

4 Galerie Daniel Templon
MAP P2 ▪ 30 Rue Beaubourg, 75003 ▪ Open 10am–7pm Tue–Sat ▪ Closed Aug ▪ www.danieltemplon.com

A favourite among the French contemporary art establishment, this gallery exhibits cutting-edge artists.

5 Galerie Karsten Greve
MAP R2 ▪ 5 Rue Debelleyme, 75003 ▪ Open 10am–7pm Tue–Sat ▪ www.galerie-karsten-greve.com

A leading international gallery with top names in modern and contemporary art and photography.

6 Galerie Patrick Seguin
MAP H4 ▪ 5 Rue des Taillandiers, 75011 ▪ Open 10am–7pm Mon–Sat ▪ www.patrickseguin.com

This gallery features stylish 20th-century furniture and architecture, including works by French architect and designer Jean Prouvé.

7 Galerie Thaddeus Ropac
MAP Q1 ▪ 7 Rue Debelleyme, 75003 ▪ Open 10am–7pm Tue–Sat ▪ www.ropac.net

A major contemporary gallery, Thaddeus Ropac exhibits new and influential international artists.

8 Galerie Sakura
MAP P3 ▪ 21 Rue du Bourg Tibourg, 75004 ▪ Open noon–8pm Tue–Sat, 2–7pm Sun ▪ www.galerie-sakura.com

Pop art and daring works by international photographers are showcased at this offbeat gallery.

Quirky exhibits at Galerie Sakura

9 David Zwirner
MAP Q1 ▪ 108 Rue Vieille du Temple, 75003 ▪ Open 11am–7pm Tue–Sat ▪ www.davidzwirner.com

This powerhouse contemporary art gallery represents a global roster of major artists; the Paris branch is its sixth outpost.

10 Galerie20Vosges
MAP H4 ▪ 20 Pl des Vosges 75004 ▪ Open 11am–7:30pm Wed–Sun ▪ www.galerie20vosges.com

Contemporary artists, painters and sculptors showcase their unique work under the arcades of the regal Place des Vosges.

See map on pp92–3

Fashion and Accessory Shops

Lovely decor at Merci, a fashion-forward concept store

Merci
MAP R2 ■ 111 Blvd Beaumarchais, 75003

This trendy multi-brand store stocks clothes and accessories alongside stylish homewares.

2 Anatomica
MAP P3 ■ 14 Rue du Bourg Tibourg, 75004

One of the best men's stores in the city, carrying perfectly tailored clothes, and leather shoes from cult brand Alden.

3 Eric Bompard
MAP R3 ■ 14 Rue de Sévigné, 75004

Everything is soft at this cashmere specialist – sweaters, scarves, gloves and much more.

4 Antoine et Lili
MAP Q2 ■ 51 Rue des Francs Bourgeois, 75004

Behind the bright pink shopfront, chic and easy-to-wear clothes for women are inspired by Romani and Asian styles, and made using vibrant natural fabrics. They sell children's clothes and home furnishings too.

5 Home Autour du Monde
MAP G4 ■ 8 Rue des Francs Bourgeois, 75003 ■ 01 42 77 06 08

French designer Serge Bensimon's popular concept store stocks the brand's classic canvas sneakers in bright colours, limited-edition patterns and pretty Liberty prints for kids as well as adults.

6 Monsieur Paris
MAP R1 ■ 53 Rue Charlot, 75003

This store sells delicate gold and silver jewellery. Designer Nadia Azoug is often at work in the on-site *atelier*.

7 Sessùn
MAP H5 ■ 34 Rue de Charonne, 75011

This is the flagship store of the young, French womenswear label, which has chic, edgy clothes and accessories.

8 K. Jacques
MAP Q3 ■ 16 Rue Pavée, 75004

The classic Saint-Tropez sandal, given iconic status by Brigitte Bardot and never out of fashion, is stocked here, in some 60 styles and colours.

9 Isabel Marant
MAP H5 ■ 16 Rue de Charonne, 75011

This designer is getting a lot of recognition outside France for her hip but elegant pieces.

10 Bonton
MAP R1 ■ 5 Blvd des Filles du Calvaire, 75003

A gorgeous store for kids, this has three levels of clothes, accessories, toys and even a vintage photo booth.

Specialist Shops

1 Mariage Frères
MAP Q3 ▪ 30 Rue du Bourg Tibourg, 75004

This famous tea house was founded in 1854 and sells all kinds of blends, as well as tea-making paraphernalia.

2 Jacques Genin
MAP G3 ▪ 133 Rue de Turenne, 75003

This trendy chocolatier is adored for his caramels and fruit jellies. He also bakes a fantastic *millefeuille*.

3 La Manufacture de Chocolat
MAP H4 ▪ 40 Rue de la Roquette, 75011

The *chocolaterie* of Michelin-starred chef Alain Ducasse smells divine – and has the taste to back it up.

4 Fragonard
MAP Q2 ▪ 51 Rue des Francs Bourgeois, 75004

If you can't visit this perfume-maker's factory in the south of France, pick up some soaps and scents in this fragrant boutique.

5 Liquides Bar à Parfum
MAP G3 ▪ 9 Rue Normandie, 75003

Behind its elegant black storefront in the Upper Marais, Liquides carries scents that you won't find anywhere else.

6 L'Arbre à Lettres
MAP H5 ▪ 62 Rue du Faubourg St-Antoine, 75012

This beautiful bookshop specializes in fine arts, literature and human sciences.

L'Arbre à Lettres

7 A l'Olivier
MAP H5 ▪ 23 Rue de Rivoli, 75004

Opened in 1822, this shop specializes in sourcing the finest Provençal and Mediterranean olive oils, along with other culinary delights.

8 Papier Tigre
MAP R1 ▪ 5 Rue des Filles du Calvaire, 75003

Stylish graphic notebooks, greeting cards and other quirkily designed paper products are on offer at this modern stationery shop.

9 Izraël
MAP P3 ▪ 30 Rue François Miron, 75004

Also called the "World of Spices", this tiny store is a treasure trove of cheese, wine, rum, honey, mustard and myriad other delights.

10 Village Saint Paul
MAP R4 ▪ Between Rue St-Paul and Rue des Jardins St-Paul, 75004

An intriguing maze of art galleries, fine antiques and design shops, tucked away behind Eglise St-Paul.

Soaps and scents at Fragonard

See map on pp92–3

Fashionable Hang-outs

Kitsch decor in Andy Wahloo

the Hôtel de Ville for some above-par brews. It also boasts a shop that stocks coffee beans and unusual jams, as well as a coffee-tasting school.

Pop In
MAP H4 ■ 105 Rue Amelot, 75011

This shabby-chic bar and nightclub has good-value drinks, friendly staff, a cool crowd and funky DJs. It's open seven days a week until late.

Café de l'Industrie
MAP H4 ■ 16 Rue St-Sabin, 75011

A fashionable and sizable café that has three rooms where the walls are lined with paintings and old-fashioned artifacts. The food is inexpensive but pretty good, and the later it gets the better the buzz.

Grazie
MAP H4 ■ 91 Blvd Beaumarchais, 75003 ■ 01 42 78 11 96

An Italian pizzeria with an industrial loft-style decor, Grazie serves authentic pizzas and classy cocktails, and attracts a hip crowd.

Le Panic Room
MAP H4 ■ 101 Rue Amelot, 75011

Top Parisian DJs set the tone at this quirky bar offering fancy cocktails, a smoking room and cellar dance floor.

⑨ Le Square Trousseau
MAP H5 ■ 1 Rue Antoine Vollon, 75012

This charming Bastille district brasserie, with its lovely heated terrace, is something of a media haunt, serving good food from breakfast into the early hours.

⑩ Le Progrès
MAP R2 ■ 1 Rue de Bretagne, 75003 ■ 01 42 72 01 44

The terrace of this corner café in the trendy Upper Marais is the place to be during Paris Fashion Week.

① Andy Wahloo
MAP Q1 ■ 69 Rue des Gravilliers, 75003

In one of Henri IV's former mansions, pop art and North African decor form a backdrop for some of the city's most fashionable soirées.

② Zéro Zéro
MAP H4 ■ 89 Rue Amelot, 75011

It doesn't get much cooler than this den-like bar with wood panelling and flowered wallpaper. Though not listed on the menu, cocktails are a speciality.

③ La Perle
MAP Q2 ■ 78 Rue Vieille du Temple, 75003 ■ 01 42 72 69 93

This bistro is one of Paris's most famous hang-outs. Its straightforward menu draws a fashionable crowd in the evenings.

④ La Caféothèque de Paris
MAP P4 ■ 52 Rue de l'Hôtel de Ville, 75004

Coffee enthusiasts congregate at this coffee roaster located behind

Places to Eat

 L'Ambroisie
MAP R3 ▪ 9 Pl des Vosges,
75004 ▪ 01 42 78 51 45 ▪ Closed
Sun, Mon ▪ €€€

The finest service matches the finest
of food and wine. The chocolate tart
is out of this world. Reserve ahead.

2 Marché des Enfants Rouges
MAP R1 ▪ 39 Rue de Bretagne,
75003 ▪ Closed Mon ▪ €

Food from Morocco to the Caribbean
is available at this old covered market.
It gets crowded at weekends but is
perfect for lunch during the week.

3 Carette
MAP G4 ▪ 25 Pl des Vosges,
75003 ▪ 01 48 87 94 07 ▪ €€

Salads and sandwiches, as well
as delicious cakes, feature at this
lovely patisserie and tea room
on the picturesque Place des
Vosges (see p69).

4 Chez Paul
MAP H5 ▪ 13 Rue de Charonne,
75011 ▪ 01 47 00 34 57 ▪ €€

An old-style bistro with a simple
but delicious menu and excellent
wine list. Reserve your table ahead.

Interior of Chez Paul

PRICE CATEGORIES
For a three-course meal for one with half
a bottle of wine (or equivalent meal),
taxes and extra charges
....
€ under €30   €€ €30–€50   €€€ over €50

5 Le Clown Bar
MAP H4 ▪ 114 Rue Amelot,
75011 ▪ 01 43 55 87 35 ▪ Closed
Mon & Tue ▪ €€€

Inventive dishes and natural wines
served in a circus-themed, Art
Nouveau setting. Try the meaty
pithiviers (pies).

6 Breizh Café
MAP G4 ▪ 109 Rue Vieille du
Temple, 75003 ▪ 01 42 72 13 77 ▪ €€

An award-winning crêperie offering
savoury and sweet Breton pancakes.
The selection of buckwheat galettes
includes daily specials.

7 Le Baron Rouge
MAP H5 ▪ 1 Rue Théophile
Roussel, 75012 ▪ 01 43 43 14 32
▪ Closed Mon ▪ €

Cold meats, cheeses and oysters
are served in an authentic setting
next to Marché d'Aligre (see p71).

8 Le Temps de Cerises
MAP R4 ▪ 31 Rue de la Cerisaie,
75004 ▪ 01 42 72 08 63 ▪ €€

One of the oldest restaurants in Paris,
serving bacon-wrapped scallops,
escargot and a selection of desserts.

9 Septime
MAP H5 ▪ 80 Rue de Charonne,
75011 ▪ 01 43 67 38 29 ▪ €€€

Dishes such as cress and sorrel
risotto and veal tartare are served at
this modern restaurant. Book ahead.

10 L'As du Fallafel
MAP Q3 ▪ 34 Rue des Rosiers,
75004 ▪ 01 48 87 63 60 ▪ Closed Fri D,
Sat ▪ €

This is one of the best falafel joints
in the city. The special with aubergine and spicy sauce is a must.

See map on pp92–3

🔟 Tuileries and Opéra Quarters

These two quarters were once the province of the rich and the royal, and there's still an air of luxury about them. Adjoining the lovely Tuileries Gardens is the largest museum in the world, the Louvre, while the grand Opera House gives the second quarter its name. The Place de la Concorde is one of the most historic sites in the city.

**Statue of Medea,
Jardin des Tuileries**

TUILERIES AND OPERA QUARTERS

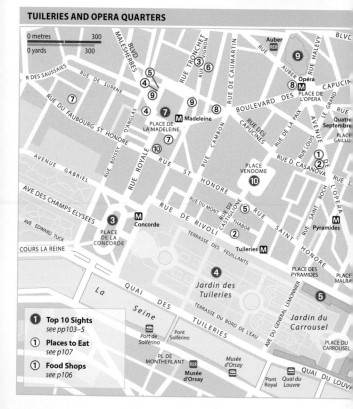

0 metres 300
0 yards 300

R DES SAUSSAIES
RUE DE SURENE
BLVD MALESHERBES
RUE DU FAUBOURG ST HONORE
RUE TRONCHET
RUE VIGNON
RUE DE CAUMARTIN
Auber RER
RUE AUBER
Opéra M
RUE HALEVY
BLVD

⑦ ⑤ ④ ⑨ ③ ⑥ ⑨ ⑧ ⑨ ⑧

PLACE DE L'OPERA
CAPUCIN
BOULEVARD DES CAPUCINES
RUE DE LA PAIX
Quatre
Septembre
PLACE
GAILLO

④ ⑦ M Madeleine
PLACE DE LA MADELEINE
RUE CAMBON
RUE DES CAPUCINES
RUE LOUIS LE GRAND
⑦ ⑩

AVENUE GABRIEL
RUE BOISSY D'ANGLAS
RUE ROYALE
RUE ST HONORE
PLACE VENDOME
⑩
RUE D. CASANOVA
① ②
RUE DE L'OPERA
RUE L

AVE DES CHAMPS ELYSEES
AVE EDWARD TUCK
COURS LA REINE
③ PLACE DE LA CONCORDE
M Concorde
RUE DE RIVOLI
RUE DU MONT
RUE DE CASTIGLIONE
RUE THABOR
⑤
TERRASSE DES FEUILLANTS
② Tuileries M
RUE SAINT ROCH
M Pyramides
SAINT HONORE
PLACE DES PYRAMIDES
PLACE MALRA

La Seine
QUAI DES TUILERIES
TERRASSE DU BORD DE L'EAU
④ Jardin des Tuileries
AVE DU GENERAL LEMONNIER
⑤ Jardin du Carrousel
PLACE DU CARROUSEL

Port de Solférino
Pont Solférino
PL DE MONTHERLANT
RER
Musée d'Orsay
Musée d'Orsay
Pont Royal
Quai du Louvre
QUAI DU LOUV

① **Top 10 Sights**
see pp103–5

① **Places to Eat**
see p107

① **Food Shops**
see p106

1 Musée du Louvre
See pp12–15.

2 Rue de Rivoli
MAP M2

Commissioned by Napoleon and named for his victory over the Austrians at Rivoli in 1797, this grand street links the Louvre with the Champs-Elysées *(see p111)*. It was intended as a backdrop for his victory marches but was not finished until the 1850s, long after the emperor's death. Along one side, railings replaced the old Tuileries walls, opening up the view, while opposite, Neo-Classical apartments sit atop the long arcades. These are now lined with a mix of shops that sell everything from luxury goods to tourist souvenirs.

Obelisk in Place de la Concorde

3 Place de la Concorde
MAP D3

This historic octagonal square, covering more than 8 ha (20 acres), was built between 1755 and 1775 as the grand setting for a statue of Louis XV; by 1792 it had become the Place de la Révolution and its central monument was the guillotine. Louis XVI, Marie-Antoinette and more than 1,000 others were executed here *(see p43)*. In 1795, in the spirit of reconciliation, it received its present name. The central obelisk, 23 m (75 ft) tall and covered in hieroglyphics, is from a 3,300-year-old Luxor temple, and was a gift from Egypt, erected in 1833. Two fountains and eight statues represent French cities. On the north side of the square are the Hôtel de la Marine and Hôtel Crillon.

4 Jardin des Tuileries
MAP J2

These gardens *(see p56)* were first laid out as part of the old Tuileries Palace, which was built for Catherine de Médicis in 1564 but burned down in 1871. André Le Nôtre redesigned them into formal French gardens in 1664. At the Louvre end is the Arc de Triomphe du Carrousel, erected by Napoleon in 1808. Also here is the entrance to an underground shopping centre, the Carrousel du Louvre. Nearby, sensuous nude sculptures by Aristide Maillol (1861–1944) adorn the ornamental pools and walkways. At the far end are the Jeu de Paume gallery *(see p53)* and the Musée de l'Orangerie *(see p52)*, famous for its giant canvases of Monet waterlilies.

STORMING OF THE TUILERIES

Visiting the Tuileries Gardens now, where children play and lovers stroll, it is hard to imagine the scenes that took place here on 20 June 1792. The palace and gardens were invaded by French citizens seeking to overthrow the monarchy. This was finally achieved on 10 August, when the Tuileries Palace was sacked and Louis XVI overthrown.

5 Musée des Arts Décoratifs

MAP M2 ▪ 107 Rue de Rivoli, 75001 ▪ Open 11am–6pm Tue–Sun (to 9pm Thu for temporary exhibitions) ▪ Adm ▪ www.madparis.fr

This huge collection covers the decorative arts from the Middle Ages to the 20th century. With over 100 rooms, its many highlights include the Medieval and Renaissance galleries, the Art Deco rooms and a superb jewellery collection. There are also displays of fashion, textiles, posters and advertising ephemera showcased in permanent and temporary exhibitions.

6 Galerie Vivienne and Galerie Colbert

MAP E3 ▪ Galerie Vivienne: 4 Rue des Petits Champs, 75002; Galerie Colbert: 4 Rue Vivienne, 75002 ▪ Galerie Vivienne: open 8:30am–8:30pm daily; Galerie Colbert: open 9am–8pm daily

These two 19th-century covered arcades are arguably the most beautiful of the few remaining passages. Built to rival each other, both feature frescoed floors and elegant lighting fixtures that entrall visitors. Today, they house shops, cafés and classes for students at the University of Paris.

7 Place de la Madeleine
MAP D3

Surrounded by 52 Corinthian columns, the Classical-style Madeleine church (see p48) commands this elegant square (see p70). On the east side a colourful flower market takes place from Monday to Saturday. Around the square are some of the most upmarket *épiceries* (food stores) and speciality shops in the city.

8 Palais-Royal

MAP L1 ▪ 8 Rue Montpensier, 75001 ▪ Open Oct–Mar: 7am–8:30pm daily (Apr–May: to 10:15pm daily, Jun–Aug: to 11pm daily, Sep: to 9:30pm daily) ▪ Public access to gardens & arcades only

In the late 18th century extensive changes were made under the dukes of Orléans. The architect Victor Louis was commissioned to build 60 uniformly styled houses around three sides of the square and the adjacent theatre, which now houses the Comédie-Française (see p65). Today the arcades house specialist shops, galleries and restaurants, and the courtyard and gardens contain modern works of art (see p45).

9 Opéra National de Paris Garnier

MAP E2 ▪ Pl de l'Opéra, 75009 ▪ 01 71 25 24 23 ▪ Open 10am–6pm daily for pre-booked, timed slots (to 2:30pm on days of matinee performances and public hols) ▪ Adm ▪ www.operadeparis.fr

Designed by Charles Garnier for Napoleon III in 1862, Paris's opulent opera house took 13 years to complete. A range of styles from Classical to Baroque incorporates stone friezes and columns, statues

Place Vendôme and Vendôme column

Performance at Opéra Garnier

and a green copper cupola. The ornate interior has a grand staircase, mosaic domed ceiling over the grand foyer and an auditorium with a ceiling by Marc Chagall. There's even an underground lake – the inspiration for Gaston Leroux's *Phantom of the Opera* – sadly closed to visitors *(see p64)*.

 Place Vendôme
MAP E3

Jules Hardouin-Mansart, the architect of Versailles *(see p155)*, designed the façades of this elegant royal square for Louis XIV in 1698. It was originally intended for foreign embassies, but bankers soon moved in and built lavish dwellings. It remains home to jewellers and financiers today. The world-famous Ritz hotel was established here at the turn of the 20th century. The column, topped by a statue of Napoleon, is a replica of the one destroyed by the Commune in 1871.

A DAY IN THE TUILERIES

▶ **MORNING**

Visiting the **Louvre** *(see pp12–15)* takes planning, and you should pre-book a timed entry slot online or in person at the ticket desk. Pick up a map as you enter so that you can be sure to see the main highlights. Enjoy a morning coffee in an elegant café in the Richelieu or Denon wings within the museum.

From the Louvre, either take a quick detour to Buren's columns in the **Jardin du Palais-Royal** *(see p56)* or stroll west along **Rue de Rivoli** *(see p103)*. Turn right onto Rue Rouget de Lisle and walk to the bottom to reach **Da Rosa**, a creative little bistro *(19 bis Rue du Mont Thabor; 01 77 37 37 87; open 11am–11:30pm daily)*.

AFTERNOON

Get some fresh air in the **Jardin des Tuileries** *(see p103)* then walk down to **Place de la Madeleine** to spend the afternoon browsing in its many gourmet stores, or visit the **Galerie Vivienne** and **Galerie Colbert**. Later, take tea in the café of one of the best shops, **Fauchon** *(see p106)*.

Walk down through **Place de la Concorde** *(see p103)* towards the 18th-century **Pont de la Concorde** to take in the views over the Seine. Look west towards the **Eiffel Tower** *(see pp24–5)* to catch a spectacular sunset panorama. Finish the day with a gastronomic dinner at two-Michelin-starred **Le Meurice** *(see p107)*.

See map on pp102–3

Food Shops

The chic Pierre Hermé café

1 Pierre Hermé
MAP E3 ■ 39 Ave de l'Opéra, 75002

Follow the rainbow of exquisite macarons in classic and more intriguing flavours at this shop.

2 Cedric Grolet Opéra
MAP E3 ■ 35 Ave de l'Opéra, 75002

Award-winning *pâtissier* Cedric Grolet's stunning cakes and fruit tarts appear as art against the minimalist decor of his shop.

3 Marquise de Sévigné
MAP D3 ■ 16 Rue Tronchet, 75008

Chocolates and *dragées* (sugar-coated almonds) are the speciality at this haven for those with a sweet tooth.

4 Caviar Kaspia
MAP D3 ■ 17 Pl de la Madeleine, 75008

The peak of indulgence. Choose from caviars from around the world, plus smoked eel, salmon and other fishy fare, along with a wide range of vodkas. Try an amazing baked potato with caviar in the upstairs dining room.

5 La Maison de la Truffe
MAP D3 ■ 19 Pl de la Madeleine, 75008

France's finest black truffles are sold here during the winter. Preserved truffles and other delicacies can be savoured in the shop or at home.

6 La Maison du Miel
MAP D3 ■ 24 Rue Vignon, 75009

The "house of honey", family-owned since 1908, is the place to try speciality honeys, to spread on your toast or your body in the form of soaps and oils.

7 Maille
MAP D3 ■ 6 Pl de la Madeleine, 75008

The retail outlet for one of France's finest mustard-makers. Fresh mustard is served in lovely ceramic jars and seasonal limited-edition mustards are also available.

8 La Maison du Chocolat
MAP E3 ■ 8 Blvd de la Madeleine, 75009

Fauchon biscuit tin

A superb chocolate shop, which offers fine chocolates and exquisite patisserie including eclairs, tarts and mouthwatering macarons.

9 Fauchon
MAP D3 ■ 11, 24–30 Pl de la Madeleine, 75008

The king of Parisian *épiceries* (grocers). The mouthwatering window displays are works of art and tempt you inside for pastries, exotic fruits and some 3,500 other items.

10 Ladurée
MAP D3 ■ 16 Rue Royale, 75008

This splendid *belle époque* tea salon has been serving some of the best macarons in Paris since 1862.

Places to Eat

 Café Marly
MAP E4 ▪ 93 Rue de Rivoli, 75001 ▪ 01 49 26 06 60 ▪ €€

Set in one of Paris's most enchanting locations, this brasserie (see p68) overlooks the glass pyramid of the Louvre. The menu is creative and irresistible.

2 Le Meurice
MAP E3 ▪ 228 Rue de Rivoli, 75001 ▪ 01 44 58 10 55 ▪ Closed Sat, Sun, Aug ▪ €€€

Try exquisite dishes with pure flavours at Alain Ducasse's splendid two-Michelin-starred venue.

3 Le Grand Véfour
MAP E3 ▪ 17 Rue de Beaujolais, 75001 ▪ 01 42 96 56 27 ▪ Closed Sat, Sun, Aug, some of Dec ▪ €€€

Guy Martin's beautiful 18th-century restaurant has two Michelin stars and is a gourmet treat.

4 Lucas Carton
MAP D3 ▪ 9 Pl de la Madeleine, 75008 ▪ 01 42 65 22 90 ▪ Closed Sun, Aug, public hols ▪ €€€

Chef Julien Dumas takes the reins at one of Paris's oldest gourmet restaurants. Superb quality food.

5 Café Castiglione
MAP E3 ▪ 235 Rue St-Honoré, 75001 ▪ 01 42 60 68 22 ▪ €€

The burgers at this classic brasserie are so popular that even the style gurus of Fashion Week will indulge.

The elegant Café Castiglione

PRICE CATEGORIES

For a three-course meal for one with half a bottle of wine (or equivalent meal), taxes and extra charges

€ under €30 €€ €30–€50 €€€ over €50

---

6 Kunitoraya
MAP E3 ▪ 1 Rue Villedo, 75001 ▪ 01 47 03 33 65 ▪ Closed Wed ▪ €

There's often a queue at this bustling udon bar serving perfect noodles in a rich broth. A larger sister restaurant is along the road at No. 5.

7 Jean-François Piège – Le Grand Restaurant
MAP D3 ▪ 7 Rue Aguesseau, 75008 ▪ 01 53 05 00 00 ▪ €€€

Located in an elite area, this chic restaurant (see p66) with striking and elegant interiors provides modern French cuisine.

8 Cafe de la Paix
MAP E3 ▪ 5 Pl de l'Opéra, 75009 ▪ 01 40 07 36 36 ▪ €€€

Step back in time at this stunning gourmet restaurant (see p68), which first opened its doors in 1862. The café boasts a beautiful frescoed interior and the menu concentrates on seasonal produce.

9 Restaurant du Palais Royal
MAP E3 ▪ 110 Galerie de Valois, 75001 ▪ 01 40 20 00 27 ▪ Closed Sun, Mon ▪ €€€

Contemporary French food is served in the bucolic setting of the Palais-Royal gardens (see p57).

10 Verjus
MAP E3 ▪ 52 Rue de Richelieu, 75001 ▪ 01 42 97 54 40 ▪ Closed Sat, Sun ▪ €€€

You need to book in advance for the set six-course gourmet dinner in the intimate dining room, but you can simply turn up to enjoy a lighter bite in the wine bar (47 Rue Montpensier), which doesn't accept bookings.

See map on pp102–3 ←

TOP 10 Champs-Elysées Quarter

The Champs-Elysées is the most famous street in Paris and the quarter that lies around it radiates wealth and power. It is home to the president of France, embassies and *haute couture* fashion houses, as well as five-star hotels and fine restaurants. The Champs-Elysées runs from Place de la Concorde to Place Charles de Gaulle, and it's here that France celebrates national events or mourns at the funeral cortèges of the great and good.

Petit Palais

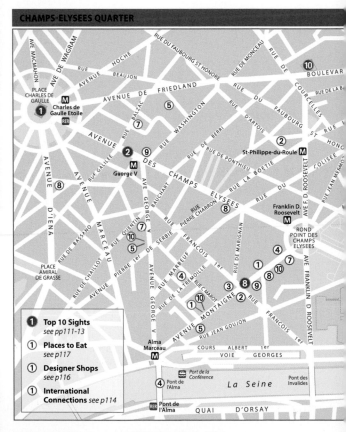

CHAMPS-ELYSEES QUARTER

1 **Top 10 Sights**
see pp111–13

1 **Places to Eat**
see p117

1 **Designer Shops**
see p116

1 **International Connections** see p114

Previous pages The Louvre viewed from the Jardin des Tuileries

1 Arc de Triomphe
See pp30–31.

2 Avenue des Champs-Elysées
MAP C3

One of the most famous avenues in the world came into being when the royal gardener André Le Nôtre planted an arbour of trees beyond the border of the Jardin des Tuileries *(see p103)* in 1667. First called the Grand Cours (Great Way), it was later renamed after the Elysian Fields. In the mid-19th century it acquired pedestrian paths, fountains, gas lights and cafés, and became a fashionable place for socializing and entertainment. Since the funeral of Napoleon in 1840, it has

Avenue des Champs-Elysées

been the route for state processions, victory parades and other city events. The Rond-Point des Champs-Elysées is the prettiest part, with chestnut trees and flowerbeds. Today, the avenue has a car-free day on the first Sunday of every month, allowing visitors to experience it without any traffic. A walk along this thoroughfare is an essential Paris experience.

3 Grand Palais
MAP D3 ▪ **3 Ave du Général-Eisenhower, 75008** ▪ **01 44 13 17 17** ▪ **Closed for renovations until 2024** ▪ **www.grandpalais.fr**

This immense *belle époque* exhibition hall was built for the Universal Exhibition in 1900. Its splendid glass roof is a landmark of the Champs-Elysées. The façade is a mix of Art Nouveau ironwork, Neo-Classical stone columns and a mosaic frieze, with bronze horses and chariots at the four corners of the roof. The Galleries du Grand Palais host temporary art exhibitions.

4 Pont Alexandre III
MAP D3

Built for the 1900 Universal Exhibition to carry visitors over the Seine to the Grand and Petit Palais, this bridge *(see p55)* is a superb example of the steel architecture and ornate Art Nouveau style popular at the time. Named after Alexander III of Russia, who laid the foundation stone, its decoration displays both Russian and French heraldry. The bridge creates a splendid thoroughfare from the Champs-Elysées to the Hôtel des Invalides.

The imposing Petit Palais

5 Petit Palais

MAP D3 ▪ Ave Winston Churchill, 75008 ▪ 01 53 43 40 00 ▪ Open 10am–6pm Tue–Sun (to 9pm Fri for temporary exhibitions) ▪ Closed 1 Jan, 1 May, 14 Jul, 25 Dec ▪ www.petitpalais.paris.fr

The "little palace" echoes its iconic neighbour, the Grand Palais, in style. It is graced with Ionic columns and a dome. The palace was initially built for the Exposition Universelle in 1900, but now it houses the Musée des Beaux Arts de la Ville de Paris *(see p72)*. The wing close to the river is used for temporary exhibitions, while the Champs-Elysées side of the palace houses the permanent collections featuring Greek and Roman artifacts, medieval and Renaissance clocks and jewellery, and furniture from the 17th, 18th and 19th centuries.

6 Place Charles de Gaulle

MAP C3 ▪ Ave des Champs-Elysées, 75008

Known as the Place de l'Etoile until the death of Charles de Gaulle in 1969, the area is still referred to simply as l'Etoile, "the star". The present *place* was laid out in accordance with Baron Haussmann's plans of 1854. For motorists, it is the ultimate challenge, as traffic laws don't really apply here.

7 Rue du Faubourg St-Honoré

MAP D3

Running parallel to the Champs-Elysées, this is Paris's equivalent of fashionable Fifth Avenue, Bond Street or Rodeo Drive. From Saint Laurent and Givenchy to Gucci and Hermès, the shopfronts read like a *Who's Who* of fashion. Even if the prices may be out of reach, window-shopping is fun. There are also elegant antiques and art galleries. Look out for swallows that nest on many of the 19th-century façades.

8 Avenue Montaigne

MAP C3

In the 19th century the Avenue Montaigne was a nightlife hotspot. Parisians danced the night away at the Mabille Dance Hall until it closed in 1870 and Adolphe Sax made music with his newly invented saxophone in the Winter Garden. Today this chic avenue is the most fashionable street and a rival to the Rue du Faubourg St-Honoré as it is home to more *haute couture* houses, such as Christian Dior and Valentino. There are also luxury hotels, top restaurants, popular cafés, and the Comédie des Champs-Elysées and Théâtre des Champs-Elysées.

LA MARSEILLAISE

The stirring French national anthem was written in 1792 by a French army engineer named Claude Joseph Rouget de Lisle. He lived for a time in this district, at 15 Rue du Faubourg St-Honoré. The rousing song got its name due to being sung by the troops from Marseille who were prominent in the storming of the Tuileries during the Revolution *(see p43)*.

⑨ Palais de l'Elysée

MAP D3 ▪ 55 Rue du Faubourg St-Honoré, 75008 ▪ Closed to the public

Built in 1718, after the Revolution this elegant palace *(see p47)* was turned into a dance hall, then, in the 19th century, became the residence of Napoleon's sister Caroline Murat, followed by his wife Empress Josephine. His nephew, Napoleon III, also lived here while plotting his 1851 coup. Since 1873 it has been the home of the president of France. For this reason, it is worth noting that the palace guards don't like people getting too close to the building.

Musée Jacquemart-André

⑩ Musée Jacquemart-André

MAP C2 ▪ 158 Blvd Haussmann, 75008 ▪ 01 45 62 11 59 ▪ Open 10am–6pm daily (to 8:30pm Mon for temporary exhibits) ▪ Adm ▪ www.musee-jacquemart-andre.com

This fine display of art and furniture, once belonging to avid collectors Edouard André and his wife Nélie Jacquemart, is housed in a late-19th-century mansion. It is best known for its Italian Renaissance works, including frescoes by Tiepolo and Paolo Uccello's *St George and the Dragon* (c.1435). The reception rooms feature the art of the 18th-century "Ecole française", with paintings by François Boucher and Jean-Honoré Fragonard. A charming period tearoom overlooks the gardens.

A DAY OF SHOPPING

Arc de Triomphe
Avenue des Champs Elysées
Prince de Galles
Le Cinq
1 km (0.5 miles)
Ladurée
Avenue Georges V
Avenue Montaigne
Grand Palais
Bar des Théâtres

▶ MORNING

The Champs-Elysées quarter is a good area for leisurely walks. Start the morning strolling the grounds of the belle époque **Grand Palais** *(see p111)*. The galleries host excellent exhibitions.

Make your way to the **Avenue Montaigne** for exquisite window-shopping – Prada and Dior, among others, have their flagship stores here. Take a break in the **Bar des Théâtres** *(44 Rue Jean Goujon; 01 45 62 04 91; closed Sun D)*, where fashion names and the theatre crowd from the Comédie des Champs-Elysées hang out.

Call ahead for a table at **Le Cinq** *(see p117)* to splurge on lunch, and head up the elegant **Avenue Georges V**, which is lined with luxury boutiques including Armani and Kenzo, and grande-dame hotels such as legendary **Prince de Galles** *(see p173)*.

AFTERNOON

Walk to and along the **Champs Elysées** *(see p111)*, with French chanteur Joe Dassin's jaunty 1969 tune in mind. The flagship stores of lots of high-end brands are here, along with luxury car showrooms and fast-food outlets – housed in some notable buildings.

For tea and cakes en route, **Ladurée** *(see p106)* is a wonderfully elegant experience.

Take the underpass to the **Arc de Triomphe** *(see pp30–31)* and climb to the top to admire Baron Haussmann's star-shaped town grid and other views, which are superb at dusk when the avenues light up.

See map on pp110–11

International Connections

1 Avenue de Marigny
MAP C3

American author John Steinbeck lived here for five months in 1954 and described Parisians as "the luckiest people in the world".

2 8 Rue Artois
MAP C2

Here, in September 2001, legendary Belgian mobster François Vanverbergh – godfather of the French Connection gang – fell victim to a drive-by assassin as he took his afternoon mineral water.

3 37 Avenue Montaigne
MAP C3

Having wowed Paris with her comeback performances, iconic German actress and singer Marlene Dietrich spent her reclusive final years in a luxury apartment here.

4 Pont de l'Alma
MAP C3

Diana, Princess of Wales, was killed in an accident in the underpass here in 1997. Her unofficial memorial, the Liberty Flame (see p54) attracts thousands of visitors each year.

5 31 Avenue George V, Hôtel George V
MAP C3

A roll-call of rockers – from the Rolling Stones and Jim Morrison to J-Lo and Madonna – have made this hotel their regular Paris home-from-home.

Hôtel George V

Marcel Proust

6 102 Boulevard Haussmann
MAP D2

Hypochondriac author Marcel Proust lived in a cork-lined room (on display in the Musée Carnavalet, see p94), turning memories into a masterpiece – In Search of Lost Time.

7 37 Avenue George V
MAP C3

Franklin D. Roosevelt and his new bride Eleanor visited his aunt's apartment here in 1905. He was later commemorated in the name of a nearby avenue.

8 49 Avenue des Champs-Elysées
MAP C3

Author Charles Dickens may well have had "the best of times and the worst of times" when he resided here during the winter of 1855–6. Ten years earlier he had also lived at 38 Rue de Courcelles.

9 114 Avenue des Champs-Elysées
MAP C2

Brazilian aviation pioneer Alberto Santos-Dumont planned many of his amazing aeronautical feats – notably that of circling the Eiffel Tower in an airship in 1901 – from this address.

10 Hôtel Elysée-Palace
MAP C3

Mata Hari, the Dutch spy and exotic dancer, set up her lair in Room 113 before finally being arrested outside 25 Avenue Montaigne.

Events on the Champs-Elysées

 1616
Paris's grand avenue was first laid out when Marie de Médicis, wife of Henri IV, had a carriage route, the Cours-la-Reine (Queen's Way), constructed through the marshland along the Seine.

2 1667
Landscape gardener Le Nôtre lengthened the Jardin des Tuileries to meet the Cours-la-Reine, and opened up the view with a double row of chestnut trees, creating the Grand Cours.

 1709
The avenue was renamed the Champs-Elysées (Elysian Fields). In Greek mythology, the Elysian Fields were the "place of ideal happiness", the abode of the blessed after death.

4 1724
The Duke of Antin, overseer of the royal gardens, extended the avenue to the heights of Chaillot, the present site of the Arc de Triomphe *(see pp30–31)*.

5 26 August 1944
Parisians celebrated the liberation of the city from Nazi Occupation with triumphant processions and festivities.

 30 May 1968
The infamous demonstrations of May 1968, when student protests against state authority spilled over into massive gatherings and riots. De Gaulle and his supporters held a huge counter-demonstration on the Champs-Elysées, marking a turning point in the uprising.

7 12 November 1970
The death of President Charles de Gaulle was an immense event in France, as he had been a dominant French political figure for 30 years. He was honoured by a silent parade along the Champs-Elysées.

 14 July 1989
The parade on Bastille Day marking the bicentennial of the Revolution was a dazzling display of folk culture and avant-garde theatre. It was a distinct change from the usual military events, and was organized by Mitterand's Culture Minister, Jack Lang.

9 8 May 2016
In a series of environmentally friendly measures, the mayor of Paris decreed that the Champs-Elysées would be car-free on the first Sunday of each month, starting May 2016. This also allows pedestrians to experience the beautiful avenue without traffic.

Traffic-free Arc de Triomphe

 15 July 2018
 Exactly 20 years after France's first World Cup victory in 1998, Les Bleus brought the trophy back home. To mark the day thousands of fans thronged the streets to celebrate France winning the cup, echoing its previous victory.

See map on pp110–11

Designer Shops

Chanel boutique window

1 Chanel
MAP C3 ■ 51 Ave Montaigne, 75008

Chanel classics, from the braided tweed jackets to two-toned shoes, as well as Lagerfeld's more daring designs, are displayed in this branch of the main rue Cambon store.

2 Christian Dior
MAP C3 ■ 30–32 Ave Montaigne, 75008

The grey and white decor, with silk bows on chairs, makes a chic backdrop for fashions from lingerie to evening wear.

3 Givenchy
MAP C3 ■ 28 Rue du Faubourg St-Honoré, 75008

This famous fashion house has been synonymous with Parisian style since the 1930s. Shop for women's and men's ready-to-wear outfits here.

4 Balenciaga
MAP C3 ■ 57 Ave Montaigne, 75008

This world-famous label is known for its modern creations, which are now designed by Demna Gvasalia.

5 Prada
MAP C3 ■ 10 Ave Montaigne, 75008

The iconic Italian designer's stylish boutique displays clothes and accessories from the latest collection.

6 Hermès
MAP C3 ■ 24 Rue du Faubourg St-Honoré, 75008

For timeless chic apparel, handbags and accessories head to this well-known luxury brand. Shop for beautiful silk scarves here.

7 Jil Sander
MAP C3 ■ 56 Ave Montaigne, 75008

A minimal and modern store, just like the clothes it sells. Sander's trouser suits, cashmere dresses and overcoats in neutral colours are displayed on two floors.

8 Chloé
MAP C3 ■ 50 Ave Montaigne, 75008

Simple, classy, ready-to-wear designer women's clothes and accessories are sold in this minimalist temple to feminine chic.

9 Eres
MAP C3 ■ 40 Ave Montaigne, 75008

A range of luxury but understated swimwear and lingerie, in subtle colours, is beautifully displayed in this elegant boutique. Everything has a certain Parisian sensuality.

10 Barbara Bui
MAP C3 ■ 50 Ave Montaigne, 75008

High-end Parisian fashion designer Barbara Bui has been creating elegant womenswear and accessories since the 1980s. Her collection is made from colourful, luxury fabrics.

Barbara Bui bag

Places to Eat

PRICE CATEGORIES

For a three-course meal for one with half a bottle of wine (or equivalent meal), taxes and extra charges

€ under €30   €€ €30–€50   €€€ over €50

① Alain Ducasse au Plaza Athénée

MAP C3 ■ Plaza Athénée, 25 Ave Montaigne, 75008 ■ 01 58 00 22 43 ■ Closed Mon–Wed L, Sat, Sun, Aug, part of Dec ■ €€€

The menu at Alain Ducasse's flagship three-Michelin-starred restaurant *(see p67)* focuses on sustainable fish, cereals and vegetables.

② Le Jardin du Petit Palais

MAP D3 ■ Petit Palais, Ave Winston Churchill, 75008 ■ 01 40 07 11 41 ■ Closed Mon, 1 Jan, 1 May, 14 Jul, 25 Dec ■ €

Take a light lunch in the casual café of the Petit Palais, which opens onto a charming enclosed garden.

③ Honor

MAP D3 ■ 54 Rue du Faubourg St-Honoré, 75008 ■ 07 82 52 93 63 ■ Closed Mon–Sat D, Sun ■ €

A good option for breakfast or a light lunch, this friendly courtyard café has toasted wraps, homemade crumpets and craft coffees.

④ Bellota Bellota

MAP C3 ■ 11 Rue Clément Marot, 75008 ■ 01 47 20 03 13 ■ Closed Sun ■ €

This intimate tapas bar and Spanish deli is a great place for excellent tapas, luxurious carvings of *jamón ibérico* and glasses of Spanish wine.

⑤ Taillevent

MAP C3 ■ 15 Rue Lamennais, 75008 ■ 01 44 95 15 01 ■ Closed Sat, Sun, Aug ■ €€€

One of the city's best dining *(see p66)* experiences. The menu changes often, relying on fresh, seasonal ingredients.

⑥ Epicure

MAP D2 ■ 112 Rue du Faubourg St-Honoré, 75008 ■ 01 53 43 43 40 ■ €€€

In Hôtel Le Bristol's elegant dining room or on the garden terrace, diners can choose from chef Eric Frechon's three-Michelin-starred menu.

Interior of Epicure

⑦ Gagnaire

MAP C3 ■ 6 Rue Balzac, 75008 ■ 01 58 36 12 50 ■ Closed Sat, Sun, Aug, 1 week Dec–Jan ■ €€€

Celebrated for his artistry in blending flavours, Pierre Gagnaire *(see p67)* has three Michelin stars to his name.

⑧ Le 116

MAP B3 ■ 2 Rue Auguste Vacquerie, 75116 ■ 01 47 20 10 45 ■ €€

Wagyu beef burgers and excellent cocktails are on the menu at this off-shoot of the Michelin-starred Pages.

⑨ L'Atelier des Chefs

MAP D2 ■ 10 Rue de Penthièvre, 75008 ■ 01 53 30 05 82 ■ Closed Mon ■ www.atelierdes chefs.fr ■ €

This cooking school offers a range of classes in French and you get to eat the meal you've made after a session.

⑩ Le Cinq

MAP C3 ■ 31 Ave George V, 75008 ■ 01 49 52 71 54 ■ €€€

The George V's *(see p114)* three-Michelin-starred restaurant serves French cuisine with a modern twist.

See map on pp110–11

ᴛᴏᴩ**10** Invalides and Eiffel Tower Quarters

Two of Paris's best-known landmarks, the golden-domed Hôtel des Invalides and the Eiffel Tower, are found in these quarters. Large parts of the district were created in the 19th century, when there was still room to construct wide avenues and grassy esplanades. To the east of Les Invalides are stately mansions, now converted into embassies, and the French parliament. Jean Nouvel's Musée du Quai Branly – Jacques Chirac is a striking feature beside the Seine.

The top of the Eiffel Tower

INVALIDES AND EIFFEL TOWER QUARTERS

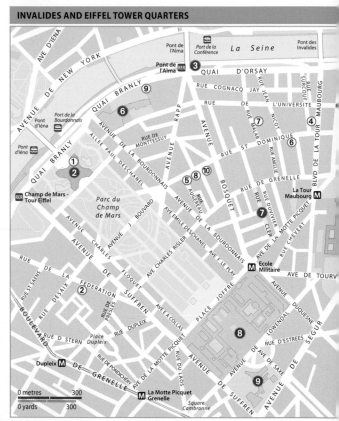

1 **Hôtel des Invalides**
See pp38–9.

2 **Eiffel Tower**
See pp24–5.

3 **Musée des Egouts**
MAP C4 ■ Opposite 93,
Quai d'Orsay, 75007 ■ 01 53 68
27 81 ■ Adm

In a city of glamour and grandeur, the sewers *(égouts)* of Paris are an incongruously popular attraction. They date from the Second Empire (1851–70), when Baron Haussmann was transforming the city *(see p43)*. The sewers, which helped to sanitize and ventilate Paris, are considered one of his finest achievements.

Engineer Eugène Belgrand provided the designs for the ambitious project. The 2,100-km (1,300-mile) network covers the area from Les Halles to La Villette – if laid end-to-end it would stretch from Paris to Istanbul. An hour-long tour includes a walk through some of the tunnels. The museum, which is situated in the sewers beneath the Quai d'Orsay on the Left Bank, tells the story of the city's water and sewers, from their beginnings to the present day through exhibits and an audio-visual show. The museum reopened in 2020 after extensive renovations.

4 **Musée de l'Armée**
MAP C4 ■ Hôtel des Invalides,
75007 ■ Open 10am–6pm daily (to
9pm Tue for temporary exhibitions)
■ Closed 1 Jan, 1 May, 25 Dec ■ Adm

The Army Museum *(see pp38–9)* contains one of the largest and most comprehensive collections of arms, armour and displays on military history in the world, offering a rich and varied visit. The range of weapons on display includes examples from prehistoric times to those used during World War II. Housed in the Hôtel des Invalides, the galleries occupy the old refectories in two wings on either side of the courtyard. The museum's ticket price includes entry to the Musée des Plans-Reliefs, the Historial Charles de Gaulle, the Musée de l'Ordre de la Libération and Napoleon's Tomb.

Courtyard of the Musée de l'Armée

5 Musée Rodin

MAP C4 ■ 77 Rue de Varenne, 75007 ■ Open 10am–6:30pm Tue–Sun ■ Closed 1 Jan, 1 May, 25 Dec ■ Adm ■ www.musee-rodin.fr

An impressive collection of works by Auguste Rodin (1840–1917) is housed in the 18th-century Hôtel Biron *(see p122)*, where the sculptor and artist spent the last nine years of his life. The museum showcases Rodin's preparatory sketches, watercolours, and bronze and marble masterpieces, including *The Kiss* and *Eve*. Exhibits are displayed chronologically and thematically, showing the creative processes behind the artist's finished sculptures – works that arguably paved the way for modern sculpture. The Musée Rodin is also home to the third-largest private garden in Paris, where works such as *The Thinker*, *Monument to Balzac* and *The Gates of Hell* stand amid the lime trees and rose bushes.

6 Musée du Quai Branly – Jacques Chirac

MAP B4 ■ 37 Quai Branly, 75007 ■ Open 10:30am–7pm Tue–Sun (to 10pm Thu) ■ Closed 1 May, 25 Dec ■ Adm ■ www.quaibranly.fr

The purpose of this museum is to showcase the arts of Africa, Asia, Oceania and the Americas. The collection boasts nearly 300,000 artifacts, of which 3,500 are on display, including a fantastic array of African instruments,

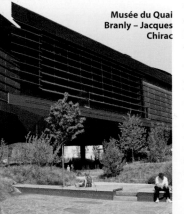

Musée du Quai Branly – Jacques Chirac

YOUNG NAPOLEON

The most famous alumnus of the Ecole Militaire was Napoleon Bonaparte, who was admitted as a cadet, aged 15, in 1784 and was deemed "fit to be an excellent sailor". He graduated as a lieutenant in the artillery, and his passing-out report stated that "he could go far if the circumstances are right". The rest, as they say, is history.

Gabonese masks, Aztec statues and 17th- century painted animal hides from North America (once the pride of the French royal family). Designed by Jean Nouvel, the building is an exhibit in itself: glass is ingeniously used to allow the surrounding greenery to act as a natural backdrop to the collection.

7 Rue Cler

MAP C4

The pedestrianized cobblestone road that stretches south of Rue de Grenelle to Avenue de lLa Motte-Picquet is the most exclusive market street in Paris. Here greengrocers, fishmongers, butchers and wine merchants sell top-quality produce to the well-heeled residents of the area. Tear yourself away from the mouthwatering displays of cheeses and pastries, however, to feast your eyes on the Art Nouveau building at No. 23, also home to a pleasant café.

8 Ecole Militaire

MAP C5 ■ 1 Pl Joffre, 75007 ■ Open during Journée de la Patrimoine (Sep) by special permission only (apply in writing)

At the urging of his mistress Madame Pompadour, Louis XV approved the building of the Royal Military Academy in 1751. Its purpose was to educate the sons of impoverished officers. A grand edifice was designed by Jacques-Ange Gabriel, architect of the Place de la Concorde *(see p103)* and the Petit Trianon at Versailles, and completed in 1773. The central pavilion with its quadrangular dome and Corinthian pillars is a splendid example of the French Classical style. An early cadet was Napoleon, whose passing-out report stated that "he could go far if the circumstances are right". The massive complex is still in use as a military school today.

Façade of the Ecole Militaire

9 UNESCO

MAP C5 ▪ 7 Pl de Fontenoy, 75007 ▪ 01 45 68 10 00 ▪ Open by appointment only, book online at www.cultival.fr

The headquarters of the United Nations Educational, Scientific and Cultural Organization (UNESCO) was built in 1958 by an international team of architects from France, Italy and the United States. It is a Y-shaped building of concrete and glass, which showcases 20th-century works by renowned international artists and is well worth a visit. There is a huge mural by Picasso, ceramics by Joan Miró, and a 2nd-century mosaic from El Djem in Tunisia. Outside is a giant mobile by Alexander Calder and a peaceful Japanese garden.

10 Assemblée Nationale

MAP D4 ▪ 126 Rue de l'Université, 75007 ▪ Open for tours only (passport required); advance reservation required, see www.assemblee-nationale.fr

Built for the daughter of Louis XIV in 1722, the Palais-Bourbon has housed the lower house of the French parliament since 1827. The Council of the Five Hundred met here during the Revolution, and it was the head-quarters of the German Occupation during World War II.

A DAY AROUND THE INVALIDES QUARTER

Musée du Quai Branly – Jacques Chirac, Les Ombres

Pont Alexandre III

Eiffel Tower, Le Jules Verne

Les Cocottes

Musée de l'Armée

Hôtel des Invalides

Musée Rodin

▶ MORNING

Begin the day with a visit to the **Musée Rodin**. A magnificent collection of Rodin's works is displayed both indoors, and outside in the attractive garden. Stop for a coffee on the leafy terrace of the garden café.

Alternatively, stroll through the Esplanade des Invalides, with the Hôtel des Invalides (see pp38–9) as a grand backdrop. Pause to watch the *pétanque* players who gather in the shade of the trees along the eastern and western sides. Stop in to see **Napoleon's Tomb** (see p39) and the **Musée de l'Armée** (see p119). Towards the Seine, admire the splendid **Pont Alexandre III** (see p55) before heading towards rue Saint-Dominique for lunch at **Les Cocottes** (see p123), top chef Christian Constant's breezy, informal bistro.

AFTERNOON

After lunch, follow the Rue de l'Université to the **Musée du Quai Branly – Jacques Chirac** and enjoy the fascinating collections of tribal art and superb modern architecture. Café Jacques, located in the museum's gardens, is the perfect place to relish a cup of tea.

Make sure you book ahead for a late afternoon visit to the **Eiffel Tower** (see pp24–5). The views are spectacular at dusk. Splash out on dinner at the world-famous **Le Jules Verne** (see p66) on level 2, or head back to **Musée du Quai Branly – Jacques Chirac's** rooftop restaurant, **Les Ombres** (see p123). Book in advance for both.

See map on pp118–19 ←

Mansions

Façade of the elegant Hôtel Biron

1 Hôtel Biron
Built in 1730, from 1904 this elegant mansion was transformed into state-owned artists' studios. Among its residents was Auguste Rodin (1840–1917). After the sculptor's death the house became the Musée Rodin *(see p120)*.

2 Hôtel de Villeroy
MAP D4 ▪ 78–80 Rue de Varenne, 75007 ▪ Closed to the public
Built in 1724 for Comédie-Française actress Charlotte Desmarnes, this is now the Ministry of Agriculture.

3 Hôtel de Matignon
MAP D4 ▪ 57 Rue de Varenne, 75007 ▪ Closed to the public
One of the most beautiful mansions in the area is now the official residence of the French prime minister.

4 Hôtel de Boisgelin
MAP D4 ▪ 47 Rue de Varenne, 75007 ▪ Call 01 49 54 03 00 for appointment
Built in 1732 by Jean Sylvain Cartaud, this mansion has housed the Italian Embassy since 1938.

5 Hôtel de Gallifet
MAP D4 ▪ 50 Rue de Varenne, 75007 ▪ Galleries: open 10am–1pm, 3–6pm Mon–Fri
This attractive mansion was built between 1776 and 1792 in Classical style. It is now the Italian Cultural Institute.

6 Hôtel d'Estrées
MAP B5 ▪ 79 Rue de Grenelle, 75007 ▪ Closed to the public
Three floors of pilasters feature on the 1713 former Russian embassy. Tsar Nicolas II lived here in 1896. It is now the residence of the Russian ambassador.

7 Hôtel d'Avaray
MAP B5 ▪ 85 Rue de Grenelle, 75007 ▪ Closed to the public
Dating from 1728, this mansion belonged to the Avaray family for nearly 200 years. It is now owned by the Dutch government.

8 Hôtel de Brienne
MAP D4 ▪ 14–16 Rue St Dominique, 75007 ▪ Closed to the public
This mansion houses the Ministry of Defence. Napoleon's mother lived here from 1806 to 1817.

9 Hôtel de Noirmoutiers
MAP B5 ▪ 138–140 Rue de Grenelle, 75007 ▪ Closed to the public
Built in 1724, this was once the army staff headquarters. It now houses ministerial offices.

10 Hôtel de Monaco de Sagan
MAP D4 ▪ 57 Rue St-Dominique, 75007 ▪ Closed to the public
Now the Polish ambassador's house, this 1784 mansion served as the British Embassy until 1825.

Places to Eat

1 Le Jules Verne
MAP B4 ▪ 2nd Level, Eiffel Tower, 75007 ▪ 01 45 55 61 44
▪ €€€

Book a window table for the view and then sit back and enjoy fine food from the kitchen of Frédéric Anton. A reservation is required for dinner.

2 Le Casse-Noix
MAP B5 ▪ 56 Rue de la Fédération, 75015 ▪ 01 45 66 09 01
▪ Closed Sat & Sun ▪ €€

A charming restaurant serving classic desserts such as *île flottante* (a poached meringue "island" floating on a "sea" of vanilla custard).

3 Arpège
MAP D4 ▪ 84 Rue de Varenne, 75007 ▪ 01 47 05 09 06 ▪ Closed Sat & Sun ▪ €€€

Among the best restaurants in the city. Chef Alain Passard produces exquisite food.

4 David Toutain
MAP D4 ▪ 29 Rue Surcouf, 75007 ▪ 01 45 50 11 10 ▪ Closed Sat & Sun ▪ €€€

Awarded two Michelin stars, Chef David Toutain delivers eclectic cuisine that showcases fine seasonal produce and includes vegetarian dishes. The set lunch menu offers good value.

David Toutain interior

5 Café Constant
MAP C4 ▪ 139 Rue St-Dominique, 75007 ▪ 01 47 53 73 34 ▪ Closed Tue, Wed ▪ €€

This classic Parisian establishment serves seasonal, modern French fare popular with locals and tourists alike.

6 Thoumieux
MAP C4 ▪ 79 Rue St-Dominique, 75007 ▪ 01 47 05 79 00
▪ Closed Aug ▪ €€€

Classic brasserie fare, such as tartare of beef and profiteroles, is served in an Art Deco-inspired dining room.

7 L'Ami Jean
MAP C4 ▪ 27 Rue Malar, 75007
▪ 01 47 05 86 89 ▪ Closed Sun & Mon
▪ €€€

Inventive dishes include marinated scallops with ewe's milk cheese.

8 Les Cocottes
MAP C4 ▪ 135 Rue St-Dominique, 75007 ▪ 01 45 50 10 28 ▪ Closed Sun & Mon ▪ €€

Star chef Christian Constant's fun French take on a diner – albeit one that serves lobster bisque.

9 Les Ombres
MAP B4 ▪ 27 Quai Branly, 75007 ▪ 01 47 53 68 00 ▪ €€€

Stylish rooftop restaurant offering fine food. At night it's a great spot for watching the Eiffel Tower twinkle.

10 La Fontaine de Mars
MAP C4 ▪ 129 Rue St-Dominique, 75007 ▪ 01 47 05 46 44 ▪ €€€

The rich, hearty cuisine of southwest France can be found here, such as cassoulet and duck confit.

TOP 10 St-Germain, Latin and Luxembourg Quarters

St-Germain-des-Prés is a synonym for Paris's café society, made famous by the writers and intellectuals who held court here in the first half of the 20th century. The Latin Quarter has been the scholastic centre of Paris for more than 700 years, and continues to buzz with student bookshops, cafés as well as jazz clubs. The area's western border is the bustling Boulevard St-Michel; to the south is the tranquil greenery of the Luxembourg Quarter.

Jardin du Luxembourg

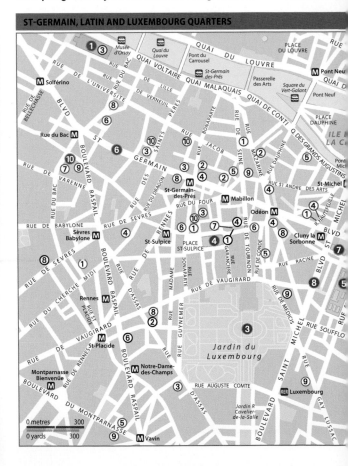

ST-GERMAIN, LATIN AND LUXEMBOURG QUARTERS

Musée d'Orsay
See pp16–19.

 The Panthéon
See pp34–5.

3 Jardin du Luxembourg
MAP L6 ■ Rue de Médicis–Rue
de Vaugirard, 75006 ■ Open dawn–
dusk daily

This 25-ha (60-acre) park (see p56) is
a swathe of green on the very urban
Left Bank. The formal gardens are set
around the Palais du Luxembourg
(see p45), with broad terraces circling
the central octagonal pond. A highlight
of the garden is the beautiful Medici

Palais du Luxembourg

Fountain (see p57). Statues, erected in
the 19th century, include the painter
Eugène Delacroix and St Geneviève,
patron saint of Paris. There is also a
children's playground, open-air café,
a bandstand, tennis courts, a puppet
theatre and a bee-keeping school.

4 St-Sulpice
MAP L5 ■ 2 Rue Palatine,
Pl St-Sulpice, 75006 ■ Open 7:30am–
7:30pm daily

Begun in 1646, this vast church took
134 years to build. Its Classical façade
features a two-tiered colonnade and
two incongruously matched towers.
The two holy water fonts by the front
door are made from huge shells
given to François I by the Venetian
Republic. The restored *Jacob Wrestling
with the Angel* and other fine murals
by Delacroix (1798–1863) are in the
chapel to the right of the main door.

5 La Sorbonne
MAP M5 ■ 1 Rue Victor Cousin,
75005 ■ 01 40 46 23 48 ■ Group tours
only, 10:30am & 2:30pm Mon, Wed–Fri
(advance booking) ■ Adm

This famous university (see p45) was
founded in 1253 as a theology college
for poor students. It soon became
the country's main centre for religious
studies. Philosophers Thomas Aquinas
(c.1226–74) and Roger Bacon (1214–
92) taught here, Italian poet Dante
(1265–1321), founder of the Jesuits
St Ignatius Loyola (1491–1556), and
church reformer John Calvin (1509–
64) are among its list of alumni. Its
tradition for conservatism led to
its closure during the Revolution (it
was reopened by Napoleon in 1806)
and also the student riots of 1968.

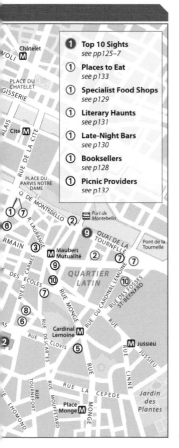

PLACE DU
CHATELET
GISSERIE

Cité **M**

RUE DE LA CITÉ

PLACE DU
PARVIS NOTRE
DAME

Q. DE MONTEBELLO

Pont de
Montebello

RMAIN

QUAI DE LA
TOURNELLE

Pont de la
Tournelle

Maubert
Mutualité **M**

QUARTIER
LATIN

DES CARMES

RUE DES ECOLES

RUE MONGE

RUE DU CARDINAL LEMOINE

RUE DES FOSSES
ST-BERNARD

Cardinal
Lemoine **M**

RUE DESCARTES

RUE CLOVIS

M Jussieu

RUE JUSSIEU

RUE LINNÉ

RUE
TOURNEFORT

RUE LA CEPEDE

Jardin
des
Plantes

Place
Monge **M**

RUE MOUFFETARD

RUE MONGE

LHOMOND

6 Boulevard St-Germain
MAP J3

This famous Left Bank boulevard runs for more than 3 km (2 miles), anchored by the bridges of the Seine at either end. At its heart is the church of St-Germain-des-Prés, established in 542, although the present church dates from the 11th century. Beyond the famous literary cafés, Flore and Les Deux Magots (see p131), the boulevard runs west past galleries, bookshops and designer boutiques

to the Pont de la Concorde. To the east, it cuts across the Latin Quarter, running through the pleasant street market in the place Maubert, to join the Pont de Sully, which connects to the Ile St-Louis (see p80).

7 Musée National du Moyen Age
MAP N5 ■ 28 Rue du Sommerard, 75005 ■ Check website for opening hours ■ Closed 1 Jan, 1 May, 25 Dec ■ Adm ■ www.musee-moyenage.fr

Also known as the Musée de Cluny, this mansion was built by the abbots of Cluny at the end of the 15th century and now houses a magnificent collection of art, from the Gallo-Roman period to the 15th century. It adjoins the ruins of 2nd-century Roman baths (thermes) with their huge vaulted frigidarium (cold bath). Nearby are the 21 carved stone heads of the kings of Judea from Notre-Dame, decapitated during the Revolution. The highlight is the exquisite Lady and the Unicorn tapestry series, representing the five senses (see p50), and the Book of Hours, which shows the Labours of the Months, accompanied by the relevant sign of the zodiac. Since 2016, the museum has been undergoing extensive renovation to modernize the space and improve its accessibility. It is scheduled to reopen to the public in autumn 2021.

Visitors on the fashionable Boulevard St-Germain

8 Boulevard St-Michel
MAP M4

The main drag of the Latin Quarter was created in the late 1860s as part of Baron Haussmann's citywide makeover (see p43), and named after a chapel that once stood near its northern end. It is now lined with lively cafés, clothes shops and restaurants. To the east are rues de la Harpe and de la Huchette, dating back to medieval times. The latter forms an enclave of the city's Greek community, with *souvlaki* stands and Greek restaurants. Place St-Michel was a pivotal spot during the Nazi occupation and in the student riots of 1968. Its huge bronze fountain depicts St Michael slaying Satan.

Statue of St Michael

9 Quai de la Tournelle
MAP P5

From this riverbank, just before the Pont de l'Archevêché, there are lovely views across to Notre-Dame. The main attraction of this and the adjacent Quai de Montebello, however, are the dark-green stalls of the *bouquinistes* (see p128). The Pont de la Tournelle also offers splendid views up and down the Seine.

10 Musée Maillol
MAP J4 ▪ 59–61 Rue de Grenelle, 75007 ▪ Open only for exhibitions: 10:30am–6:30pm daily (to 8:30pm Fri) ▪ www.museemaillol.com

Dina Vierny, who modelled for the artist Aristide Maillol (1861–1944) from the age of 15 to 25, went on to set up this foundation dedicated largely to his works. Located in an 18th-century mansion, it features sculpture, paintings, engravings and terracotta works. The museum puts on two temporary exhibitions per year, highlighting modern and contemporary art in its many forms.

A DAY ON THE LEFT BANK

▶ MORNING

This area is as much about atmosphere as sightseeing, so take time to soak up some of that Left Bank feeling. Begin on the **Quai de la Tournelle**, strolling by the booksellers here and on the adjacent **Quai de Montebello**, which runs parallel to Rue de la Bûcherie, home to **Shakespeare and Company** (see p128).

From here head south down any street away from the river to the busy **Boulevard St-Germain**. Turn right for two famous cafés, **Café de Flore** (see p68) and **Les Deux Magots** (see p131), and stop for a break at either one, joining the locals talking the morning away.

Cut your way south to the Rue de Grenelle and the **Musée Maillol**, a truly delightful, lesser-known museum. Then enjoy lunch at **Dupin** (see p133), a popular bistro that attracts a mix of locals and tourists.

AFTERNOON

Pre-book a timed entry to the **Musée d'Orsay** (see pp16–19) and spend an hour or two browsing the collections. The most popular works on display are those of the Impressionists, on the upper level.

When you've finished exploring the museum, you can rest and enjoy tea and cake in the stylish **Café Campana** (see p17) or, if it's dinner time, walk over to **L'Atelier de Joël Robuchon** (see p133), having booked in advance, to splurge on the Michelin-starred chef's take on modern French cuisine.

See map on pp124–5 ←

Booksellers

Shakespeare and Company

1 Shakespeare and Company
MAP N5 ■ 37 Rue de la Bûcherie, 75005

Bibliophiles spend hours in the rooms and narrow passageways of Paris's renowned English-language bookshop. There are regular author events and readings in English and French. The café next door serves great coffee and cakes.

2 Bouquinistes
MAP N5

The green stalls of the second-hand booksellers (bouquinistes) on the quays of the Left Bank are a landmark. Pore over old postcards, books, posters, comics and sheet music.

3 Musée d'Orsay Bookshop
As well as its wonderful collections, the museum (see pp16–19) has a remarkably large and comprehensive art bookshop.

4 YellowKorner La Hune
MAP L4 ■ 16 Rue de l'Abbaye, 75006

Part gallery, part bookstore, this reincarnation of the St-Germain-des-Prés institution focuses on photography.

5 Gibert Jeune
MAP F5 ■ 5 Pl St-Michel, 27 Quai St-Michel, 75006

A couple of bookshops that sell everything from travel guides and French literature to cookery books and children's stories.

6 Album
MAP L4 ■ 8 Rue Dante, 75005

One of several shops on this street selling a wide range of specialist comic books (big business in France) from Tintin to erotica, as well as related merchandise.

7 Librairie Présence Africaine
MAP P6 ■ 25 bis, Rue des Ecoles, 75005 ■ Closed Aug

A specialist on books about Africa, as the name suggests. It's an excellent information point, too, if you want to find out where to eat African food or hear African music.

8 San Francisco Book Co.
MAP M5 ■ 17 Rue Monsieur le Prince, 75006

This hodge-podge of all genres carries exclusive used English books as well as collectibles and a carefully chosen selection of new titles and classics. If you have books to sell, there is usually a buyer on duty.

9 The Red Wheelbarrow
MAP N5 ■ 9 Rue de Médicis, 75006

French and English language books here range from contemporary literature to gastronomy.

10 Abbey Bookshop
MAP N5 ■ 29 Rue de la Parcheminerie, 75005

This quirky, Canadian-owned shop in the Latin Quarter stocks books in French and English and serves coffee with maple syrup.

Abbey Bookshop

Specialist Food Shops

 Patrick Roger
MAP F5 ▪ 108 Blvd St-Germain, 75006
One of the new generation of *chocolatiers*, Patrick Roger already has legions of fans thanks to his lifelike sculptures and ganache-filled chocolates.

 Henri Le Roux
MAP L4 ▪ 1 Rue de Bourbon le Château, 75006 ▪ Closed Aug
The award-winning *chocolatier* offers his trademark salted butter caramels and other delicacies such as cacao marshmallows.

3 Jean-Paul Hévin
MAP E6 ▪ 3 Rue Vavin, 75006 ▪ Closed Sun, Mon, Aug
Another distinguished *chocolatier* with elegant, minimalist presentation and superb flavour combinations.

4 Poilâne
MAP E5 ▪ 8 Rue du Cherche-Midi, 75006 ▪ Closed Sun
Founded in the 1930s, this tiny, delicious-smelling bakery produces rustic, naturally leavened loaves in a wood-fired oven.

5 La Dernière Goutte
MAP E5 ▪ 6 Rue de Bourbon le Château, 75006
The English-speaking owners of this wine shop, which specializes in bottles from small producers, also run the nearby wine bar Fish La Boissonnerie.

6 Pierre Hermé
MAP L5 ▪ 72 Rue Bonaparte, 75006
This boutique sells some of the city's very finest cakes and pastries, including innovative flavoured macarons.

 Ryst Dupeyron
MAP N5 ▪ 79 Rue du Bac, 75007 ▪ Closed Sun, Mon (am)
The atmospheric Ryst Dupeyron wine shop specializes in fine Bordeaux, rare spirits and vintage Champagne.

 Sadaharu Aoki
MAP E5 ▪ 35 Rue de Vaugirard, 75006 ▪ Closed Mon
Aoki cleverly incorporates Japanese flavours such as yuzu, green tea and black sesame into intoxicating classic French pastries that taste as good as they look.

9 Barthélémy
MAP J4 ▪ 51 Rue de Grenelle, 75007 ▪ Closed Sun & Mon
Gorgeous farmhouse cheeses are piled high in this charming neighbourhood *fromagerie*.

10 Debauve & Gallais
MAP K4 ▪ 30 Rue des Sts-Pères, 75007 ▪ Closed Sun
This exquisite shop dates from 1800, when chocolate was sold for medicinal purposes.

Historic interior of Debauve & Gallais chocolatier

See map on pp124–5

Late-Night Bars

1 Café de la Mairie
MAP K5 ■ 8 Pl St-Sulpice, 75006

This is an old-fashioned Parisian café *(see p69)*, which offers great views of St-Sulpice church from its busy pavement terrace. It is open until 2am daily except Sunday.

2 Prescription Cocktail Club
MAP L4 ■ 23 Rue Mazarine, 75006

The expertly mixed drinks are the main attraction at this chic and hip cocktail bar.

3 Le Comptoir des Canettes – Chez Georges
MAP E5 ■ 11 Rue des Canettes, 75006

Night owls flock to this old-school bar, which has been serving cheap beer and wine since 1952. The vaulted basement holds parties till 2am.

4 Castor Club
MAP M4 ■ 14 Rue Hautefeuille, 75006 ■ Closed Sun, Mon

Clandestine cocktail bar with a great menu and a downstairs section.

5 Le 10 Bar
MAP L5 ■ 10 Rue de l'Odéon, 75006 ■ Closed Sun

This atmospheric sangria bar, with an old jukebox, has been a neighbourhood institution since 1955. Happy hour is 6–8pm.

The Bombardier pub

6 The Bombardier
MAP F5 ■ 2 Pl du Panthéon, 75005

Sip drinks until late at this *franglais* pub, which offers great views of the Panthéon.

7 Compagnie des Vins Surnaturels
MAP E5 ■ 7 Rue Lobineau, 75006

This cosy, candlelit bar has a superb wine list that features several thousand wines. Enjoy a glass with a selection of delicious small plates.

8 Le Piano Vache
MAP N6 ■ 8 Rue Laplace, 75005

Popular with a young crowd, this relaxed, trendy bar, with walls covered in posters, has themed nights dedicated to jazz, rock, punk and pop.

9 Le Bar du Marché
MAP E5 ■ 75 Rue de Seine, 75006

This corner bar, with a popular terrace, appeals to locals and tourists alike, mostly due to its reasonably priced drinks and jovial waiters.

10 O'Neil
MAP E5 ■ 20 Rue des Canettes, 75006

Artisanal beers, from light, bubbly blondes to thick brown ales, are made on the premises of this pub. Don't forget to tuck in to sweet and savoury *flammekuechen* (Alsacien cream-topped pizza), served until midnight.

Interior of Le 10 Bar

Literary Haunts

1 La Palette
MAP L4 ■ 43 Rue de Seine, 75006 ■ Open 7am–2am daily
This café has been patronized by the likes of Henry Miller, Apollinaire and Jacques Prévert.

2 Les Deux Magots
MAP K4 ■ 6 Pl St-Germain-des-Pres, 75006 ■ 01 45 48 55 25 ■ Open 7:30am–1am daily
This was home to the literary and artistic élite of Paris, such as Albert Camus and Picasso (see p68).

3 Café de Flore
MAP K4 ■ 172 Blvd St-Germain, 75006 ■ 01 45 48 55 26 ■ Open 7:30am–1:30am daily
Guillaume Apollinaire founded his literary magazine, *Les Soirées de Paris*, here (see p68) in 1913.

4 Le Procope
MAP L4 ■ 13 Rue de l' Ancienne Comédie, 75006 ■ Open 12pm–midnight daily (to 1am Thu–Sat)
The oldest café in Paris, this was a meeting place for writers such as Voltaire, Balzac and Zola.

5 Le Select
MAP E6 ■ 99 Blvd du Montparnasse, 75006 ■ Open 7am–2am daily (to 3am Fri & Sat)
F. Scott Fitzgerald and Truman Capote are among many American writers who have drunk in this café.

6 Hotel Pont Royal
MAP J3 ■ 5–7 Rue de Montalembert, 75007 ■ Open 11am–midnight daily
Henry Miller drank at the bar here at the time of writing his *Tropic of Capricorn* and *Tropic of Cancer*.

7 Shakespeare and Company
This renowned bookshop (see p128) was once described by novelist Henry Miller as a "wonderland of books".

Beautiful Brasserie Lipp

8 Brasserie Lipp
MAP L4 ■ 151 Blvd St-Germain, 75006 ■ Open 9am–12:45am daily
Ernest Hemingway pays homage to this café in *A Moveable Feast*, and André Gide was also a customer. It sponsors an annual literary prize.

9 La Coupole
MAP E6 ■ 102 Blvd du Montparnasse, 75014 ■ Open 8:30am–midnight (to 11pm Sun & Mon)
This former coal depot became a lavish Art Deco brasserie frequented by Françoise Sagan.

10 Le Petit St-Benoît
MAP K3 ■ 4 Rue St-Benoît, 75006 ■ Open noon–2:30pm & 6:30–10:30pm Mon–Sat
Albert Camus, Simone de Beauvoir and James Joyce once took their daily coffee here.

See map on pp124–5 ←

Picnic Providers

 1 Saint Germain Market

MAP L5 ■ 4–6 Rue Lobineau, 75006 ■ Closed Mon

Find cheeses, charcuterie, foie gras and fresh produce all under one roof in this 19th-century covered market.

 2 Judy Market

MAP K6 ■ 18 Rue de Fleurus, 75006

Cold-pressed juices and colourful salads are among the healthy takeaway options at this smart canteen.

3 Maubert Market

MAP N5 ■ Pl Maubert, 75006

This small market specializes in organic produce every Tuesday, Thursday and Saturday morning. A good place to pick up olives, cheese, tomatoes and fruit.

4 Maison Mulot

MAP L4 ■ 76 Rue de Seine, 75006 ■ Closed Mon

Tarts, sandwiches and good breads from this up-market patisserie and deli make for a chic picnic.

 5 Naturalia

MAP N6 ■ 36 Rue Monge, 75005 ■ Closed Sun pm

For a fully organic picnic, look no further than this grocery store: breads, wines, cheeses, hams, fruits, desserts and much more.

 6 Marché Raspail

MAP J4 ■ Blvd Raspail, 75006

Superb but pricey produce can be found at this food market held in the morning on Tuesday, Friday and Sunday (when it is all organic).

7 La Rôtisserie d'Argent

MAP P5 ■ 19 Quai de la Tournelle, 75005

Place an advance takeaway order of spit-roasted heritage chicken and other luxe picnic options at this bistro.

8 La Grande Epicerie de Paris

MAP D5 ■ Le Bon Marché, 38 Rue de Sèvres, 75007

Hunt for treasures such as Breton seaweed butter and *coucou de Rennes* at the food hall in Le Bon Marché *(see p71)*.

9 Le Pirée

MAP N5 ■ 47 Blvd St-Germain, 75005

Delicious, freshly prepared Greek and Armenian specialities, such as stuffed vegetables and honey-soaked cakes, are sold here.

 10 Kayser

MAP P6 ■ 8 Rue Monge, 75005 ■ Closed Mon

If you don't want to make up your own picnic then try a ready-made sandwich from this bakery. Mouthwatering combinations include goat's cheese with pear.

Interior of Kayser

Places to Eat

PRICE CATEGORIES
For a three-course meal for one with half
a bottle of wine (or equivalent meal),
taxes and extra charges
....
€ under €30 €€ €30–€50 €€€ over €50

 Dupin
MAP J5 ■ 11 Rue Dupin, 75006
■ 01 42 22 64 56 ■ Closed Sun, Mon
■ €€€
Dishes such as scallops and wild
mushrooms or confit aubergine are
sublime – reserve a table in advance.

2 Baieta
MAP P5 ■ 5 Rue de Pontoise,
75005 ■ 01 42 02 59 19 ■ Closed Sun,
Mon ■ €€€
Michelin-starred Niçoise chef Julia
Sedefdjian cooks with verve at her
friendly bistro. Try the bouillabaisse.

3 Clover Green
MAP E4 ■ 5 Rue Perronnet,
75007 ■ 01 75 50 00 05 ■ Closed Sun,
Mon ■ €€
Jean-François Piège's inventive
modern cuisine focuses on vegetables and is served in this minimalist
cosy bistro with an open kitchen.

4 Le Comptoir du Relais
MAP L5 ■ 9 Carrefour de
l'Odéon, 75006 ■ 01 44 27 07 97 ■ €€
Yves Camdeborde's much-praised
restaurant serves excellent bistro
lunches and prix-fixe dinners.

5 Lapérouse
MAP M4 ■ 51 Quai des Grands
Augustins, 75006 ■ 01 43 26 68 04
■ Closed Sat L, Sun, Mon L, Aug ■ €€€
Classic French cuisine is served
in a setting that has remained
unchanged since 1766.

6 La Crèmerie
MAP L5 ■ 9 Rue des Quatre
Vents, 75006 ■ 01 43 54 99 30
■ Closed Mon L, Sun ■ €€
Beyond the charming façade of this
intimate wine bar and informal bistro,

chef Tsuyoshi Yamakawa creates new
interpretations of French classics. His
small plates let natural flavours shine.

La Tour d'Argent

7 La Tour d'Argent
MAP P5 ■ 15 Quai de la
Tournelle, 75005 ■ 01 43 54 23 31
■ Closed Sun, Mon, Aug ■ €€€
This historic restaurant with fine
views of Notre-Dame serves
duckling as its speciality.

**8 L'Atelier de Joël
Robuchon**
MAP E4 ■ 5 Rue de Montalembert,
75007 ■ 01 42 22 56 56 ■ €€€
Sample mouthwatering French
gastronomic cuisine by Joël
Robuchon at this atelier (see p67).

9 Les Papilles
MAP F6 ■ 30 Rue Gay Lussac,
75005 ■ 01 43 25 20 79 ■ Closed Sun,
Mon, Aug, 25 Dec–1 Jan ■ €€
Choose your wine straight off the
shelves to accompany the great-
value Market or Bistro menus.

10 Au Moulin à Vent
MAP P6 ■ 20 Rue des Fossés
St-Bernard, 75005 ■ 01 43 54 99 37
■ Closed Sat L, Sun, Mon L, Aug ■ €€€
One of the best bistros in Paris. Try
the frogs' legs sauteed in garlic.

See map on pp124–5 ←

🔟 Jardin des Plantes Quarter

This is traditionally one of the most peaceful areas of Paris. The medicinal herb gardens that give the quarter its name were established here in 1626. Near the gardens is the Arènes de Lutèce, a well-preserved Roman amphitheatre. Rue Mouffetard, a lively cobbled street winding down the hill from the bustling place de la Contrescarpe, dates from medieval times. The area is also home to a sizable Muslim community, focused on the Paris Mosque and the Institut du Monde Arabe cultural centre.

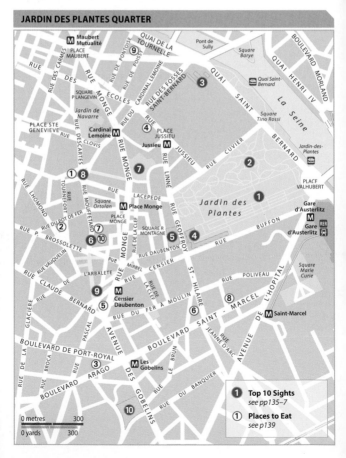

JARDIN DES PLANTES QUARTER

	Top 10 Sights
❶	see pp135–7
①	Places to Eat
	see p139

Flowers in the Jardin des Plantes

1 Jardin des Plantes

MAP G6 ▪ 57 Rue Cuvier, 75005
▪ 01 40 79 56 01 ▪ Open 8am–8pm
daily (to 5:30pm in winter)

The 17th-century royal medicinal
herb garden *(see p138)* was planted
by two physicians to Louis XIII.
Opened in 1640, it flourished under
the curatorship of Comte de Buffon.
It contains some 6,500 species, and
10,000 plants. There's a Cedar of
Lebanon, planted in 1734, a hillside
maze, and Alpine gardens.

2 Ménagerie

MAP G6 ▪ Jardin des Plantes,
75005 ▪ Open summer: 9am–6pm
(to 6:30pm Sun & hols); winter: 9am–
5pm (to 5:30pm Sun & hols) ▪ Adm
▪ www.zoodujardindesplantes.fr

The country's oldest public zoo
(see p60) was founded during the
Revolution to house the surviving
animals from the royal menagerie
at Versailles. Other animals were
donated from circuses around the
world. However, during the Siege
of Paris in 1870–71 *(see p43)*, most
of the unfortunate creatures were
eaten by hungry citizens. A favourite
with children, the zoo has since
been restocked.

3 Institut du Monde Arabe

MAP G5 ▪ 1 Rue des Fossés
St-Bernard, Pl Mohammed V, 75005
▪ 01 40 51 38 38 ▪ Open 10am–6pm
Tue, Wed & Fri (to 7pm Thu, Sat & Sun)
▪ Adm ▪ www.imarabe.org

This institute was founded in 1980 to
promote cultural relations between
France and the Arab world. The
stunning building (1987) designed
by architect Jean Nouvel *(see p120)*
features a southern wall of 240 ornate
photo-sensitive metal screens that
open and close like camera apertures
to regulate light entering the building.
The design is based on the traditional
latticed wooden screens of Islamic
architecture. Inside is a museum
featuring Islamic artworks, from
9th-century ceramics to contemporary art, as well as a tea salon
and restaurant.

4 Muséum National d'Histoire Naturelle

MAP G6 ▪ Jardin des Plantes,
75005 ▪ Open 10am–6pm Wed–
Mon (advance booking required)
▪ Closed 1 Jan, 1 May, 25 Dec
▪ Adm ▪ www.mnhn.fr

The Jardin des Plantes houses varied
natural history exhibits. The Grande
Galerie de l'Evolution *(see p60)* has
stuffed African mammals, a massive
whale skeleton and an endangered
species exhibit *(see p50)*.

Muséum National d'Histoire Naturelle

5 Grande Mosquée de Paris

MAP G6 ▪ 2 bis Pl du Puits de l'Ermite, 75005 ▪ Open 9am–6pm Sat–Thu; call 01 45 35 78 17 to book a guided tour ▪ Closed Islamic hols ▪ Adm

Built in 1922–6, this mosque is the spiritual centre for Parisian Muslims *(see p49)*. The Hispano-Moorish decoration, especially the grand patio, was inspired by the Alhambra in Spain. The minaret soars nearly 33 m (100 ft). The complex has an Islamic school, tearoom and a hammam reminiscent of North Africa.

Tearoom, Grande Mosquée de Paris

6 Rue Mouffetard

MAP F6

Although Rue Mouffetard is most famous today for its lively street market held every Tuesday to Sunday *(see p71)*, it has an equally colourful past. In Roman times this was the main road from Paris to Rome. Some say its name comes from the French word *mouffette* (skunk), as a reference to the odorous River Bièvre (now covered over) where waste was dumped by tanners and weavers from the nearby Gobelins tapestry factory. Though no longer poor nor bohemian, the neighbourhood still has lots of character, with its 17th-century mansard roofs, old-fashioned painted shop signs and affordable restaurants. In the market you can buy everything from Auvergne sausage to horsemeat and perfectly ripened cheeses.

7 Arènes de Lutèce

MAP G6 ▪ 49 Rue Monge, 75005 ▪ Open summer: 9am–8:30pm daily; winter: 8am–6pm daily

The remains of the 2nd-century Roman amphitheatre from the settlement of Lutetia *(see p42)* lay buried for centuries and were only discovered in 1869 during construction of Rue Monge. The novelist Victor Hugo, concerned with the preservation of his city's historic buildings, including Notre-Dame *(see p23)*, led the campaign for its restoration. The original arena would have had 35 tiers and could seat 15,000 spectators for theatrical performances and gladiator fights.

8 Place de la Contrescarpe

MAP F5

This bustling square has a village community feel, with busy cafés and restaurants and groups of students from the nearby Lycée Henri-IV hanging out here after dark. In medieval times, it lay outside the city walls, a remnant of which still stands on Rue Clovis. Notice the memorial plaque above the butcher's at No. 1, which marks the site of the old Pine Cone Club, a café where François Rabelais and other writers gathered in the 16th century.

FRENCH NORTH AFRICA

France has long had close connections with North Africa, though not always harmonious. Its annexation of Algeria in 1834 led to the long and bloody Algerian War of Liberation (1954–62). Relations with Tunisia, which it governed from 1883 to 1956, and Morocco, also granted independence in 1956, were better. Many North Africans now live in Paris.

Façade of St-Médard church

⑨ St-Médard

MAP G6 ▪ 141 Rue Mouffetard, 75005 ▪ Open 5–7:30 pm Mon; 8am–12:30pm & 2:30–7:30pm Tue–Sat; 9am–12:30pm & 4–8:15pm Sun

The church at the bottom of Rue Mouffetard dates back to the 9th century, when it was a parish church dedicated to St Médard, counsellor to the Merovingian kings. The present church, completed in 1655, is a mixture of Flamboyant Gothic and Renaissance styles. Among the fine paintings inside is the 17th-century *St Joseph Walking with the Christ Child* by Francisco de Zurbarán. The churchyard became notorious as it was the scene of hysterical fits in the 18th century, when a cult of *convulsionnaires* sought miracle cures at the grave of a Jansenist deacon.

⑩ La Manufacture des Gobelins

42 Ave des Gobelins, 75013 ▪ Open 1am–6pm Tue–Sun for temporary exhibitions; book a guided tour at www.cultival.fr

This world-renowned tapestry factory was originally a dyeing workshop, founded by the Gobelin brothers in the mid-15th century. In 1662, Louis XIV's minister Colbert set up a royal factory here and gathered the greatest craftsmen of the day to make furnishings for the palace at Versailles *(see p155)*. Visitors can observe the traditional weaving process on a guided tour, which usually takes place on Wednesday afternoons.

A DAY IN THE GARDENS

Institut du Monde Arabe
Le Buisson Ardent
Arènes de Lutèce
Muséum National d'Histoire Naturelle
Place de la Contrescarpe
Jardin des Plantes
Grande Mosquée de Paris
Grande Galerie de l'Evolution
St-Médard
Café-Restaurant de la Mosquée
Rue Mouffetard

▶ MORNING

Start the day by browsing the stalls at the fabulous market on **Rue Mouffetard**, which gets going by about 8am. Working upwards from the bottom of the street and the church of **St-Médard**, you'll find plenty here to make up a delicious breakfast, whether from the many market stalls or from the grocers and cafés that dot the street. Don't forget to take your eyes off the tempting produce every now and then to see the splendid old buildings on this medieval street.

Follow Rue Mouffetard up to the café-lined **Place de la Contrescarpe**, then head to the **Muséum National d'Histoire Naturelle** *(see p135)* and the excellent **Grande Galerie de l'Evolution** *(see p60)*. Stroll through the **Jardin des Plantes** *(see p135)* and take a break on one of the many benches to admire the plantings. Exit through the gate on Rue Cuvier, near Rue Linné, and make a detour to the **Arènes de Lutèce** on your way to **Le Buisson Ardent** *(see p139)* for a simple, authentic bistro lunch.

AFTERNOON

Spend part of the afternoon at the **Institut du Monde Arabe** *(see p135)*, exploring its beautiful Islamic artworks, before walking down to admire the Moorish architecture of the **Grande Mosquée de Paris**. Finish the day with a mint tea and a selection of maamoul and baklava at the **Café-Restaurant de la Mosquée** *(39 Rue Geoffroy St-Hilaire; 01 43 31 14 32; open noon–midnight daily)*.

See map on p134 ←

Jardin des Plantes Sights

1 Dinosaur Tree
One of the trees in the Botanical Gardens is a *Ginkgo biloba*, which was planted in 1795, but the species is known to have existed in exactly the same form in the days of the dinosaurs, 125 million years ago.

2 Cedar of Lebanon
This magnificent tree was planted in 1734, and came from London's Botanic Gardens in Kew, although a story grew up that its seed was brought here all the way from Syria in the hat of a scientist.

Cedar of Lebanon

3 Rose Garden
Having only been planted in 1990 and so relatively modern compared to the other gardens, the beautiful *roseraie* has some 170 species of roses and 180 rose bushes on display. Spectacular when in full bloom in spring and summer.

4 Rock Gardens
One of the stars of the Botanical Gardens, with more than 3,000 plants from the world's diverse Alpine regions. There are samples from Corsica to the Caucasus, Morocco and the Himalayas.

5 Sophora Japonica
Sent to Paris under the label "unknown Chinese tree" by a Jesuit naturalist living in China, this tree, often called a Pagoda Tree, was planted in 1747, first flowered in 1777, and still flowers today.

6 Iris Garden
An unusual feature is this designated garden which brings together more than 400 different varieties of iris.

7 Dodo Manège
The strange and exotic animals on this magical merry-go-round *(see p61)* include a dodo, a triceratops, a horned turtle and even a sivatherium, which was like a giraffe with antlers.

8 Nile Crocodile
The crocodile in the Reptile House now has a better home than he once did. It was found in 1998, when he was six months old, in the bathtub of a Paris hotel room, left behind as an unwanted pet.

9 Young Animal House
One of the zoo's most popular features for children is this house where young creatures, which for one reason or another cannot be looked after by their natural parents, are raised. Once they have reached adulthood they are returned to their natural habitat.

10 Greenhouses
Otherwise known as *Les Grandes Serres*, these 19th-century greenhouses were at one time the largest in the world. Today, they house a rainforest environment, a prickly Mexican cactus garden and a tropical winter garden which is kept at a constant 22°C (74°F) and 80 per cent humidity.

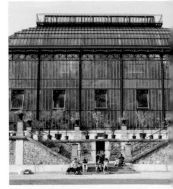

Nineteenth-century greenhouse

Places to Eat

PRICE CATEGORIES

For a three-course meal for one with half a bottle of wine (or equivalent meal), taxes and extra charges

€ under €30 ▪ €€ €30–€50 ▪ €€€ over €50

1 La Truffière
MAP F6 ▪ 4 Rue Blainville, 75005 ▪ 01 46 33 29 82 ▪ Closed Sun, Mon ▪ €€€

A 17th-century building, a wood fire and welcoming staff all make for a great little Michelin-approved bistro. Naturally, the menu features truffles.

La Truffière's vaulted interior

2 Chez Léna et Mimile
MAP F6 ▪ 32 Rue Tournefort, 75005 ▪ 01 47 07 72 47 ▪ Closed Sun, Mon ▪ €€

Those in the know avoid the touristy restaurants around Rue Mouffetard to savour a meal at this ambitious bistro with a peaceful terrace.

3 Au Petit Marguery
MAP F6 ▪ 9 Blvd de Port-Royal, 75013 ▪ 01 43 31 58 59 ▪ €€

One for meat lovers, with plenty of steak, veal and game on the menu. Boisterous atmosphere.

4 Le Buisson Ardent
MAP G6 ▪ 25 Rue Jussieu, 75005 ▪ 01 43 54 93 02 ▪ Closed Sun D (brunch only Sun) ▪ €€

This creative bistro is a romantic night-time destination serving classic French dishes with a twist. Set menus offer good value.

5 Le Bel Ordinaire
MAP F6 ▪ 5 Rue des Bazeilles, 75005 ▪ 09 81 11 72 78 ▪ Closed Sun, Mon ▪ €€

This new-generation bistro with an open kitchen and a large terrace prioritizes seasonal produce and natural wines.

6 L'Agrume
MAP G6 ▪ 15 Rue des Fossés St-Marcel, 75005 ▪ 01 43 31 86 48 ▪ Closed Sun & Mon, Tue D ▪ €€€

Seafood fresh from Brittany features on the menu at this popular bistro. There are good-value set lunches too.

7 DOSE – Dealer de Café
MAP F6 ▪ 73 Rue Mouffetard, 75005 ▪ 01 43 36 65 03 ▪ Closed Mon ▪ €

Some of the best espressos and cappuccinos in Paris are served at this coffee shop. It also offers delicious healthy salads and toasties.

8 Au Coco de Mer
MAP G6 ▪ 34 Blvd St-Marcel, 75005 ▪ 06 20 26 77 67 ▪ Closed Sun, Mon L, Aug ▪ €€

This restaurant serves spicy Seychelles cuisine and has a "beach hut" terrace with soft sand. Vegetarians should book ahead.

9 Kitchen Ter(re)
MAP G5 ▪ 26 Blvd St-Germain, 75005 ▪ 01 42 39 47 48 ▪ Closed Sun, Mon ▪ €€

Italian and Asian flavours mix at chef William Ledeuil's zesty restaurant, which specializes in homemade pasta. Good cocktails too.

10 Flocon
MAP F6 ▪ 75 Rue Mouffetard, 75005 ▪ 01 47 07 19 29 ▪ Closed Mon, Tue ▪ €€

Locals applauded the opening of this well-priced bistro, where the imaginative cooking might include dishes such as artichoke carpaccio and buttery skate.

See map on p134

TOP 10 Chaillot Quarter

Chaillot was a separate village until the 19th century, when it was swallowed up by the growing city and bestowed with wide avenues and grand mansions, many of which now house embassies. The quarter's centrepiece is the glorious Palais de Chaillot, its white-stone wings embracing the Trocadéro Gardens and its terrace facing the Eiffel Tower, across the Seine. Behind the palace is Place du Trocadéro, laid out in 1858 and ringed with smart cafés.

Fish sculpture, Aquarium de Paris

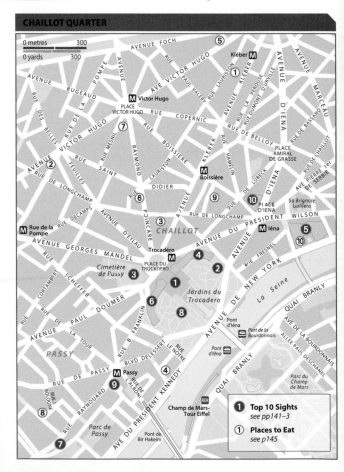

CHAILLOT QUARTER

- 1 **Top 10 Sights**
  see pp141–3
- 1 **Places to Eat**
  see p145

View from Palais de Chaillot

1 Palais de Chaillot
MAP B4
■ 17 Pl du Trocadéro, 75016

The fall of his empire scuppered Napoleon's plans for a palace for his son on Chaillot hill, but the site was later used for the Trocadéro palace, built for the Universal Exhibition of 1878. It was replaced by the present Neo-Classical building with its colonnaded wings for the prewar exhibition of 1937. The two pavilions house three museums, including the Musée de l'Homme. The broad terrace is the domain of souvenir sellers and skateboarders by day, while at night tourists come to admire the splendid view of the Eiffel Tower across the Seine. Two bronzes, *Apollo* by Henri Bouchard and *Hercules* by Pommier, stand at the front of the terrace. Beneath the terrace is the 1,200-seat Théâtre National de Chaillot.

2 Aquarium de Paris
MAP B4 ■ 5 Ave Albert de Mun, 75016 ■ Open 10am–7pm daily (to 10pm Sat) ■ Closed 14 Jul ■ Adm (advance booking required) ■ www.aquariumdeparis.com

Originally constructed in 1878 for the Universal Exhibition, this aquarium is home to over 10,000 species, including seahorses, stonefish and some sharks and rays. Built into a former quarry, the site has been designed to blend in with the Chaillot hillside. There is also a futuristic cinema complex showing nature films, and a modern French restaurant.

3 Cimetière de Passy
MAP A4 ■ Pl du Trocadéro (entrance Rue du Commandant Schloesing), 75016

This small cemetery established in 1820 covers only 1 ha (2.5 acres), yet many famous people *(see p144)* have been laid to rest here with the Eiffel Tower as their eternal view. It is worth a visit just to admire the striking sculptures on the tombs.

4 Cité de l'Architecture et du Patrimoine
MAP B4 ■ Palais de Chaillot, 75116 ■ 01 58 51 52 00 ■ Open 11am–7pm Wed–Mon (to 9pm Thu) ■ Closed Tue ■ Adm (advance booking required) ■ www.citedelarchitecture.fr

Occupying the east wing of the Palais de Chaillot, this museum is an ode to French architectural heritage, showcasing its development through the ages as well as contemporary architecture. The Galerie des Moulages (Medieval to Renaissance) contains moulded portions of churches and French cathedrals including Chartres. The Galerie d'Architecture Moderne et Contemporaine includes a reconstruction of an apartment designed by Le Corbusier, and architectural designs from 1990 onwards. The gallery in the Pavillon de Tête has a collection of murals copied from medieval frescoes.

Cité de l'Architecture et du Patrimoine

GENERAL FOCH

General Ferdinand Foch (1851–1929), whose statue stands in the centre of Place du Trocadéro, was commander-in-chief of the Allied armies by the end of World War I. His masterful command ultimately led to victory over Germany in 1918, whereupon he was made a Marshal of France and elected to the French Academy. He is interred at the Hôtel des Invalides (see pp38–9).

5 Musée d'Art Moderne de la Ville de Paris

MAP B4 ■ 11 Ave du Président Wilson, 75116 ■ Open 10am–6pm Tue–Sun (to 10pm Thu during temporary exhibitions) ■ Closed public hols ■ Adm for temporary exhibitions ■ www.mam.paris.fr

This museum is housed in the east wing of the Palais de Tokyo (see p53), built for the 1937 World's Fair. Its permanent collection consists of 10,000 works and includes such masters as Chagall, Picasso, Modigliani and Léger; further highlights include Raoul Dufy's enormous mural The Spirit of Electricity (1937) and Picabia's Lovers (After the Rain) (1925). The museum also showcases the work of up-and-coming artists in the west wing.

6 Musée de l'Homme

MAP B4 ■ 17 Pl du Trocadéro, 75016 ■ Open 11am–7pm Wed–Mon ■ Closed 1 Jan, 1 May, 14 Jul, 25 Dec ■ Adm ■ www.museedelhomme.fr

This anthropological and ethnographic museum, opened in 1938, uses scientific and cultural approaches to explore the questions surrounding the human race. It is home to one of the world's most comprehensive prehistoric collections. Reopened in 2015 after 5 years of renovations, it traces the history of mankind and addresses the questions, who are we, where do we come from, what is our future? Fossils, skulls, anthropological casts and other displays help visitors understand their biological evolution as well as the development of societies and cultures over the centuries.

7 Maison de Balzac

MAP A4 ■ 47 Rue Raynouard, 75016 ■ Open 10am–6pm Tue–Sun ■ Closed public hols ■ Adm for temporary exhibitions ■ www.maisondebalzac.paris.fr

The writer Honoré de Balzac (see p48) rented an apartment here from 1840 to 1847, assuming a false name to avoid his many creditors. He worked on several of his famous novels here, including La cousine Bette and La comédie humaine. The house is now a museum displaying first editions and manuscripts, personal mementoes and letters, and paintings and drawings of his friends and family. It also houses temporary exhibitions.

8 Jardins du Trocadéro

MAP B4

Designed in 1937, the tiered Trocadéro Gardens descend gently down Chaillot hill from the palace to the Seine and the Pont d'Iéna. The centrepiece of this 10-ha (25-acre) park is the long rectangular pool lined with stone and bronze statues, including Woman by Daniel Bacqué (1874–1947). Its illuminated fountains

Aerial view, Jardins du Trocadéro

(see p57) are spectacular at night. With flowering trees, walkways and bridges over small streams, the gardens are a romantic place for a stroll.

Exhibits in the Musée du Vin

⑨ Musée du Vin
MAP A4 ■ 5 Square Charles Dickens, Rue des Eaux, 75016 ■ Open 10am–6pm Tue–Sat ■ Adm ■ www.museeduvinparis.com

The vaulted 14th-century cellars where the monks of Passy once made wine are an atmospheric setting for this wine museum. Waxwork figures recreate the history of the wine-making process, and there are displays of wine paraphernalia. The museum also has tasting sessions, wine for sale and an excellent restaurant.

⑩ Musée National des Arts Asiatiques–Guimet
MAP B3 ■ 6 Pl d'Iéna, 75116 ■ Open 10am–6pm Wed–Mon (to 9pm Thu in summer) ■ Closed 1 Jan, 1 May, 25 Dec ■ Adm ■ www.guimet.fr

Founded in 1889, Musée National des Arts Asiatiques–Guimet is one of the world's foremost museums of Asian art, and the largest European museum devoted to the subject. The Khmer Buddhist temple sculptures from Angkor Wat are the highlight of a fine collection of Cambodian art. Emile Guimet's collection tracing Chinese and Japanese religion from the 4th to 19th centuries is also on display, as are rare artifacts from Afghanistan, India, Indonesia and Vietnam.

A DAY IN CHAILLOT

Etude
Café Carette
Musée National des Arts Asiatiques–Guimet
Café du Trocadéro
Cité de l'Architecture
Cimetière de Passy
Palais de Chaillot
Jardins du Trocadéro
Musée de l'Homme
Eiffel Tower, Le Jules Verne

▶ MORNING

It would be hard to imagine a better start to a day in Paris than going to the **Palais de Chaillot** *(see p141)* and taking in its perfect view of the **Eiffel Tower** *(see pp24–5)* across the Seine. Afterwards, explore the tree-lined paths of the **Jardins du Trocadéro**, or tour the fascinating collections of the **Cité de l'Architecture** *(see pp142)* or the **Musée de l'Homme** *(see p141)*.

Have lunch at the **Café du Trocadéro** *(8 Pl du Trocadéro; 01 44 05 37 00; open 7am–2am daily)* and watch the comings and goings in the square. Or, for something a little fancier – and having made a reservation well in advance – walk up to the excellent **Etude** *(see p145)*.

AFTERNOON

In good weather, take a stroll through the **Cimetière de Passy** *(see p141)*, where the extravagant tombstones and statuary speak to the good fortunes of the members of the 19th-century upper class buried here *(see p144)*. Or, if it is wet out, pop into the **Musée National des Arts Asiatiques–Guimet** for its remarkable Eastern artifacts and artworks – don't miss the stunning Riboud collection of rare textiles from India, Japan, China and Indonesia.

Take tea, with éclairs, at **Café Carette**, back at the Place du Trocadéro *(01 47 27 98 85; open 7am–11:30pm daily)*, or have an unforgettable dinner at the stylish **Le Jules Verne** *(see p123)*. Be sure to book a table in advance.

See map on p140 ←

Graves in Cimetière de Passy

Edouard Manet

Edouard Manet
Born in Paris in 1832, Manet became the most notorious artist in the city when works such as *Olympia* and *Le Déjeuner sur l'Herbe (see p16)* were first exhibited. He died in Paris in 1883.

Claude Debussy
The French composer (1862–1918) achieved fame through works such as *Prélude à l'Après-midi d'un Faune* and *La Mer*, and was regarded as the musical equivalent of the Impressionist painters.

Berthe Morisot
The French Impressionist artist was born in Paris in 1841, posed for Edouard Manet and later married his lawyer brother Eugène. One of the mainstays of the Impressionist movement, Morisot died in Paris in 1895.

Fernandel
The lugubrious French film actor known as Fernandel was born Fernand Contandin in Marseille in 1903. He made more than 100 films in a career that lasted from 1930 until his death in Paris in 1971.

Marie Bashkirtseff
This Russian artist became more renowned as a diarist after her death from tuberculosis in 1884. Despite living for only 24 years she produced 84 volumes of diaries and their posthumous publication created a sensation due to their intimate nature.

Marie-Louise Jay
A former Bon Marché shopgirl, Jay founded the historic Parisian department store La Samaritaine with her husband, Ernest Cognacq. The couple's fine art collection forms the heart of the Musée Cognacq-Jay (see p93).

Comte Emmanuel de Las Cases
Born in 1766, this historian and friend of Napoleon shared the emperor's exile on the island of St Helena and recorded his memoirs. Las Cases himself died in Paris in 1842.

Gabriel Fauré
The French composer, probably best known today for his *Requiem*, was a great influence on the music of his time. He died in Paris in 1924, at the age of 79.

Octave Mirbeau
The satirical French novelist and playwright was also an art critic and a journalist. Born in 1848, he died in Cheverchemont in 1917 and his body was brought to Passy for burial.

Henri Farman
The French aviator was born in Paris in 1874 and died here in 1958. He was the first man to make a circular 1-km (0.5-mile) flight, and the first to fly cross-country in Europe. His gravestone shows him at the controls of a primitive plane.

Grave of Henri Farman

Places to Eat

1 Alan Geaam

MAP B2 ▪ 19 Rue Lauriston, 75016 ▪ 01 45 01 72 97 ▪ Closed Sun, Mon ▪ €€€

In this refined restaurant, Michelin-starred chef Alan Geaam combines classic French cuisine with bright Lebanese flavours to create dishes such as langoustine cooked with *soujouk* spices.

2 Le Stella

MAP A3 ▪ 133 Ave Victor Hugo, 75116 ▪ 01 56 90 56 00 ▪ €€€

This jovial neighbourhood institution, with an almost retro charm, is a traditional Parisian brasserie in style and atmosphere. Le Stella serves fantastic seafood platters.

3 Mokus l'Ecureuil

MAP B3 ▪ 116 Ave Kléber, 75016 ▪ 01 42 56 23 56 ▪ €€

This trendy pizzeria and burger bar is set in an industrial-inspired dining room, complete with neon lights and brick walls. It is a great place for comfort food. The menu also features several options for vegetarians.

4 Astrance

MAP B4 ▪ 4 Rue Beethoven, 75116 ▪ 01 40 50 84 40 ▪ Closed Sat–Mon ▪ €€€

Pascal Barbot serves fusion food at its best. Book at least a month in advance to secure a table.

5 Prunier

MAP B3 ▪ 16 Ave Victor Hugo, 75016 ▪ 01 44 17 35 85 ▪ Closed Sun, Mon ▪ €€€

Fish dishes reign at this restaurant, with its dazzling Art Deco interior.

6 Bistrot Paul Chêne

MAP B3 ▪ 123 Rue Lauriston, 75116 ▪ 01 43 59 45 47 ▪ Closed Sun, Mon D ▪ €€

Located near Trocadéro, this typically Parisian bistro offers quality food impeccably served.

7 Le Petit Rétro

MAP B3 ▪ 5 Rue Mesnil, 75016 ▪ 01 44 05 06 05 ▪ Closed Sun ▪ €€

There's a cosy atmosphere and affordable prices at this 1900s bistro. The *blanquette de veau* is delicious.

8 Le Bistrot des Vignes

MAP B4 ▪ 1 Rue Jean Bologne, 75016 ▪ 01 45 27 76 64 ▪ €€

An unpretentious little bistro of the type everyone hopes to find in Paris.

9 Etude

MAP B3 ▪ 14 Rue du Bouquet de Longchamp, 75116 ▪ 01 45 05 11 41 ▪ Closed Sat L, Sun, Mon ▪ €€€

Chef Keisuke Yamagishi has been awarded a Michelin star for his perfectly balanced Franco-Japanese tasting menus. The restaurant prepares vegan menus as well, with advance notice.

Monsieur Bleu terrace

10 Monsieur Bleu

MAP B4 ▪ 20 Ave de New York, 75116 ▪ 01 47 20 90 47 ▪ €€

A glamorous modern brasserie within the Palais de Tokyo, near the Musée d'Art Moderne *(see p142)*. Nibbles from the bar menu are perfect for enjoying on the terrace facing the Eiffel Tower.

See map on p140

🔟 Montmartre and Pigalle

In the 19th and early 20th centuries, painters and poets put the "art" in Montmartre, and it will forever be associated with their bohemian lifestyle. Throngs of tourists climb the hill for the view from Sacré-Coeur, but you can still discover village-like charms in the winding back streets. Pigalle, once home to dance halls and cabarets, is now better known for its adult shows and sex shops.

Church of St-Pierre de Montmartre

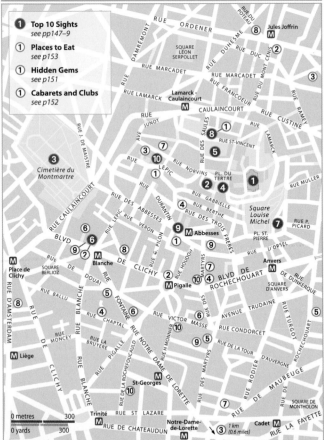

MONTMARTRE AND PIGALLE

1 **Top 10 Sights**
see pp147–9

1 **Places to Eat**
see p153

1 **Hidden Gems**
see p151

1 **Cabarets and Clubs**
see p152

1 Sacré-Coeur
See pp26–7.

2 Dalí Paris
MAP F1 ■ 11 Rue Poulbot, 75018 ■ Open 10am–6:30pm daily ■ Adm ■ www.daliparis.com

The Dalí works here may not be the artist's most famous, but this museum is still a must for any fan of the Spanish Surrealist *(see p150)*. The impressive private collection – France's largest – of Dalí's paintings, sculptures, engravings, objects and furniture reveals the dramatic char- acter of the 20th-century Catalan genius. Look out for the bronzes of his memorable "fluid" clocks.

3 Cimetière de Montmartre
MAP E1 ■ 20 Ave Rachel, 75018

The main graveyard for the district lies beneath a busy road in an old gypsum quarry, though it's more restful than first appears when you actually get below street level. The illustrious tombs, many with ornately sculpted monuments, packed tightly into this intimate space, reflect the artistic bent of the resi- dents, who include composers Berlioz and Offenbach, writers Stendhal and Dumas, Russian dancer Nijinsky as well as the iconic film director François Truffaut.

Cimetière de Montmartre

Portrait artist in the Place du Tertre

4 Place du Tertre
MAP F1

At 130 m (430 ft), Montmartre's old village square, whose name means "hillock", is the highest point in the city. Any picturesque charm it might once have had is now sadly hidden under the tourist-trap veneer of overpriced restaurants and portrait artists hawking their services, although the fairy lights at night are still atmospheric. No. 21 houses the Old Montmartre information office, with details about the area. Nearby is the church of St-Pierre de Montmartre, all that remains of the Benedictine abbey which stood here from 1133 until the Revolution.

5 Musée de Montmartre
12 Rue Cortot, 75018 ■ Open 10am–6pm daily (Apr–Sep: to 7pm) ■ Adm ■ www.museede montmartre.fr

The museum is set in Montmartre's finest town house, known as Le Manoir de Rosimond after the 17th-century actor who once owned it. From 1875 it provided living quarters and studios for numerous artists. Using drawings, photographs and all sorts of memorabilia, the museum presents the history of the Montmartre area, from its 12th- century convent days to the present, with an emphasis on the bohemian lifestyle of the *belle époque*. There is even a recreated 19th-century bistro, as well as lovely gardens where Renoir painted.

Cancan dancers on stage at the Moulin Rouge

6 Moulin Rouge

MAP E1 ■ 82 Blvd de Clichy, 75018 ■ Shows daily at 9pm & 11pm (dinner at 7pm) ■ www.moulinrouge.fr

The Moulin Rouge ("red windmill") is the most famous of the *belle époque* dance halls *(see pp64–5)* that once scandalized respectable citizens and attracted Montmartre's artists and other bohemian characters. Henri de Toulouse-Lautrec immortalized the era with his sketches and posters of dancers such as Jane Avril, some of which now grace the Musée d'Orsay *(see p17)*. Cabaret shows are still performed here.

7 Halle Saint Pierre

MAP F1 ■ 2 Rue Ronsard, 75018 ■ Open 11am–6pm Mon–Fri, 11am–7pm Sat, noon–6pm Sun ■ Closed public hols, Aug weekends ■ Adm ■ www.hallesaintpierre.org

The former covered market is now a cultural centre, which hosts temporary exhibitions of Art Brut. Coined by the painter Jean Dubuffet in 1945, the concept of Art Brut encompasses works created outside the boundaries of "official" culture, often by psychiatric patients, prisoners and children. The centre also has a permanent collection of native folk art. It stages avant-garde theatre and musical productions and holds literary evenings and debates.

8 Au Lapin Agile

MAP F1 ■ 22 Rue des Saules, 75018 ■ Open 9pm–1am Tue–Sun ■ www.au-lapin-agile.com

This *belle époque* restaurant and cabaret *(see p152)* was a popular hang-out for Picasso and Renoir, and poets Apollinaire and Paul Verlaine. It took its name from a humorous painting by André Gill of a rabbit *(lapin)* leaping out of a cooking pot, called the *Lapin à Gill*. In time it became known by its current name ("nimble rabbit").

***Lapin à Gill* by André Gill**

9 Place des Abbesses
MAP E1

This pretty square lies at the base of the Butte Montmartre. Visit it via the metro station of the same name to appreciate one of the few original Art Nouveau stations left in the city. Designed by the architect Hector Guimard in 1900, it features green wrought-iron arches, amber lanterns and a ship shield, the symbol of Paris. Along with Porte Dauphine, it is the only station entrance to retain its original glass roof. A mural painted by local artists winds around the spiral staircase at the entrance. But don't walk to the platform, take the elevator – it's the deepest station in Paris, with 285 steps.

THE MONTMARTRE VINEYARDS

It's hard to imagine it today, but Montmartre was once a French wine region said to match the quality of Bordeaux and Burgundy. There were 20,000 ha (50,000 acres) of Parisian vineyards in the mid-18th century, but today just 1,500 bottles of wine are made annually from the remaining 2,000 vines in Montmartre (below), and are sold in aid of charity.

10 Moulin de la Galette
MAP E1 ■ T-junction at Rue Tholozé and Rue Lepic, 75018

Montmartre once had more than 30 windmills, used for pressing grapes and grinding wheat; this is one of only two still standing. During the siege of Paris in 1814 its owner, Pierre-Charles Debray, was crucified on its sails by Russian soldiers. It became a dance hall in the 19th century and inspired paintings by Renoir and Van Gogh (see p150). Another windmill on the same street, the Moulin Radet, houses a restaurant confusingly called Le Moulin de la Galette.

A DAY IN MONTMARTRE

▶ MORNING

As with all the city's attractions, the sooner you get to **Sacré-Coeur** (see pp26–7) the more you will have it to yourself – it opens at 6am. Later in the morning, enjoy the bustle of Montmartre, and watch tourists having their portraits painted by the area's street artists in the **Place du Tertre** (see p147). There are plenty of places to choose for a coffee, but the one most of the artists frequent is the **Clairon des Chasseurs** (3 Pl du Tertre; 01 42 62 40 08; open 7am–2am daily).

For art of a more surreal kind, visit **Dalí Paris** (see p147). Head down Rue des Saules to continue the artistic theme with lunch at **La Maison Rose** (2 Rue de l'Abreuvoir; 01 42 64 49 62). Utrillo once painted this pretty pink restaurant.

AFTERNOON

Musée de Montmartre (see p147) is close by, as are the Montmartre Vineyards, and also the little **Cimetière de St-Vincent** where you will find Maurice Utrillo's grave.

Walk back up to Rue Lepic, which is a great place to shop. Next, see the **Moulin de la Galette** before heading towards the **Place des Abbesses**, one of Paris's most picturesque squares. Don't miss seeing the famous entrance to the Art Nouveau metro station.

To the south is a great bar for an apéritif, **La Fourmi** (74 Rue des Martyrs; 01 42 64 70 35). Then finish off the day in style with a show at the world-famous **Moulin Rouge** cabaret.

See map on p146 ←

Artists who Lived in Montmartre

Reclining Nude by Suzanne Valadon

1 Suzanne Valadon

Suzanne Valadon (1865–1938) was one of the first female painters to find success in Montmartre. Today her bold masterpieces, challenging the conventions of the nude, are on display in France and even at the Met in New York.

2 Salvador Dalí

The Catalan painter (1904–89) came to Paris in 1929 and held his first Surrealist exhibition that year. He kept a studio in Montmartre, and his work is now celebrated in Dalí Paris *(see p147)*.

3 Vincent van Gogh

The Dutch genius (1053–90) lived for a time on the third floor of 54 Rue Lepic. Many of his early paintings were inspired by the Moulin de la Galette windmill *(see p149)*.

4 Edgar Degas

The French artist Edgar Degas was born in Paris in 1834 and lived in the city for the whole of his life, most of the time in Montmartre, painting many of its street scenes and characters. He died here in 1917 and is buried in Montmartre cemetery *(see p147)*.

5 Louise Weber

Popularly known as La Goulue, Weber (1866–1929) was a well-known dancer at the Moulin Rouge, famous for her performances of the traditional cancan. Her fall from fame was almost as talked about as her rise to stardom.

6 Maurice Utrillo

Maurice Utrillo (1883–1955) lived with his artist mother, Suzanne Valadon, at 12 Rue Cortot, now the Musée de Montmartre *(see p147)*. His painted cityscapes include many atmospheric depictions of old Montmartre.

7 Henri de Toulouse-Lautrec

More than any other artist, Toulouse-Lautrec (1864–1901) is associated with Montmartre for his sketches and posters of dancers at the Moulin Rouge and other dance halls *(see p17)*. For most people, they epitomize the era to this day.

Toulouse-Lautrec

8 Dalida

France's disco queen, Dalida (1933–87) performed over 700 songs in several languages, which are still popular today.

9 Amedeo Modigliani

The Italian painter and sculptor (1884–1920) arrived in Paris in 1906, when he was 22, and was greatly influenced by Toulouse-Lautrec and the other famous bohemian artists on the Montmartre scene.

10 Pierre-Auguste Renoir

Renoir (1841–1919) is another artist who found inspiration in the Moulin de la Galette, when he lived at 12 Rue Cortot. For a time he laid tables at Au Lapin Agile *(see p148)*.

Hidden Gems

 1 **St-Jean l'Evangéliste de Montmartre**

MAP E1 ■ 19 Rue des Abbesses, 75018 ■ Open daily

This 1904 church is a clash of styles, from Moorish to Art Nouveau.

2 **18th-Arrondissement City Hall**

1 Pl Jules Joffrin, 75018 ■ Metro Jules Joffrin

On display in this building are two Utrillo paintings.

3 **Hameau des Artistes**

MAP E1 ■ 11 Ave Junot, 75018

This little hamlet of artists' studios is private, but no one will mind if you take a quiet look round.

 4 **Musée de la Vie Romantique**

MAP E1 ■ 16 Rue Chaptal, 75009 ■ Open 10am–6pm Tue–Sun ■ Adm for temporary exhibitions

George Sand was a frequent visitor to this house, which is now devoted to the writer.

 5 **Rue des Martyrs**

MAP E1

Filled with cute shops and cafés, this hilly street leading up to Montmartre is mostly full of locals and travellers looking for a reprieve.

 6 **Cité Véron**

MAP E1 ■ 92 Blvd de Clichy, 75018

This bucolic cul-de-sac is home to the Académie des Arts Chorégraphiques, a prestigious dance school.

 7 **Square Suzanne Buisson**

MAP E1

Named after a World War II Resistance fighter, this square is a quiet spot to unwind and relax.

 8 **Rue du Poteau**

Metro Jules Joffrin

A great market street with an authentic local feel.

9 **Crypte du Martyrium de St-Denis**

MAP E1 ■ 11 Rue Yvonne Le Tac, 75018 ■ 01 42 23 48 94 ■ Open 3–6pm Fri, 1st Sat & Sun of the month

A simple 19th-century chapel, this is said to be on the spot where St Denis, the patron saint of Paris, was beheaded by the Romans in AD 250.

10 **Musée Gustave Moreau**

MAP E2 ■ 14 Rue de La Rochefoucauld, 75009 ■ Open 10am–6pm Wed–Mon ■ Adm ■ www.musee-moreau.fr

The former home of Symbolist artist Moreau displays a large collection of his imaginative works.

Musée Gustave Moreau

See map on p146

Cabarets and Clubs

Old photograph of Au Lapin Agile

1 Au Lapin Agile
Poets and artists not only drank in this cabaret club *(see p148)*, some – such as Renoir and Verlaine – also laid tables. Picasso even paid his bill with one of his Harlequin paintings.

2 Moulin Rouge
MAP E1 ■ 82 Blvd de Clichy, 75018

As old as the Eiffel Tower (1889) and as much a part of the Parisian image, today's troupe *(see p148)* of 60 Doriss Girls are the modern versions of Jane Avril and La Goulue.

3 Silencio
MAP F3 ■ 142 Rue Montmartre, 75002 ■ 01 40 13 12 33

David Lynch's club, which opens to the general public from 11pm, mixes art, theatre and music in one of Paris's most eclectic nightlife venues.

4 La Cantine de la Cigale
MAP E1 ■ 124 Blvd de Rochechouart, 75018 ■ 01 55 79 10 10

A popular brasserie by day, this lively hangout, next to the famed La Cigale theatre, hosts DJ sets on Friday and Saturday nights.

5 La Nouvelle Eve
MAP E1 ■ 25 Rue Pierre Fontaine, 75009 ■ 01 48 74 69 25

One of the lesser-known cabaret venues produces professional shows that feature colourful displays of the celebrated French cancan.

6 Le Bus Palladium
MAP E1 ■ 6 Rue Pierre Fontaine, 75009 ■ 01 45 26 80 35 ■ Closed Sun

This 1960s club, which was graced by The Beatles, now hosts concerts with an alternative/rock vibe.

7 Cabaret Michou
MAP E1 ■ 80 Rue des Martyrs, 75018 ■ 01 46 06 16 04

With outrageous drag artists and a compère whose behaviour can never be predicted, this place is close to the original spirit of Montmartre cabaret.

Cabaret Michou

8 Les Trois Baudets
MAP E1 ■ 64 Blvd de Clichy, 75018 ■ 01 42 62 33 33

Famous French singer Serge Gainsbourg got his start at this venue.

9 La Machine du Moulin Rouge
MAP E1 ■ 90 Blvd de Clichy, 75018 ■ 01 53 41 88 89

Next to the Moulin Rouge, this venue hosts both club nights and concerts.

10 Le Divan du Monde
MAP E1 ■ 75 Rue des Martyrs, 75018 ■ 07 68 78 68 01 ■ Combined ticket with Madame Arthur

World music gigs and a drag cabaret act coexist at this quirky spot.

Places to Eat

PRICE CATEGORIES

For a three-course meal for one with half a bottle of wine (or equivalent meal), taxes and extra charges

....

€ under €30   €€ €30–€50   €€€ over €50

 Coq Rico
MAP E1 ▪ 98 Rue Lepic, 75018
▪ 01 42 59 82 89 ▪ €€

Poultry is the star of the show at chef Antoine Westermann's bistro. Try the rotisserie-style Bresse chicken with hand-cut fries.

2 Boullion Pigalle
MAP E1 ▪ 22 Blvd de Clichy, 75018 ▪ 01 42 59 69 31 ▪ €

A modern take on the classic French eatery, Boullion Pigalle serves well-priced traditional fare. Reservation in advance is recommended.

3 Table d'Eugène
18 Rue Eugène Sue, 75018
▪ 01 42 55 61 64 ▪ Closed Sun, Mon & Aug ▪ €€€

This chic restaurant serves fantastic gastronomic tasting menus at very reasonable prices.

4 Le Relais de la Butte
MAP E1 ▪ 12 Rue Ravignan, 75018 ▪ 01 42 23 24 34 ▪ €

A pavement café (see p69) perfect for sipping coffee, tucking into a charcuterie board or indulging in a glass of wine.

5 Pétrelle
MAP F1 ▪ 34 Rue Pétrelle, 75009 ▪ 01 42 82 11 02 ▪ Closed Sun L, Mon L, 1st week May & Aug ▪ €€€

A restaurant with offbeat, eccentric decor, an intimate atmosphere and a menu using only local produce.

6 Le Pantruche
MAP F1 ▪ 3 Rue Victor Massé, 75009 ▪ 01 48 78 55 60 ▪ Closed Sat & Sun ▪ €€

This bistro is a great go-to for French classics with fun twists.

7 Restaurant Caillebotte
MAP F2 ▪ 8 Rue Hippolyte Lebas, 75009 ▪ 01 53 20 88 70
▪ €€

Elegant yet simple dining with a contemporary edge, tucked away from Rue des Martyrs.

8 Le Vaisseau Vert
MAP E1 ▪ 10 Rue de Parme, 75009 ▪ 01 49 70 03 55 ▪ Closed Sat L, Sun & 3 weeks in Aug ▪ €€

This bistro offers innovative French dishes and a great selection of wines.

9 Hôtel Amour
MAP F2 ▪ 8 Rue de Navarin, 75009 ▪ 01 48 78 31 80 ▪ €€

The modish restaurant in this hip hotel serves internationally inspired food with a mix of French classics.

10 Buvette
MAP E1 ▪ 28 Rue Henry Monnier, 75009 ▪ 01 44 63 41 71
▪ €

Under a gorgeous tin ceiling, this comfortable New York-style bistro serves cocktails, a mouthwatering chocolate mousse and classic French dishes prepared using locally sourced ingredients. Linger over a hearty brunch at the weekend.

Buvette, with its beautiful tin ceiling

See map on p146

TOP 10 Greater Paris

Central Paris has more than enough on offer to keep any visitor occupied, but if time permits you should make at least one foray out of the centre, whether it be to the sumptuous Palace of Versailles, former home of the "Sun King" Louis XIV, or to the Magic Kingdom of Disneyland® Paris. The excellent metro system makes for easy day trips to the area's two main parks, the Bois de Boulogne and the Bois de Vincennes, for a wide range of outdoor activities, from boating to horse riding or cycling, or just strolling amid pleasant greenery. In contrast to these bucolic pleasures is the cutting-edge modern architecture of La Défense. Visually stunning, it comprises Paris's high-rise business district, with added attractions in its exhibition centres. Two large cemeteries outside the centre are worth a visit for their ornate tombs.

The Grande Arche de la Défense

GREATER PARIS

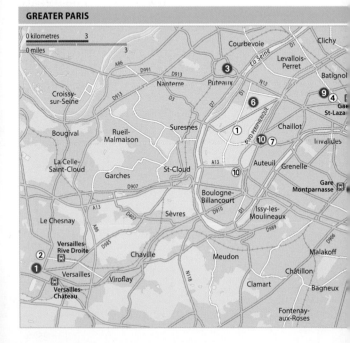

Fountain at Versailles

1 Versailles

Place d'Armes, 78000 Versailles ■ RER line C to Versailles-Château–Rive Gauche ■ Château: open Apr–Oct: 9am–6:30pm Tue–Sun (Nov–Mar: to 5:30pm Tue–Sun); gardens: open 8am–8:30pm daily (winter: 8am–6pm) ■ Closed public hols ■ Adm ■ www.chateauversailles.fr

The top day trip from Paris has to be Versailles. This stunning chateau, begun by Louis XIV around 1662, is overwhelming in its opulence and scale. Plan what you want to see and arrive early, as even a full day may not be long enough. If you'd like to spend a few days exploring, opt for the two-day passport, which includes one musical fountain show (Apr–Oct). Pre-booking your ticket online is essential.

2 Disneyland® Paris

Marne-la-Vallée ■ RER line A to Marne-la-Vallée Chessy/Disneyland ■ See website for opening times and prices ■ www.disneylandparis.com

Since its opening in 1992, this theme park still draws more people than the Louvre and the Eiffel Tower combined. In the shadow of the extravagant Château de la Belle au Bois Dormant (Sleeping Beauty Castle), visitors – whether young or young-at-heart – will enjoy the high-tech workings and imagination behind such attractions as the multisensory, 4D Ratatouille ride and the rollicking Pirates of the Caribbean. At the adjacent Walt Disney Studios® Park, dedicated to Disney's movies and television shows, visitors can experience the thrill of special-effects rides and professional stunt shows. Marvel, Star Wars and Frozen attractions are the latest additions to the park.

3 La Défense

Metro Esplanade de la Défense or RER line A to La Défense–Grande Arche

French vision and flair coupled with Parisian style are clearly shown by this modern urban development. This business and government centre was purposely built to the west of the city to allow the centre to remain unmarred by skyscrapers. More than just offices, however, the area is also an attraction in its own right, with stunning sights such as the Grande Arche, a cube-like structure with a centre large enough to contain Notre-Dame, and surrounded by artworks, a fountain, cafés and restaurants.

1 **Top 10 Sights**
see pp155–7

1 **Places to Eat**
see p161

4 Bois de Vincennes

94300 Vincennes ■ Metro Château de Vincennes/RER Vincennes ■ Park open 24 hours daily; château open Sep–May: 10am–5pm (Jun–Aug: to 6pm) ■ Closed public hols ■ www.chateau-vincennes.fr

Southeast of the city lies the Bois de Vincennes (see p58), which has several lakes with boating facilities, beautiful formal gardens, a Buddhist centre, a zoo and children's play areas. The Château de Vincennes was a royal residence before Versailles and has the tallest keep in Europe. The more energetic can walk here all the way from the Bastille along Promenade Plantée, which follows, part way, a former railway viaduct.

5 Parc de la Villette

211 Ave Jean-Jaurès, 75019 ■ Metro Porte de Pantin ■ 01 40 03 75 75 ■ Opening times vary depending on the attraction ■ Adm for certain attractions ■ www.lavillette.com

More than just a park, this landscape (see p60) was created in 1993 to a futuristic design. It provides the usual park features of paths and gardens, but modern sculptures, zany park benches and several major attractions offer a different edge. These include the Philharmonie de Paris concert hall and museum, the interactive science museum, the Cité des Sciences et de l'Industrie, and an Omnimax cinema in a geodesic dome. There are also play areas for children. In the summer, the park holds an open-air film festival.

Parc de la Villette's Géode

6 Bois de Boulogne

MAP A2

This enormous park is Parisians' favourite green retreat, especially on summer weekends when its 865 ha (2,135 acres) can become crowded. There is plenty to do here, apart from simply walking and picnicking, such as cycling, horse riding, boating or visiting the various attractions – including parks within the park, two race courses and the striking Frank Gehry-designed Fondation Louis Vuitton (see p159) contemporary arts centre. The park is open 24 hours a day, but is best avoided after dark.

7 Montparnasse

■ Cemetery: open 8am–6pm Mon–Fri, 8:30am–6pm Sat, 9am–6pm Sun (mid-Nov–mid-Mar: to 5:30pm) ■ Tour Montparnasse: www.tourmontparnasse56.com

The area of Montparnasse is always recognisable due to the 210-m (689-ft) Tour Montparnasse, which offers spectacular views. It is set to undergo extensive renovation for the 2024 Olympics. Five minutes' walk away is the area's main draw, the Montparnasse Cemetery, where the great writers Maupassant, Sartre, de Beauvoir, Baudelaire and Samuel Beckett are buried. Nearby, too, the Catacombs (see p58) offer an intriguing underground experience of the city.

8 Père Lachaise Cemetery

8 Blvd de Ménilmontant ■ Metro Père-Lachaise ■ 01 55 25 82 10 ■ Open 8am–5:30pm Mon–Fri, 8:30am–5:30pm Sat, 9am–5:30pm Sun (Mar–Nov: to 6pm)

This is the most visited cemetery in the world, largely due to rock music fans who come from around the world to see the grave of the legendary singer Jim Morrison of The Doors. There are about one million other graves here, and some 70,000 different tombs, including those of Chopin, Oscar Wilde, Balzac, Edith Piaf, Colette, Molière and Delacroix. There are maps posted around the cemetery to help you find the most famous graves *(see p160)*, and it's also possible to download a map from www.paris.fr/cimetieres.

Père Lachaise Cemetery

⑨ Parc Monceau
Blvd de Courcelles, 75008
■ Metro Monceau

This civilized little park *(see p56)* is no further from the city centre than Montmartre, yet it goes unnoticed by many visitors. It was created in 1778 by the Duc de Chartres and is still frequented by well-heeled residents. The park grounds are full of statues.

⑩ Musée Marmottan Monet
2 Rue Louis-Boilly, 75016 ■ Metro La Muette ■ Open 10am–6pm Tue–Sun (to 9pm Thu) ■ Adm ■ www.marmottan.fr

Paul Marmottan was an art historian and his 19th-century mansion now houses the world's largest collection of works by Claude Monet, including his *Impression, Soleil Levant*, which gave the Impressionist movement its name. The collection was donated by the artist's son in 1966, and includes Monet's own collection of works by Renoir and Gauguin.

THE TREATY OF VERSAILLES

France, Great Britain, the USA, Italy and Germany negotiated this agreement after World War I at Versailles, which required Germany to demilitarize parts of its territory, reduce the size of its army, abolish conscription, cease trading in military equipment and to pay compensation. The Treaty was signed on 28 June 1919.

A DAY IN THE BOIS DE VINCENNES

▶ **MORNING**

To immerse yourself in a swathe of greenery, head to the **Bois de Vincennes**. Take metro line 1 to **Château de Vincennes**, stopping off at **Le Drapeau** brasserie *(18 Ave de Paris; 01 43 65 17 94; open 7:30am–midnight Mon–Fri, from 8:30am Sat & Sun)* for a cup of coffee.

Cross over the road (or follow signs from the metro if you skipped coffee) to the medieval castle that was at the heart of the French monarchy until 1682, when Louis XIV decided to settle in Versailles. Look out for the ornate gate and stained-glass windows of the Gothic **Sainte-Chapelle**.

For lunch, try **La Rigadelle** *(23 Rue de Montreuil; 01 43 28 04 23; open Wed–Sun L & D)*, just outside the fortress, which specializes in fish and seafood dishes.

AFTERNOON

Walk off lunch amid the flowers and botanical plants in the **Parc Floral de Paris** *(see p59)* within the Bois, then head for the charmingly kitsch mini-golf course featuring models of Parisian monuments. Afterwards, if you're still feeling energetic, stroll to **Lac Daumesnil**, where you can rent a boat to row around the lake's two islands.

Time to rejoin urban life? From the **Porte Dorée metro** station, near the Art Deco Palais de la Porte Dorée, take the metro westward to the hubbub of the Aligre quarter. Get out at **Ledru-Rollin** metro station and walk to the lively **Baron Rouge** *(see p101)* for a well-earned aperitif.

Versailles Sights

 The Hall of Mirrors
The spectacular 70-m- (233-ft-) long Galerie des Glaces has been magnificently restored. It was in this room that the Treaty of Versailles was signed in 1919, formally ending World War I.

 Chapelle Royale
The Royal Chapel is regarded as one of the finest Baroque buildings in the country. Finished in 1710, its elegant, white marble Corinthian columns and numerous murals make for an awe-inspiring place of prayer.

 Salon de Venus
In this elaborate room, which is decorated predominantly in marble, a statue of Louis XIV, the creator of Versailles, stands centre stage, exuding regal splendour beneath the fine painted ceiling.

 Queen's Bedchamber
Nineteen royal infants were born in this opulent room, which has been meticulously restored to exactly how it appeared when it was last used by Marie-Antoinette in 1789.

Queen's Hamlet
Behind the Petit Trianon is the Queen's Hamlet, a life-size model village, built for Marie-Antoinette, that was also a functioning farm. The cottages, inspired by rural French architecture, have rustic exteriors, but the interiors are richly furnished.

Cottages in the Queen's Hamlet

Salon d'Apollon

 Salon d'Apollon
Louis XIV's throne room is, naturally, one of the palace's centrepieces, and features a suitably regal portrait of the great Sun King. Dedicated to the god Apollo, it strikingly reflects the French monarchy's divine self-image.

L'Opéra Royal
The opulent opera house was built in 1770 for the marriage of the *Dauphin*, the future Louis XVI, to Marie-Antoinette. The floors were designed so that they could be raised to stage level during special festivals.

Le Domaine de Trianon
In the southeast corner of the gardens, Louis XIV and Louis XV had the Grand and Petit Trianon palaces built as "private" retreats. Marie-Antoinette was given the Petit Trianon by Louis XVI.

Palace Gardens
The palace gardens feature many walkways, landscaped topiary, fountains, pools, statues and the Orangery, where exotic plants were kept in the winter. The magnificent Fountain of Neptune is situated to the north of the North Wing.

Royal Stables
The magnificent stables have been restored and they now house the famous Bartabas Academy of Equestrian Arts.

Bois de Boulogne Features

 Parc de Bagatelle
Differing garden styles feature in this park, including English and Japanese, though for most visitors the major attraction is the huge rose garden, best seen in June.

 Jardin du Pré-Catelan
This park-within-a-park is at the very centre of the Bois. Its lawns and wooded areas include a magnificent 200-year-old beech tree and the idyllic eponymous restaurant (see p161).

 Jardin d'Acclimatation
The main children's area (see p61) of the Bois incorporates a small amusement park, a zoo with a farm and a pets' corner, and a Herb Museum aimed especially at children.

 La Grande Cascade
This artificial waterfall was a major undertaking when the park was built, requiring concrete to be shipped down the Seine.

5 Lakes
Two long, thin lakes adjoin each other. The larger of the two, confusingly called Lac Inférieur (the other is Lac Supérieur) has boats for hire and a motor boat to take you to the islands.

Boats for hire in the Bois de Boulogne

6 Fondation Louis Vuitton
A thrilling example of modern architecture, this spectacular glass Frank Gehry-designed building (see p53) is a cultural centre dedicated to modern art. It hosts regular art events and exhibitions.

7 Château de Longchamp
While he redesigned central Paris (see p43), Baron Haussmann landscaped the Bois de Boulogne. This chateau was given to him as a thank-you by Napoleon III.

8 Shakespeare Garden
In the Jardin du Pré-Catelan is a little garden planted with all the trees, flowers and herbs mentioned in the plays of Shakespeare. There is a lovely open-air theatre.

9 Jardin des Serres d'Auteuil
This 19th-century garden has a series of greenhouses where ornamental hothouse plants are grown. In the centre is a palm house with tropical plants.

10 Horse-Racing
The Bois is home to two race courses. To the west is the Hippodrome de Longchamp, where flat racing takes place, including the Qatar Prix de l'Arc de Triomphe (see p75); in the east, the Hippodrome d'Auteuil holds steeplechases.

Notable Graves

1 Jim Morrison, Père Lachaise Cemetery

The American lead singer of The Doors rock band spent the last few months of his life in Paris and died here in 1971. Fans still hold vigils at his grave, which is covered with scrawled messages from those who come from all over the world.

2 Oscar Wilde, Père Lachaise Cemetery

The Dublin-born author died in 1900, after allegedly uttering: "My wallpaper and I are fighting a duel to the death. One or the other of us has to go." His tomb is unmissable, with a huge monument by Jacob Epstein.

3 Frédéric Chopin, Père Lachaise Cemetery

The Polish composer was born in 1810 and died in Paris at the age of 39. The statue on his tomb represents "the genius of music sunk in grief".

4 Edith Piaf, Père Lachaise Cemetery

The iconic French *chanteuse*, known as the "little sparrow", was born in poverty in the Belleville district of

Edith Piaf's gravestone

Paris in 1915, less than 1,500 m (5,000 ft) from where she was buried in 1963 in a simple black tomb.

5 Marcel Proust, Père Lachaise Cemetery

The ultimate chronicler of the city, Proust was born in Paris in 1871. He *(see p48)* is buried in the family tomb.

6 Samuel Beckett, Montparnasse Cemetery

The Irish-born Nobel Prize-winning writer *(see p49)* settled in Paris in 1937, having previously studied here. He died in 1989 and his gravestone is a simple slab, reflecting the writer's enigmatic nature.

7 Jean-Paul Sartre and Simone de Beauvoir, Montparnasse Cemetery

Joined together in death as in life, even though they never actually lived together, their joint grave is a remarkably simple affair. Both of these philosophers were born, lived and died in Paris.

8 Sarah Bernhardt, Père Lachaise Cemetery

A world-famous actress, Bernhardt played characters from *Hamlet* to *Cleopatra* in the late 19th and early 20th centuries, and was one of the first dramatic artists to star on screen.

9 Rosa Bonheur, Père Lachaise Cemetery

A leading Realist artist featured in the Musée d'Orsay, Bonheur was one of the 19th century's most prominent painters, allowing her to publicly wear trousers before most French women could.

10 Colette, Père Lachaise Cemetery

One of France's most respected writers, her novel *Gigi* was adapted for the stage, when Colette famously picked a young Audrey Hepburn to play the leading role.

Places to Eat

PRICE CATEGORIES

For a three-course meal for one with half a bottle of wine (or equivalent meal), taxes and extra charges

€ under €30 €€ €30–€50 €€€ over €50

Le Pré Catelan

Route de Suresnes, Bois de Boulogne, 75016 ■ Metro Porte Maillot ■ 01 44 14 41 14 ■ Closed Sun, Mon, 2 weeks Feb, 3 weeks Aug, 1 week Nov ■ €€€

Tucked away in the Bois de Boulogne (see p156) is this high-class dining pavilion in a romantic setting with elegant service.

2 Gordon Ramsay au Trianon

1 Blvd de la Reine, 78000 Versailles ■ RER line C to Versailles ■ 01 30 84 50 18 ■ Closed Mon, Tue–Sat L, Sun, Jan, Aug ■ €€€

Gordon Ramsay's protegé Frédéric Larquemin is the chef at this Michelin-starred restaurant.

3 La Fontaine de Belleville

31–33 Rue Juliette Dodu, 75010 ■ 09 81 75 54 54 ■ €

This corner café (see p69) has had a facelift by Paris's hippest coffee roaster. Craft coffee, innovative cocktails, and fresh food are all excellent.

4 Le Camondo

MAP D2 ■ 61 bis Rue de Monceau, 75008 ■ 01 45 63 40 40 ■ Closed Sun ■ €€€

Set in the Musée Nissim de Camondo (see p59), this restaurant serves modern dishes in an elegant courtyard.

5 La Closerie des Lilas

MAP E6 ■ 171 Blvd du Montparnasse, 75006 ■ 01 40 51 34 50 ■ €€

With its piano bar and terrace, this is a Montparnasse institution. The brasserie is cheaper than the main restaurant. The steak tartare is recommended.

6 Simonetta

32 Quai de la Marne, 75019 ■ 01 42 81 32 63 ■ €€

Locals and families flock to this excellent canal-side pizzeria close to the Parc de la Villette. Eat on the terrace while watching life on the water.

7 La Gare

19 Chaussée de la Muette, 75016 ■ Metro La Muette ■ 01 42 15 15 31 ■ €€

Any visit to the Bois de Boulogne, should include a stop at this stylish brasserie in a former railway station.

Interior of La Gare

8 Le Baratin

3 Rue Jouye-Rouve, 75020 ■ Metro Pyrénées ■ 01 43 49 39 70 ■ Closed Sun & Mon ■ No vegetarian options ■ €€

A local favourite in Belleville, this bistro serves modern French cuisine with excellent wines. The fixed-price lunch is particularly popular.

9 Le Perchoir

14 Rue Crespin du Gast, 75020 ■ Metro Ménilmontant ■ 01 83 62 64 22 ■ Closed Sun D, Mon, Tue, Wed–Sat L ■ €€

Rooftop restaurant, with an open-air cocktail bar, offering innovative French dishes for dinner and Sunday brunch.

10 Brasserie Urbaine

13 Rue Nungesser et Coli, 75016 ■ Metro Michel Ange Molitor ■ 01 56 07 08 50 ■ €€

Housed in the Art Deco Hotel Molitor, Brasserie Urbaine is famous for French classics with modern twists.

See map on pp154–5

Streetsmart

Art Nouveau entrance to
St-Michel metro station

Getting Around

Arriving by Air

Three aiports serve Paris. **Roissy-Charles-de-Gaulle Airport (CDG)**, 23 km (14 miles) northeast of central Paris, is the arrival point for most international flights. Its main terminals are some distance apart, so check which one you need in advance. For more information regarding flights, download the free **Aeroports de Paris** app.

CDG is connected to central Paris by **Le Bus Direct** and the **RATP Roissybus** services, as well as, the easiest option, the RER train line B3. This links with Gare du Nord, Les Halles and St-Michel. A taxi costs €53 from CDG to the Right Bank and €58 to the Left Bank for up to four people.

Orly Airport is 14 km (8.5 miles) south of the city centre and is used by French domestic services and some international airlines. The airport is divided into four main separate zones – Orly 1, 2, 3 and 4 – each with its own arrivals and departures area.

Le Bus Direct runs from Orly to and from Etoile, Invalides and Montparnasse metro and mainline stations. The high-speed Orlyval shuttle train serves both of Orly's terminals from Antony on RER line B4. Metro signs to Orly on RER C refer to Orly town (not Orly Airport). Taxi journey times generally take about 30 minutes and cost €37 to the Right Bank and €32 to the Left Bank.

Beauvais Airport is some 70 km (43 miles) north of Paris and is used mainly by budget airlines. There is a connecting bus link with Porte Maillot metro station. It is wise to book the 90-minute journey in advance online.

The **Airport Shuttles** website searches the best offers for services, including shared rides and private drivers, between the airports and your destination. It provides up-to-date prices for buses, taxis and all other options, allowing travellers to find what fits their budget.

International Train Travel

Regular high-speed trains connect Paris's six international railway stations to numerous major cities across Europe. Reservations for these services are essential, as seats get booked up quickly, particularly during peak times.

You can buy tickets and passes for multiple international journeys from **Eurail** or **Interrail**; however, you may need to pay an additional reservation fee. Always check carefully before boarding that your pass is valid on the service you wish to use.

Eurostar runs a fast, regular service from London to central Paris via the Channel Tunnel.

Thalys runs a high-speed service between Paris, Brussels and Amsterdam ten times a day, with a variety of special offers, package deals and half-price last-minute discounts.

Students and those under 26 can benefit from discounted rail travel both to and within France. For more information on discounted travel, visit the Eurail or Interrail website.

Domestic Train Travel

Paris has a number of main train stations situated at various locations right across the city, all of which serve different regions.

The French state railway, **OUI SNCF**, has two services in Paris: the Banlieue suburban service and the Grandes Lignes, or long-distance service. The suburban service operates within the five-zone network. The long-distance service operates throughout France. The TGV offers a reliable high-speed service which should be booked in advance. There are also a number of budget high-speed trains, such as **Ouigo**.

Before boarding a train, remember to time-punch (composter) tickets to validate your journey; this does not apply for e-tickets. Tickets for city transport cannot be used on Banlieue trains, with the exception of some RER tickets to stations with both SNCF and RER lines.

Public Transport

The metro, RER, buses and trams are all run

by **RATP** (Régie Autonome des Transports Parisiens). Safety and hygiene measures, timetables, ticket information, transport maps and more can be found on their website.

Tickets

The Paris metropolitan area is divided into five ticket zones. Central Paris is zone 1, Roissy-Charles-de-Gaulle Airport is in zone 5, and Orly Airport and Versailles are in zone 4. The metro network serves zones 1–3.

To avoid buying paper tickets you can get a **Navigo** pass, a rechargeable smart card that can be used on the metro, RER and buses. The Navigo Easy costs €2 for the pass and can be topped up with credit and with as many standard fares as you like. A ten-journey top-up will cost less on the Navigo Easy than when bought as a paper *carnet*. The Passe Navigo Découverte costs €5 for the pass and can then be loaded with a week's unlimited travel in zones 1–5. You will need a passport-sized photo and to add your signature to the pass.

Visitors can also enjoy unlimited travel on the metro, RER and Paris buses with a Paris Visite pass, valid for 1, 3 or 5 consecutive days in zones 1–3, or a Mobilis card, valid in the zones of your choice for one day. Both of these are available from the RATP. Children aged 11 and under travel free.

Bus-only paper tickets can be purchased on board from the driver. All bus tickets must be validated using the machine on the bus. Anyone travelling without a valid ticket on any mode of transport may be fined.

Metro and RER

The Paris metro has 14 main lines and two minor lines. The RER is a system of five lines of commuter trains that travel underground in central Paris and above ground in outlying areas. The two systems overlap in the city centre. RER trips outside the city centre require special tickets; fares to suburbs and nearby towns vary.

Buses and Trams

Most buses must be flagged down at designated stops. Your ticket may be used for transfers to other bus and tramway lines for 90 minutes (between the first and last validation). Each time you change buses or trams, you must validate your ticket again. Exceptions to this rule are the Balabus, Noctambus, Orlybus and Roissybus services, and lines 221, 297, 299, 350 and 351.

There are 48 night bus lines, called Noctilien, serving Paris and its suburbs. The terminus for most lines is Châtelet.

Eight tram lines, T1 to T8, operate in Paris, mainly servicing the outskirts of the city. You can travel on the trams using regular metro tickets and passes. They don't run past the most major tourist attractions but can be a pleasant way to see the outer reaches of Paris.

Long-Distance Bus Travel

Two major coach operators, **FlixBus** and **BlaBlaBus**, link Paris to other towns in France and destinations throughout Europe. Between the two companies – low-cost alternatives to planes and trains – travellers from Paris can reach London, Brussels, Amsterdam, Milan and Barcelona, as well as Warsaw, Zagreb and Bucharest, among other cities.

Taxis

Taxis can be hailed in the street or from one of the 500 or so taxi ranks dotted all over the city. The meter will show an initial starting charge (around €2.60). There is generally an additional charge for more than three passengers and for luggage weighing more than 5 kg and bulky items (but not for wheelchairs).

Vélo taxis are motorized tricycle rickshaws that offer a green alternative to traditional taxis. **G7 Taxis** has a large fleet of electric and hybrid cars. If you're after a motorcycle taxi, book with **CityBird**. Taxi apps such as Uber, Free Now and Bolt also operate in Paris.

Driving to Paris

Autoroutes (motorways) converge on Paris from all directions. For those travelling from Britain to Paris by road, the simplest way is to use the Eurotunnel trains that run between the terminals at Folkestone and Calais, which both have direct motorway access. Paris is surrounded by an outer ring road called the Boulevard Périphérique. All motorways leading to the capital link in to the Périphérique, which separates the city from the suburbs. Each former city gate, called a *porte*, now corresponds to an exit onto or from the Périphérique. Arriving motorists should take time to check their destination address and consult a map of central Paris to find the closest corresponding *porte*.

To take your own car into France you will have to carry proof of registration, valid insurance documents, a full and valid driving licence, and passport at all times.

Driving in Paris

Driving in Paris is not recommended. Traffic is often heavy, there are many one-way streets and parking can be notoriously difficult, not to mention expensive.

For those who must drive in the city, Paris is a limited traffic zone and it is compulsory for all vehicles to display a Crit'Air sticker with a number ranging from 1 to 5, which denotes the level of pollution in ascending order. In the event of high pollution levels, vehicles with certain stickers may be banned from the road. The stickers can be purchased from the **Air Quality Certificate Service**.

Park in areas with a large "P" or *payant* sign on the pavement or road, and pay at the parking meter with *La Paris Carte* (available from any kiosk), a credit or debit card, or by using the **PaybyPhone** app.

Paris has numerous underground car parks, signposted by a white "P" on a blue background.

Car Rental

To rent a car in France you must be 21 years old or over and have held a valid driver's licence for at least a year. You will also need to present a credit card to secure the rental deposit. Check the regulations regarding the type of driving licence you will need to drive in France with your local automobile association before you travel.

Ada.Paris is a self-service car rental firm that operates throughout Paris and the Paris region. You can pick up a car from one parking station, make your journey and park at any other station in the region.

Rules of the Road

Always drive on the right. Unless otherwise signposted, vehicles coming from the right have right of way. Cars on a roundabout usually have right of way, although the Arc de Triomphe is a hair-raising exception because cars give way to traffic on the right.

At all times, drivers must carry a valid driver's licence, registration and insurance documents. The wearing of seat belts is compulsory, and it is prohibited to sound your horn in the city. For motorbikes and scooters, the wearing of helmets and protective gloves is compulsory. In the city centre, it is against the law to use the bus lanes at all times. France strictly enforces its drink-drive limit of 0.05 percent BAC (blood alcohol content).

Boats and Ferries

Several companies run regular passenger and vehicle ferry services from the UK.

P&O Ferries offers services from Dover to Calais, **Condor Ferries** operates between Poole and St-Malo and **DFDS Seaways** runs routes from Newhaven to Dieppe and from Dover to Dunkirk. **Brittany Ferries** makes crossings from Plymouth to Roscoff, from Poole and Portsmouth to Cherbourg, and from Portsmouth to Le Havre and Caen. They also run an overnight service from Portsmouth to St-Malo. Driving to Paris from Cherbourg takes about four hours; from Dieppe

or Le Havre, about two and a half hours; and from Calais, two hours.

Paris by Boat

Paris's riverboat shuttle, the hop-on-hop-off **Batobus**, runs every 20 to 45 minutes, with more frequent services in spring and summer. Tickets can be bought at Batobus stops and at RATP and tourist offices.

Cycling

Paris is reasonably flat, manageably small and has many backstreets where traffic is restricted. You can hire a bicycle and download a free map of the city's cycle lanes at **Paris à Vélo**. **Allovelo** has a selection of electic bikes for hire.

The **Vélib'** shared bike scheme is available 24 hours a day. There are some 1,400 Vélib' docking terminals dotted throughout the city; payment is made via the smartphone

app or by credit card at the terminals. For regular bikes, the first half-hour is free, increasing by €1 for every additional half-hour; for electric bikes the first half-hour is €1, increasing by €2 for every additional half-hour.

Bicycle Tours

Fat Tyre Tours offers trips to Paris's most famous landmarks, while Paris à Vélo runs multi-lingual tours to more offbeat locations. **Bike About Tours** organizes small group tours around Paris and Versailles.

Walking

Walking is by far the most agreeable way to explore central Paris and the best way to experience its beauty and culture. Most sights are only a short distance apart. The **Office du Tourisme et des Congrès de Paris** has walking itineraries on their website.

DIRECTORY

LONG-DISTANCE BUS TRAVEL

BlaBla Bus
🆆 blablacar.fr/bus

Flixbus
🆆 global.flixbus.com

TAXIS

CityBird
🆆 city-bird.com

G7 Taxis
🆆 taxisg7.com

DRIVING IN PARIS

Air Quality Certificate Service
🆆 certificat-air.gouv.fr

PaybyPhone
🆆 paybyphone.fr

CAR RENTAL

Ada.Paris
🆆 ada.fr

BOATS AND FERRIES

Brittany Ferries
🆆 brittany-ferries.co.uk

Condor Ferries
🆆 condorferries.co.uk

DFDS Seaways
🆆 dfdsseaways.co.uk

P&O Ferries
🆆 poferries.com

PARIS BY BOAT

Batobus
🆆 batobus.com

CYCLING

Allovelo
🆆 allovelo.paris

Paris à Vélo
🆆 paris.fr/velo

Vélib
🆆 velib-metropole.fr

BICYCLE TOURS

Bike About Tours
🆆 bikeabouttours.com

Fat Tyre Tours
🆆 fattiretours.com

WALKING

Office du Tourisme et des Congrès de Paris
🆆 parisinfo.com

Practical Information

Passports and Visas

For entry requirements, including visas, consult your nearest French embassy or check the **France-Visas** website. EU nationals and citizens of the UK, US, Canada, Australia and New Zealand do not need a visa for a stay of up to three months as long as their passport is valid for at least three months beyond the end of their stay.

Government Advice

Now, more than ever, it is important to consult both your and the French government's advice before travelling. The **UK Foreign and Commonwealth Office**, the **US Department of State**, the **Australian Department of Foreign Affairs and Trade** and **Gouvernement France** offer the latest information on security, health and local regulations.

Customs Information

You can find information on the laws relating to goods and currency taken in or out of France on the official **France Tourism** website. For EU citizens there are no limits on goods that can be taken into or out of France, provided they are for your personal use.

Insurance

We recommend that you take out a comprehensive policy covering theft, loss of belongings, medical care, cancellations and delays, and read the small print carefully. EU citizens are eligible for free emergency medical care in France, provided they have a valid **EHIC** (European Health Insurance Card).

Health

France has a world-class healthcare system. Emergency medical care is free for all EU nationals with an EHIC card. Be sure to present this as early on as possible. You may have to pay for treatment and reclaim the money later. For other visitors, payment of medical expenses is the patient's responsibility. It is therefore important to arrange comprehensive medical insurance before travelling.

Paris hospitals are listed on the **Assistance Publique** website. The most centrally located hospital is the **Hôtel Dieu**.

In the case of a dental emergency, **SOS Dentaire** will provide a prompt house call, but be prepared to pay a substantial fee for this visit. A dental practice can be found at the **Centre Médical Europe**.

A green cross (usually in flashing neon) indicates a pharmacy (chemist). They are usually open 9am–7pm Monday to Saturday. At other times, the address of the duty pharmacy will usually be displayed. Pharmacies will advise on minor health problems and

can give details of the nearest doctor.

Unless stated otherwise, tap water in France is safe to drink. No vaccinations are needed for France.

Smoking, Alcohol and Drugs

Smoking is prohibited in all public places, but is allowed on restaurant, café and pub outside terraces, as long as they are not enclosed.

The possession of narcotics is prohibited and could result in a prison sentence.

Unless stated otherwise, alcohol consumption on the streets is permitted.

ID

There is no requirement for visitors to carry ID, but in the event of a routine check you may be asked to show your passport. If you don't have it with you, the police may escort you to wherever your passport is being kept.

Personal Security

Paris is generally a safe city to visit. Petty theft is as common here as in most major cities. Pickpockets often frequent tourist spots and wander the metro system and RER so guard your belongings at all times. To report a theft, go to the nearest police station (commissariat de police). A list of police stations can be found on the **Office du Tourisme et des Congrès de Paris** website. Get a copy of the crime report in order to make an insurance claim. If you have your passport stolen, contact your embassy.

For emergency **police, fire department** or **ambulance** services call 112 – the operator will ask which service you require. For medical emergencies you can also dial 15 for **SAMU (ambulance)**. The direct number for the **police** is 17 and for the **fire department** it is 18.

When travelling late at night, avoid long transfers in metro stations such as Châtelet-Les-Halles and Montparnasse. The last RER trains to and from outlying areas should also be avoided.

Paris is a diverse, multicultural city. As a rule, Parisians are accepting of all people, regardless of their race, gender or sexuality. Same-sex marriage was legalized in 2013 and France recognized the right to legally change your gender in 2016. Paris has a thriving LGBT+ scene, centred in the Marais district. The **Centre LGBT Paris Ile-de-France** offers advice and hosts regular events. It also has a library and bar.

Events in recent years have led to an increased army and police presence in Paris, which should be regarded as normal. Expect bag checks at most major attractions. Small groups of armed guards patrolling are common scenes.

Travellers with Specific Requirements

Paris's historic buildings and cobbled streets can make the city tricky to navigate. However, most of Paris's top attractions are wheelchair-accessible and there are a number of organizations working to further improve accessibility throughout France's capital.

The Office du Tourisme et des Congrès de Paris lists easily accessible sights, adapted public toilets and routes for visitors with mobility, visual or hearing impairment, while **Jaccede** has details of accessible museums, hotels, bars, restaurants and cinemas.

The **Vianavigo** website provides detailed information on accessible public transport, including a route planner that can be tailored to your specific needs. SNCF's **Accès Plus** website is a useful source of information regarding accessible train travel.

Les Compagnons du Voyage will provide an escort for persons with limited mobility or visual or hearing impairment on public transport, for a small fee.

DIRECTORY

PASSPORTS AND VISAS

France-Visas
w france-visas.gouv.fr

GOVERNMENT ADVICE

Australian Department of Foreign Affairs and Trade
w smartraveller.gov.au

Gouvernement France
w gouvernement.fr

UK Foreign and Commonwealth Office
w gov.uk/foreign-travel-advice

US Department of State
w travel.state.gov

CUSTOMS INFORMATION

France Tourism
w ee.france.fr

INSURANCE

EHIC
w ec.europa.eu

HEALTH

Assistance Publique
w apap.fr

Centre Médical Europe
MAP E2 ■ 44 Rue d'Amsterdam, 75009
w centre-medical-europe.fr

Hôtel Dieu
MAP N4 ■ Pl du Parvis Notre Dame, 75004
C 01 42 34 82 34

SOS Dentaire
87 Blvd Port Royal, 75013
w sosdentaire.com

PERSONAL SECURITY

Centre LGBT Paris Ile-de-France
w centrelgbtparis.org

Fire Department
C 18

Office du Tourisme et des Congrès de Paris
w parisinfo.com

Police
C 17

Police, Fire Department and Ambulance
C 112

SAMU (ambulance)
C 15

TRAVELLERS WITH SPECIFIC REQUIREMENTS

Accès Plus
w accessbilite.sncf.com

Les Compagnons du Voyage
w compagnons.com

Jaccede
w jaccede.com

Vianavigo
w actus.lab.vianavigo.com

Time Zone

France operates Central European Time (CET), which is 1 hour ahead of Greenwich Mean Time (GMT), 6 hours ahead of US Eastern Standard Time (EST) and 9 hours ahead of PST (Pacific Time Zone). The clock moves forward 1 hour during daylight saving time from the last Sunday in March until the last Sunday in October. Keep in mind the French use the 24-hour clock.

Money

France's currency is the euro (€). Most establishments accept major credit, debit and prepaid currency cards, but it's always a good idea to carry some cash too. Contactless payments are widely accepted in Paris.

Tipping in restaurants is considered polite. If you are pleased with the service a tip of 5–10% of the total bill is appreciated. Hotel porters and housekeeping generally expect a tip of €1 to €2 per bag or day. It is sufficient to tip taxi drivers €1 to €2.

Electrical Appliances

Electricity runs on 220V out of double, round-pin wall sockets. You will need adaptors, and possibly a transformer (for some US electrical appliances).

Mobile Phones and Wi-Fi

Free Wi-Fi hotspots dotted all over Paris provide fast internet access in more than 260 public places, including museums, parks and libraries. These are clearly signposted with the Paris-Wifi logo. Simply select the Paris_Wi-Fi_ network on your device, fill in your details when prompted and you will then be connected to the web for free.

Cafés and restaurants usually permit free use of their Wi-Fi as long as you make a purchase, and many hotels provide free Wi-Fi to guests.

Visitors with EU tariffs will be able to use their devices abroad without being affected by data roaming charges. Users will be charged the same rates for data, SMS and voice calls as they would pay at home. Those not on EU tariffs should check roaming rates with their provider. A cheaper option may be to purchase a French SIM card (you will need to show ID).

Postal Services

The postal service in France is fast and reliable. The main post office in Paris, La Poste Paris Louvre, is located at 16 rue Etienne Marcel and has the longest opening hours.

Most post offices have self-service machines to weigh and frank your mail. For simple letters and postcards, you can buy stamps at a *tabac* (tobacconist) rather than try to find a post office (La Poste). Not all *tabacs* advertise the service, but if they sell postcards it is worth asking. Some hotels and newsagents also sell postage stamps.

Weather

Paris has a temperate and pleasant climate. Summers can be hot, with temperatures sometimes reaching 35–40°C (95–105°F). Both spring and autumn are mild, with a fair amount of rain, but there are also many bright days. Winter is cold, though the light then can be beautiful.

Opening Hours

Department stores and chain boutiques are usually open 10am–8pm Monday to Saturday. Some open on Sunday too. Independent shops often don't open up until 10 or 11am, and may be closed during the holidays, on Mondays and/or between noon and 2pm, but some open on Sundays in main tourist areas. Many food shops are open on a Sunday morning.

Museums are generally open 9/10am to 5/6pm and some have a late opening one evening a week. Most museums close either on a Monday or Tuesday. Banks are usually open Tuesday to Saturday 9am–4pm. Businesses, banks, most shops and many restaurants are closed on New Year's Day, Easter Monday, 1 May (Labour Day), 8 May (VE Day), Ascension Day (40 days after Easter), Whitsun (7th Sunday after Easter), Whit Monday (the day after Whitsun), 14 July (Bastille Day), 15 August (Assumption), 1 November (All Saints' Day), 11 November (Armistice Day) and 25 December (Christmas Day).

COVID-19 The pandemic continues to affect Paris. Some museums, tourist attractions and hospitality venues are operating on reduced or temporary opening hours, and require visitors to make advance bookings for a specific date and time. Always check ahead before visiting.

Visitor Information

The Paris tourism board, **Office du Tourisme et des Congrès de Paris**, has a very useful website. Its main information centre is located close to the Hôtel de Ville metro station. There are also information points at Gare du Nord and Beauvais Airport, on the Champs-Élysées, at the Carrousel du Louvre and near the Opéra Garnier.

Visit Paris Region serves both Paris and the wider Ile de France region, and is the best source of advice and information on visiting places outside the city. It has offices at Roissy–CDG and Orly airports, Disneyland® Paris and Galeries Lafayette.

Entry to some national and municipal museums is free on the first Sunday of each month. Visitors under 18 years of age and EU passport holders aged 18–26 years are usually admitted free of charge to national museums, and there are sometimes discounts for students and those over 60 who have ID showing their date of birth.

The **Paris Pass** offers access to more than 60 attractions for 2, 3, 4 or 6 consecutive days. It also includes unlimited travel on the metro, buses and RER within central Paris, and a ticket for a hop-on hop-off bus tour.

Local Customs

Etiquette *(la politesse)* is important to Parisians. On entering a store or café, you are expected to say *"bonjour"* to staff, and when leaving, *"au revoir"*. Be sure to add *"s'il vous plaît"* (please) when ordering something and *"pardon"* if you bump into someone accidentally.

The French usually shake hands on meeting someone for the first time. Friends and colleagues who know each other well greet each other with a kiss on each cheek. If you are unsure what's expected, wait to see if they proffer a hand or a cheek.

Language

French is the official language spoken in Paris. The French are fiercely proud of their language, but don't let this put you off. Mastering a few niceties goes a long way though you can get by without knowing the language at all.

Taxes and Refunds

VAT is around 20% in France. Non-EU residents can claim back tax on certain goods. Look out for the Global Refund Tax-Free sign, where the retailer will supply a form and issue a *détaxe* receipt. Present the goods receipt, *détaxe* receipt and passport at customs when you depart to receive your refund.

Accommodation

Paris offers a huge variety of accommodation, including luxury five-star hotels, family-run B&Bs, budget hostels and private apartments. The Office du Tourisme et des Congrès de Paris website provides an extensive list of options.

Book as far in advance as you can, as hotels get booked up quickly, especially in spring and autumn and around Christmas and New Year.

France offers more than 9,000 campsites all over the country, in hugely varied landscapes. A full list and information about facilities is available on the **Camping France** website.

All places of accommodation are obliged by law to add a tourist tax *(taxe de séjour touristique)* to their rates. This ranges from 0.5 to 5 euros per person per night.

Places to Stay

PRICE CATEGORIES
For a standard double room per night (with breakfast if included), taxes and extra charges.

€ under €150   €€ €150–€350   €€€ over €350

Boutique Hotels

Hôtel Amour
MAP E2 ■ 8 Rue Navarin, 75009 ■ 01 48 78 31 80 ■ www.hotelamourparis.fr ■ €€
Just below the hill of Montmartre, this trendy hotel and bistro has medium-sized rooms with different themes, all brightly decorated with cutting-edge photography (some erotic) and pop art. As it is on a quiet residential street, guests can experience Parisian bohemia without the usual crowds. Visitors can also stay in the sister Hôtel Grand Amour if Hôtel Amour is fully booked.

Hôtel du Temps
MAP F2 ■ 11 Rue de Montholon, 75009 ■ 01 47 70 37 16 ■ www.hotel-du-temps.fr ■ €€
Vintage furniture and textiles give this creatively decorated small hotel, near the Gare du Nord, a home-away-from-home feel. Some rooms can be snug, but the imaginative touches fill the space with charm and style.

La Maison Favart
MAP E3 ■ 5 Rue de Marivaux, 75002 ■ 01 42 97 59 83 ■ www.lamaisonfavart.com ■ €€
There is a sense of theatre at this graceful, small hotel dedicated to the colourful lives of Charles-Simon and Justine Favart, the "It" couple of the 18th-century Opéra-Comique. Well-appointed, cheerfully decorated rooms have a courtesy tray; guests also have access to the pool.

Hôtel Baume
MAP M5 ■ 7 Rue Casimir Delavigne, 75006 ■ 01 53 10 28 50 ■ www.baume-hotel-paris.com/en/ ■ €€€
Minutes from the Jardin de Luxembourg, this modern hotel has been outfitted with a glamorous Art Deco-inspired interior. On the upper floors, spacious suites with a large terrace overlook the Neo-Classical Théâtre de l'Odéon.

Hôtel Bel Ami
MAP K4 ■ 7/11 Rue St-Benoît, 75006 ■ 01 42 61 53 53 ■ www.hotel belami-paris.fr ■ €€€
Occupying a former 19th-century printing works, this bright, stylish hotel is on a small side street in the heart of lively St-Germain-des-Prés. A good choice for design-conscious families, it has connecting rooms, as well as larger rooms that include a sofabed.

Hôtel de Nell
MAP F2 ■ 9 Rue du Conservatoire, 75009 ■ 01 44 83 83 60 ■ www.hoteldenell.com ■ €€€
The sleek, minimalist rooms in this contemporary hotel are ideal for a chic Parisian stay.

Twenty minutes on foot from the Louvre, the hotel is on a quiet street away from the crowds. For a more serene experience, ask for a room facing the interior courtyard.

Hôtel Vernet
MAP C3 ■ 25 Rue Vernet, 75008 ■ 01 44 31 98 00 ■ www.hotelvernet-paris.com ■ €€€
Steps away from the Champs-Elysées, this hotel combines cutting-edge contemporary design with the elegant framework of the post-Haussmannian building that it occupies. Enjoy breakfast underneath the ornate, Gustave-Eiffel-designed glass dome.

W Paris – Opéra Hotel
MAP E2 ■ 4 Rue Meyerbeer, 75009 ■ 01 77 48 94 94 ■ www.wparisopera.com ■ €€€
Ideally located next to the Opéra National de Paris Garnier, the W brings its trendy, modern flair to Paris with 91 ultra-chic rooms and suites. Opt for a room with a view of the opera house.

Luxury Hotels

Hôtel Molitor
13 Rue Nungesser et Coli, 75016 ■ Metro Michel-Ange – Molitor ■ 01 56 07 08 50 ■ www.mltr.fr ■ €€
An immaculate and stunning hotel which breathes new life into the historic Art Deco Piscine Molitor, where the beautiful people of 1930s Paris made waves. Minutes from the elegant

botanical gardens in the Bois de Boulogne, it is within walking distance of the metro to central Paris.

Four Seasons George V

MAP C3 ■ 31 Ave George V, 75008 ■ 01 49 52 70 00 ■ www.fourseasons.com/paris ■ €€€

One of the most luxurious and fashionable hotels in Paris, the George V combines period features with modern amenities. Bedrooms are spacious, beautifully decorated and have marble bathrooms. The three-Michelin-starred restaurant, Le Cinq (see p117), is unquestionably one of the finest places to dine in the whole of Paris.

Hôtel de Crillon

MAP D3 ■ 10 Pl de la Concorde, 75008 ■ 01 44 71 15 00 ■ www.rosewoodhotels.com/en/hotel-de-crillon ■ €€€

This luxury hotel is housed in a Neo-Classical building dating from 1758. The stylish rooms feature flat-screen TVs and Nespresso machines while the en suite marble bathrooms have heated floors. Visitors can enjoy live music in the bar.

Hôtel Raphaël

MAP B3 ■ 17 Ave Kleber, 75116 ■ 01 53 64 32 00 ■ www.raphael-hotel.com ■ €€€

In a 1920s building close to the Arc de Triomphe, this fine hotel has traditionally decorated rooms with modern facilities. Rooms on higher floors have stunning city views; the rooftop's terrace restaurant and Champagne bar (open in summer) overlooks the Eiffel Tower.

Le Royal Monceau

MAP C2 ■ 37 Ave Hoche, 75008 ■ 01 42 99 88 00 ■ www.leroyalmonceau.com ■ €€€

This Paris branch of the Raffles hotel chain features interiors by Philippe Starck, two superb restaurants and a Clarins spa with a pool.

Mandarin Oriental

MAP E3 ■ 251 Rue St-Honoré, 75001 ■ 01 70 98 78 88 ■ www.mandarinoriental.com/paris ■ €€€

On one of Paris's most fashionable streets, this centrally located hotel has elegant rooms and suites, plus a top-floor four-bedroom apartment with a rooftop terrace. In addition to a two-Michelin-starred restaurant, the hotel has its own cake shop.

The Peninsula Paris

MAP B3 ■ 19 Ave Kléber, 75016 ■ 01 58 12 28 88 ■ www.peninsula.com ■ €€€

Occupying a sumptuously restored 1908 building, steps away from the Arc de Triomphe, this hotel feels modern and has some great contemporary artworks on display in its vast public areas. Among the six drinking and dining outlets in the hotel, the Oiseau Blanc restaurant stands out for its spectacular views. Gershwin wrote the musical An American in Paris here in 1928.

Prince de Galles

MAP C3 ■ 33 Ave George V, 75008 ■ 01 53 23 77 77 ■ www.princedegalles paris.com ■ €€€

Steps from the luxury and haute couture

boutiques, this gloriously restored Art Deco hotel features handsome rooms (some with a balcony or terrace), two restaurants and a cocktail bar. Guests can use the on-site spa and gym.

Ritz Paris

MAP D3 ■ 15 Pl Vendôme, 75001 ■ 01 43 16 30 30 ■ www.ritzparis.com ■ €€€

This iconic 1898 hotel enjoys a superb location overlooking the elegant Place Vendôme. The lovely, spacious rooms with French decor have exquisite antiques and marble bathrooms. The fabulous Hemingway-inspired bar is not to be missed.

Shangri-La Paris

MAP A3 ■ 10 Ave d'Iéna, 75116 ■ 01 53 67 19 98 ■ www.shangri-la.com ■ €€€

Housed in the former home of Napoleon's grand-nephew, this fabulous hotel is located in the elegant 16th arrondissement. Most of the rooms have views of the Eiffel Tower.

The Westin Paris

MAP E3 ■ 3 Rue de Castiglione, 75001 ■ 01 44 77 11 11 ■ www.westin.marriott.com ■ €€€

The Westin is a world away from the usual anonymity of chain hotels due to its location in a 19th-century building designed by Charles Garnier. The original atmosphere has been retained, but the rooms offer everything you would expect from a hotel of this class.

Romantic Hotels

Five Hotel
3 Rue Flatters, 75005
■ Metro Les Gobelins
■ 01 43 31 74 21 ■ www.
thefivehotel.com ■ €€
Fibre-optic lighting creates a glittering atmosphere in this boutique hotel's 24 rooms. The rooms come in nine colours and boast five "olfactory ambiences" by Esteban. The Five has already established a reputation as the perfect lovers' hideaway hotel.

Hôtel Bellechasse
MAP J2 ■ 8 Rue de Bellechasse, 75007
■ 01 45 50 22 31 ■ www.lebellechasse.com ■ €€
The opulent rooms at this boutique hotel – all rich colours, plush fabrics and decorated ceilings – were designed by Christian Lacroix. Evening cocktails may be followed by breakfast in bed. The Musée d'Orsay is a few minutes' walk away.

Hôtel Bourg Tibourg
MAP P3 ■ 19 Rue du Bourg Tibourg, 75004
■ 01 42 78 47 39 ■ www.bourgtibourg.com ■ €€
The rooms in this hotel are furnished with antiques and luxurious fabrics. Public spaces are hung with tapestries, and there is a library lounge. Most rooms are small and even the lift is tiny but the location, in the heart of the Marais, makes up for it.

Hôtel Caron de Beaumarchais
MAP R2 ■ 12 Rue Vieille du Temple, 75004 ■ 01 42 72 34 12 ■ www.carondebeaumarchais.com ■ €€
Wooden beams, a log fire, candlelight, charming decor and sparkling crystal chandeliers evoke the essence of 18th-century romance here. Rooms facing the street have large French windows; others overlook the quiet inner courtyard.

Hôtel d'Aubusson
MAP M4 ■ 33 Rue Dauphine, 75006 ■ 01 43 29 43 43 ■ www.hoteldaubusson.com ■ €€
The rooms in this 17th-century building are spacious and many of them have beams. The hotel's café doubles as a chic jazz bar, which regularly hosts concerts and events.

Hôtel Costes
MAP E3 ■ 239–241 Rue St-Honoré, 75001 ■ 01 42 44 50 00 ■ www.hotelcostes.com ■ €€€
Book a first-floor room overlooking the courtyard for a romantic place to stay. Low lighting and dark furniture add to the seductive mood, as does the swimming pool, live music and trendy restaurant.

Hôtel Particulier Montmartre
MAP E1 ■ 23 Ave Junot, Pavillon D, 75018 ■ 01 53 41 81 40 ■ www.hotelparticulier.com ■ €€€
This hotel is a romantic hideaway right in the heart of Montmartre, housed in a former private residence between the picturesque Avenue Junot and Rue Lepic. The five suites are individually decorated by artists in quirky and decadent style.It is surrounded by a vast, beautiful garden, abundant with vegetation.

Le Relais Christine
MAP M4 ■ 3 Rue Christine, 75006 ■ 01 40 51 60 80 ■ www.relais-christine.com ■ €€€
This historic mansion with a spa offers a quiet side-street escape from the St-Germain bustle. Guests can opt for a terraced room overlooking the secluded garden and take breakfast in the vaulted dining room, which was once the refectory of an abbey.

L'Hôtel
MAP E4 ■ 13 Rue des Beaux-Arts, 75006 ■ 01 44 41 99 00 ■ www.l-hotel.com ■ €€€
This hotel has come up in the world since Oscar Wilde expired here, having uttered the famous words, "My wallpaper and I are fighting a duel to the death. One or the other of us has to go." Fashionable as it has become, with its stylish decor by Jacques Garcia as well as a bookable private hammam, the hotel still retains its quirky charm.

Hotels in Great Locations

Hôtel Brighton
MAP K1 ■ 218 Rue de Rivoli, 75001 ■ 01 47 03 61 61 ■ www.paris-hotel-brighton.com ■ €€
Enjoy the Rue de Rivoli, within walking distance of numerous attractions, without paying the usual prices associated with this location. The venerable Hôtel Brighton was a famous stop on many a Briton's Grand Tour. Ask for a room with a view over the Tuileries gardens opposite or of the Eiffel Tower.

Hôtel de la Place du Louvre

MAP M2 ■ 21 Rue des Prêtres-St-Germain-l'Auxerrois, 75001 ■ 01 42 33 78 68 ■ www.paris-hotel-place-du-louvre.com ■ €€

The 20 rooms in this neat little hotel may be small, but many of them offer a superb view onto the colonnade of the Louvre museum. The decor is bright and fresh, and cleverly mixes classic and modern influences.

Hôtel des Deux-Îles

MAP Q5 ■ 59 Rue St-Louis-en-l'Île, 75004 ■ 01 43 26 13 35 ■ www.deuxiles-paris-hotel.com ■ €€

To stay on one of the Seine islands is a treat, and to do it in this hotel is a double treat. The bedrooms may be small, due to the building's 17th-century origins, but the cheerful decor, the intimacy (only 17 rooms) and the hidden patio with its flowers and fountain more than compensate.

Hôtel d'Orsay

MAP J2 ■ 93 Rue de Lille, 75007 ■ 01 47 05 85 54 ■ www.paris-hotel-orsay.com ■ €€

Art-lovers will enjoy this hotel in an 18th-century building near the magnificent Musée d'Orsay. The hotel's bright and modern decor is strikingly offset with choice items of elegant antique furniture here and there. Several more expensive suites are also available. A buffet breakfast is served in a light and airy room under a glass roof.

Hôtel du Jeu de Paume

MAP Q5 ■ 54 Rue St-Louis-en-l'Île, 75004 ■ 01 43 26 14 18 ■ www.jeudepaumehotel.com ■ €€

Tucked away on the Île St-Louis is this characterful old building with ancient beamed ceilings. Some rooms overlook a peaceful courtyard, and all are quite small, but the welcoming atmosphere makes up for that.

Hôtel Edouard VII

MAP E3 ■ 39 Ave de l'Opéra, 75002 ■ 01 42 61 56 90 ■ www.hoteledouard7-paris.fr ■ €€

An elegant boutique hotel with eclectic design features and oodles of charm. Most rooms have the bonus of breath-taking balcony views over the spectacular Opéra National de Paris Garnier. The bar serves tailor-made cocktails and a range of snacks, and the restaurant offers inventive seasonal cuisine.

Hôtel Les Dames du Panthéon

MAP N6 ■ 19 Pl du Panthéon, 75005 ■ 01 43 54 32 95 ■ www.hotellesdamesdupantheon.com ■ €€

This retro-inspired hotel has great views across to the Panthéon, and the feel of an 18th-century townhouse – some rooms have four-poster beds and spacious bathrooms.

Castille

MAP E3 ■ 33–37 Rue Cambon, 75001 ■ 01 44 58 44 58 ■ www.castille.com ■ €€€

This elegant hotel is located near Place Vendôme. The bedrooms are decorated in either a contemporary style or classic 1930s French, depending on which wing you stay in. The hotel also boasts an Italian restaurant, l'Assaggio.

Hôtel Le Bristol Paris

MAP D3 ■ 112 Rue du Faubourg St-Honoré, 75008 ■ 01 53 43 43 00 ■ www.lebristolparis.com ■ €€€

Prices reflect the level of luxury and the location, on the Rue du Faubourg St-Honoré. Rooms are spacious, and fitted out with antique furniture. They offer indulgently large marble bathrooms, as well as all the latest modern facilities. There are also two restaurants.

Pavillon de la Reine

MAP R3 ■ 28 Pl des Vosges, 75003 ■ 01 40 29 19 19 ■ www.pavillon-de-la-reine.com ■ €€€

This may well be the finest hotel in the Marais, right on the Place des Vosges. It offers lovely rooms, a spa and a quiet courtyard. The list of famous guests includes Georges Simenon and Victor Hugo.

Rooms with a View

Artus Hôtel

MAP L4 ■ 34 Rue de Buci, 75006 ■ 01 43 29 07 20 ■ www.artushotel.com ■ €€

Indulge yourself in the food shops of the Rue de Buci, then pamper yourself even more back in this hotel – especially if you have booked the suite with a Jacuzzi, from which there are views of the rooftops of the Latin Quarter.

For a key to hotel price categories see p172

Bourgogne & Montana

MAP D4 ■ 3 Rue de Bourgogne, 75007 ■ 01 45 51 20 22 ■ www. bourgogne-montana. com ■ €€

A stylish hotel, with the Musée d'Orsay as well as the Invalides close by. Rooms feature Empire-style furnishings and Kenzo-designed wallpaper. Some top-floor rooms have views across the Seine.

Hôtel des Grands Hommes

MAP N6 ■ 17 Pl du Panthéon, 75005 ■ 01 46 34 19 60 ■ www.hoteldes grandshommes.com ■ €€

Enjoy great upper-floor views of the Panthéon from this intimate 30-room hotel in an 18th-century house. Rooms are a good size.

Hôtel du Quai Voltaire

MAP K2 ■ 19 Quai Voltaire, 75007 ■ 01 42 61 50 91 ■ www.quaivoltaire.fr ■ No air conditioning ■ €€

Impressionist artist Camille Pissarro (1830–1903) painted the view of the Seine and Notre-Dame visible from most of the guest rooms here. Rooms are small, but the warm welcome and the location make up for that.

Hôtel Notre-Dame St-Michel

MAP N4 ■ 1 Quai St-Michel, 75005 ■ 01 43 54 20 43 ■ www.hotelnotre dameparis.com ■ €€

Located right by the Seine with magnificent views of Notre-Dame. Rooms may be small, but they have been lavishly decorated by Christian Lacroix.

Hotel Square

MAP A5 ■ 3 Rue de Boulainvilliers, 75016 ■ 01 44 14 91 90 ■ www. hotelsquare.com ■ €€

The Square is an ultra-chic boutique hotel with 22 rooms and views over Paris. The dramatic architecture includes a four-storey exhibition wall featuring a regularly changing display of works by modern artists. Classic and inventive cuisine is served at the sleek Zebra brasserie, and there is also a spa.

Les Rives de Notre-Dame

MAP N4 ■ 15 Quai St-Michel, 75005 ■ 01 43 54 81 16 ■ www.rivesde notredame.com ■ €€

The views of Notre-Dame from this 10-room Latin Quarter hotel are arguably the best in Paris. The spacious and airy rooms feature charming wooden ceiling beams.

Terrass Hôtel

MAP E1 ■ 12–14 Rue Joseph de Maistre, 75018 ■ 01 46 06 72 85 ■ www. terrass-hotel.com ■ €€

Located in Montmartre, the Terrass has fabulous views over the city from its rooftop bar and restaurant. All the bedrooms are stylish and modern, but the best rooms and suites look over treetops and rooftops to the Eiffel Tower.

Hôtel Régina

MAP K1 ■ 2 Pl des Pyramides, 75001 ■ 01 42 60 31 10 ■ www.regina-hotel.com/en ■ €€€

Across the Rue de Rivoli from the Louvre, with views of the museum and the Tuileries, this old hotel has been used as a backdrop for a number of films. The rooms are elegantly decorated and there's a terrace for alfresco dining. The bar is reminiscent of Victorian England, with its oak panelling and plush sofas.

Le Metropolitan

MAP A3 ■ 10 Pl de Mexico, 75116 ■ 01 56 90 40 04 www.hotelle metropolitan paris.com ■ €€€

Five upper suites offer striking views of the Eiffel Tower; the best has a giant bull's-eye window. Lower-floor rooms have good, but less spectacular, balcony views.

Family-Friendly Hotels

Hôtel des Arts

MAP F2 ■ 7 Cité Bergère, 6 Rue du Faubourg Montmartre, 75009 ■ 01 42 46 73 30 ■ www. hoteldesarts.fr ■ €

This hotel is great for families on a budget, with triple rooms and cots available. It's tucked away in the Grand Boulevards district – home to many restaurants and shops.

Ibis Paris Bastille Faubourg Saint Antoine

MAP H5 ■ 13 Rue Trousseau, 75011 ■ 01 48 05 55 55 ■ www.ibis. com ■ €

A popular budget option, this hotel in the Ibis chain is a five-minute walk from the bustling Marché d'Aligre. Triple rooms and smartly designed duplex rooms are perfect for families.

Yooma Urban Lodge

MAP B5 ▪ 51 Quai de Grenelle, 75015 ▪ 01 44 09 00 13 ▪ www.yooma-hotels.com ▪ €

A 15-minute riverside walk from the Eiffel Tower, this fun, modern hotel has colourful, well-priced bedrooms that can accommodate up to six people. Cooking classes for the entire family can be organized, and remote child monitoring is available, too, so parents can have a night out.

Gardette Park Hotel

MAP H4 ▪ 1 Rue du Général Blaise, 75011 ▪ 01 47 00 57 93 ▪ www.hotelgardettepark.com ▪ €€

The tastefully decorated junior suites at this hotel, on a leafy square with a playground, accommodate up to four people. There are plenty of resturants nearby and the Marais is a short walk away.

Hôtel St-Jacques

MAP N5 ▪ 35 Rue des Ecoles, 75005 ▪ 01 44 07 45 45 ▪ www.paris-hotel-stjacques.com ▪ €€

Numerous Left Bank attractions are within walking distance of this comfortable hotel with triple-bed rooms and cots available. The Toulouse-Lautrec Bar serves excellent cocktails.

Relais du Louvre

MAP M2 ▪ 19 Rue des Prêtres-St-Germain-l'Auxerrois, 75001 ▪ 01 40 41 96 42 ▪ www.relais dulouvre.com ▪ €€

Right by the Louvre, this great family hotel offers several family suites and connecting rooms, as well as a host of extras for children, including baby kits with cots, bottle warmers and anti-slip mats for the bathrooms.

Relais St-Germain

MAP L4 ▪ 9 Carrefour de l'Odéon, 75006 ▪ 01 44 27 07 97 ▪ www.hotel-paris-relais-saint-germain.com ▪ €€

A delightful 17th-century property, this St-Germain-des-Prés townhouse hotel has rooms and family-friendly suites dedicated to famous writers. The Louvre, Musée d'Orsay and Notre-Dame cathedral are all within walking distance, as is the Jardin du Luxembourg, with its sailboats and playground. Babysitting can be arranged.

Résidence Nell

MAP E2 ▪ 60 Rue Richer, 75009 ▪ 01 53 24 98 98 ▪ www.residencenell.com ▪ €€

The 17 chic, understated apartments and suites in this handsomely renovated building range from studios to luxury living spaces and each has a kitchenette so families can stock up at the grocery shops and bakeries nearby. Large families should ask for adjoining suites.

Sofitel Paris Baltimore Tour Eiffel

MAP B3 ▪ 88 bis, Ave Kléber, 75016 ▪ 01 44 34 54 54 ▪ www.sofitel.com ▪ €€

Part of the Accor hotel chain and located in the most beautiful district, between the Trocadéro and the Arc de Triomphe, this boutique hotel caters well for families, with good facilities and a friendly, helpful ambience. Rooms as well as suites are elegant.

Medium-Priced Hotels

Hôtel d'Angleterre

MAP N5 ▪ 44 Rue Jacob, 75006 ▪ 01 42 60 34 72 ▪ www.hotel-dangleterre.com ▪ No air conditioning ▪ €€

Hemingway once stayed at this hotel. Most of the rooms have high ceilings, and some are furnished with antiques. Standard rooms can be on the small side, but more spacious superior rooms can be reserved at an extra cost.

Hôtel de Banville

166 Blvd Berthier, 75017 ▪ 01 42 67 70 16 ▪ www.hotelbanville.fr ▪ €€

This wonderful 1927 mansion may be away from the centre but it blends old-world charm with contemporary furnishings in a very modern and stylish way. Once a month on Thursdays, there is live music in the hall. Several bedrooms have balconies.

Hôtel de l'Abbaye

MAP K5 ▪ 10 Rue Cassette, 75006 ▪ 01 45 44 38 11 ▪ www.hotel abbayeparis.com ▪ €€

This delightful, quiet hotel, in a 16th-century former convent, is set around a leafy cobbled courtyard near St-Sulpice. It is perfect for exploring much of the Left Bank, and is a haven to return to. The 44 rooms are all different. The top-floor suites have rooftop views.

Hôtel des Trois Poussins

MAP E1 ■ 15 Rue Clauzel, 75009 ■ 01 53 32 81 81 ■ www.les3poussins.com ■ €€

This hotel is in the Pigalle area but well away from the sleazier side of the district. Some rooms are small, but the higher up they are, the better the view of the city becomes. The decor is modern with warm colours and each room has a quirky artwork on the wall.

Hôtel Jeanne d'Arc

3 Rue de Jarente, 75004 ■ Metro St-Paul ■ 01 48 87 62 11 ■ www.hotel jeannedarc.com ■ No air conditioning ■ €€

Visitors could easily spend a whole weekend in Paris without wandering far from this charming, well-equipped hotel, surrounded as it is by the many Marais district attractions.

Hôtel le Senat

MAP M5 ■ 10 Rue de Vaugirard, 75006 ■ 01 43 54 54 54 ■ www.hotel senat.com ■ €€

Just a few steps away from the Jardin de Luxembourg, this small modern hotel is smartly decorated in cheerful colours. Some rooms can accommodate families and the two duplex terrace suites on the top floors have fantastic panoramic views.

Hôtel Notre-Dame Paris Maître Albert

MAP N5 ■ 19 Rue Maître Albert, 75005 ■ 01 43 26 79 00 ■ www.hotel-notredame-charmeparis. com ■ €€

Situated in a quiet street opposite Notre-Dame,

close to the Latin Quarter and the Marais, this hotel combines sleek modern design and high-tech facilities with the odd old beam or stone wall.

Hôtel Saint-Paul

MAP M5 ■ 43 Rue Monsieur-le-Prince, 75006 ■ 01 43 26 98 64 ■ www. hotelsaintpaulparis.com ■ €€

This 17th-century building features antique furniture, beamed ceilings and even some four-poster beds. Several rooms have great views over Paris and the Sorbonne. Breakfast is served in a cellar with a vaulted ceiling.

La Régence Etoile Hôtel

MAP B2 ■ 24 Ave Carnot, 75017 ■ 01 58 05 42 42 ■ www.hotelregence etoile.com ■ €€

Very reasonably priced considering its standard of luxury and its location (just a short walk away from the Arc de Triomphe), the Régence Etoile features handsome public spaces with classic decor and plush modern bedrooms with plasma TVs, mini-bars as well as safes.

Le Citizen

MAP H2 ■ 96 Quai de Jenmapes, 75010 ■ 01 83 62 55 50 ■ www.lecitizen hotel.com ■ €€

This modern eco-hotel is within walking distance of Place de la Republique, Gare du Nord and Gare de l'Est. It boasts views over Canal St-Martin. Each of the 12 rooms and suites offers guests a complimentary minibar and use of an iPad. There is a wide choice of restaurants nearby, too.

Budget Hotels

Generator Hostel

MAP E2 ■ 9-11 Pl du Colonel Fabien, 75010 ■ 01 70 98 84 00 ■ www. staygenerator.com ■ €

With attractive options for budget travellers looking for a more grown-up vibe, Paris's Generator hostel has it all. A great location, private rooms and a number of dining options make it a good choice for solo travellers.

Henriette

9 Rue des Gobelins, 75013 ■ Metro Les Gobelins ■ 01 47 07 26 90 ■ www. hotelhenriette.com ■ €

On a quiet street close to many Left Bank sights, this relaxed, family-friendly hotel has smartly deco-rated, modern bedrooms and a sunny inner court-yard for breakfasts.

Hôtel Arvor Saint-Georges

MAP E2 ■ 8 Rue Laferrière, 75009 ■ 01 48 78 60 92 ■ hotelarvor.com ■ No air conditioning ■ €

This boutique hotel at the foot of Montmartre has comfortable rooms, many boasting views across Paris. Two-room suites, one in the attic and one opening onto a small patio, are suitable for families.

Hôtel Chopin

MAP F2 ■ 46 Passage Jouffroy, 75009 ■ 01 47 70 58 10 ■ www.hotelchopin. fr ■ No air conditioning ■ €

This characterful, historic hotel dating from 1846 has rooms with plenty of charm. Top-floor rooms have picture-perfect roof-top views, while others overlook the atmospheric Passage Jouffroy.

Hôtel de Nesle
MAP L4 ▪ 7 Rue de Nesle, 75006 ▪ 01 43 54 62 41 ▪ www.hoteldenesleparis. com ▪ €
Centrally located, this atmospheric hotel, complete with a large courtyard garden, is colourfully decorated with murals and vintage wallpaper. Not all rooms are en-suite.

Hôtel de Nice
MAP Q3 ▪ 42 bis Rue de Rivoli, 75004 ▪ 01 42 78 55 29 ▪ www. hoteldenice.com ▪ No air conditioning ▪ €
A ten-minute walk to Notre-Dame cathedral, and even less to the shops and cafés of the Marais, this quirky small hotel with antique furnishings has a romantic, 19th-century charm.

Hôtel des Grandes Ecoles
MAP P6 ▪ 75 Rue du Cardinal Lemoine, 75005 ▪ 01 43 26 79 23 ▪ www. en.hoteldesgrandes ecoles.com ▪ No air conditioning ▪ €
A secret hideaway in a lovely part of Paris, the three buildings that make up this 51-room family-run hotel are set around a beautiful garden. Floral wallpaper abounds in the reasonably sized rooms, which have a country cottage feel. The location is perfect for exploring the Latin Quarter.

Hôtel du Cygne
MAP N1 ▪ 3–5 Rue du Cygne, 75001 ▪ 01 42 60 14 16 ▪ www.hotelducygne.fr ▪ No air conditioning ▪ €
This lovely hotel is housed in a restored late-17th-century building, just five minutes' walk away from Forum des Halles. The cosy, cheerful rooms all have free Wi-Fi.

Hôtel Familia
MAP P6 ▪ 11 Rue des Ecoles, 75005 ▪ 01 43 54 55 27 ▪ www.familia hotel.com ▪ €
This good-value option in the heart of the Latin Quarter is a friendly hotel housed in an 1865 building within walking distance of many landmarks. The best rooms have a charming wrought-iron balcony.

Hôtel Joyce
MAP E2 ▪ 29 Rue la Bruyère, 75009 ▪ 01 55 07 00 01 ▪ www.astotel. com ▪ €
Located at the crossroads of the theatre district, Place St Georges and South Pigalle, this wittily decorated modern hotel has a fresh, informal feel and well-equipped rooms with organic toiletries. Room rates include a good-value buffet breakfast.

Hôtel Le Clos Médicis
MAP M5 ▪ 56 Rue Monsieur-le-Prince, 75006 ▪ 01 43 29 10 80 ▪ www. closmedicis.com ▪ €
This was built in 1773 for the Médici family; historic features now seamlessly combine with modern design. Rooms are small, but compensations are the garden, bar, and the location, in a quiet street off Boulevard St-Michel.

Hôtel Regyn's Montmartre
MAP E1 ▪ 18 Pl des Abbesses, 75018 ▪ 01 42 54 45 21 ▪ www.paris-hotels-montmartre.com ▪ No air conditioning ▪ €
Colourful decor livens up the smallish rooms in this budget hotel, well-placed in the heart of Montmartre and just minutes away on foot from Sacré-Coeur. The amenities are basic, but the stunning views of the Eiffel Tower from the upper floors are priceless.

Le Caulaincourt Square Hostel
2 Square Caulaincourt, 75018 ▪ 01 46 06 46 06 ▪ www.caulaincourt.com ▪ No air conditioning ▪ €
This is one part budget hotel, one part hostel, with a warm, friendly atmosphere and easy access to the sights of Montmartre. It is just a few minutes' walk to Moulin Rouge and Sacré-Coeur.

L'Ermitage Sacré-Coeur
MAP E1 ▪ 24 Rue Lamarck, 75018 ▪ 06 12 49 05 15 ▪ www. ermitagesacrecoeur.fr ▪ No credit cards ▪ No air conditioning ▪ €
A wonderful family-run hotel in Montmartre. Some rooms have views over the city, others overlook a garden, and the furniture is antique or retro.

Mama Shelter East
109 Rue de Bagnolet, 75020 ▪ Metro Gambetta ▪ 01 43 48 48 48 ▪ www. mamashelter.com ▪ €
Created by world-famous designer Philippe Starck, this hotel close to Père Lachaise cemetery offers ultra-stylish yet affordable rooms. The lively restaurant is very popular, and there's a rooftop sundeck offering panoramic views of the city.

For a key to hotel price categories see p172

General Index

Acknowledgments

Author
Donna Dailey and Mike Gerrard are award-winning journalists, specializing in travel, food and wine and have written more than 30 guidebooks between them. Mike Gerrard's *Time for Food* guide to Paris for Thomas Cook won the Benjamin Franklin Award for the best new guidebook in 2001. Their work has appeared in international publications such as the *Times*, *Washington Post* and *Global Adventure*.

Additional contributors
Ruth Reisenberger, M Astella Saw

Publishing Director Georgina Dee

Publisher Vivien Antwi

Design Director Phil Ormerod

Editorial Michelle Crane, Rachel Fox, Fay Franklin, Fíodhna Ní Ghríofa, Freddie Marriage, Sally Schafer, Christine Stroyan

Cover Design Maxine Pedliham, Vinita Venugopal

Design Tessa Bindloss, Richard Czapnik, Marisa Renzullo

Picture Research Phoebe Lowndes, Susie Peachey, Ellen Root, Oran Tarjan

Cartography Mohammad Hassan, Suresh Kumar, Casper Morris, Simonetta Giori

DTP Jason Little, George Nimmo

Production Nancy-Jane Maun

Factchecker Bryan Pirolli

Proofreader Kate Berens

Indexer Patricia Baker

Illustrator Chris Orr & Associates

Commissioned Photography Max Alexander, Neil Lukas, Eric Meacher, Rough Guides/Lydia Evans, Rough Guides/James McConnachie, Jules Selmes, Valerio Vincenzo, Peter Wilson.

Revisions Avanika, Hansa Babra, Parnika Bagla, Marta Bescos, Subhadeep Biswas, Anna Brooke, Aishwarya Gosain, Mohammad Hassan, Sumita Khatwani, Shikha Kulkarni, Bandana Paul, Kanika Praharaj, Rada Radojicic, Lucy Richards, Rohit Rojal, Ankita Sharma, Farah Sheikh, Azeem Siddiqui, Beverly Smart, Hollie Teague, Manjari Thakur, Priyanka Thakur, Stuti Tiwari Bhatia, Richa Verma, Åsa Westerlund, Tanveer Zaidi

First edition created by Book Creation Services Ltd, London

Picture Credits

Serge001 112tl; Lee Snider 57tl; Sognolucido 54bc; Tinamou 93tr; Topdeq 20–21c; Vitalyedush 124tr; Vogelsp 142br; Adam Wasilewski 4cl; Yulan 155tl.
Epicure: 117cra.
Fotolia: JL 31tl; lornet 30br; 111tr; petunyia 34–5c.
Four Seasons Hotel George V: 114bl.
Fragonard Parfumeur: 99bl.
Galerie Sakura: 97cr.
Getty Images: Alinari Archives 23tl; DEA/G. DAGLI ORTI 17tl; Fernand Ivaldi 32–3c; Keystone-France 22br; Patrick Kovarik 148t; Leemage 15tl; Print Collector 42cr; Yvan Travert 149clb.
iStockphoto.com: asab974 73tr; neirfy 1
Kayser: Thierry Samuel 132b.
L'Atelier de Joel Robuchon: 67tr.
La Rose de France: 83tr.
La Truffiere: 138cl.
Lockwood Paris: 90tl.
Merci: 98t.
Ministere Français de la Culture et de la Communication: 74br.
Monsieur Bleu: Adrien Dirand 145crb.
Musée de la Magie et des Automates: Mikelkl 60tl.
Palais de Tokyo: Photography Studio Tomás Saraceno, 2018 53b.
Parc de la Villette: Marie-Sophie Leturcq 60br, 156bl.
Paris Tourist Office: Marc Bertrand 72br.
Restaurant Chez Paul: 101bl.
Restaurant David Toutain: Thai Toutain 123bl.
Restaurant La Tour d'Argent: 133cra.
Restaurant Septime: François Flohic 66br.
Shakespeare and Company: Tobias Staebler 128tl.
SuperStock: Peter Willi 14tr.
Le Taillevent: Arnaud Meyer 66t.

Cover

Front and spine: **iStockphoto.com:** neirfy.
Back: **Dreamstime.com:** Cmarkou tr, Dennis Dolkens tr, Ekaterinabelova tl, Mistervlad crb, Vitalyedush cla; **iStockphoto.com:** neirfy.

Pull Out Map Cover

iStockphoto.com: neirfy.

All other images are © Dorling Kindersley.
For further information see www.dkimages.com.

Penguin Random House

Printed and bound in China
First Edition 2002
First published in Great Britain by
Dorling Kindersley Limited
DK, One Embassy Gardens, 8 Viaduct
Gardens, London, SW11 7BW, UK
Published in the United States by
DK US, 1450 Broadway, Suite 801,
New York, NY 10018, USA
Copyright © 2002, 2021 Dorling
Kindersley Limited
A Penguin Random House Company
20 21 22 23 10 9 8 7 6 5 4 3 2 1

Reprinted with revisions 2003, 2004, 2005, 2006, 2007, 2008, 2009, 2010, 2011, 2012, 2013, 2014, 2016 (twice), 2017, 2018, 2019, 2021

All rights reserved.

ISSN 1479-344X
ISBN 978-0-2415-0965-4

*As a guide to abbreviations in visitor information blocks: **Adm** = admission charge; **D** = dinner; **L** = lunch.*

MIX
Paper from
responsible sources
FSC™ C018179

This book was made with Forest Stewardship Council™ certified paper – one small step in DK's commitment to a sustainable future. For more information go to www.dk.com/our-green-pledge

Phrase Book

In an Emergency

Help!	Au secours!	oh sekoor
Stop!	Arrêtez!	aret-ay
Call…	Appelez…	apuh-lay
…a doctor!	…un médecin!	uñ medsañ
…an ambulance!	…une ambulance!	oon oñboo-loñs
…the police!	…la police!	lah poh-lees
…the fire brigade!	…les pompiers!	leh poñ-peeyay

Communication Essentials

Yes/No	Oui/Non	wee/noñ
Please	S'il vous plaît	seel voo play
Thank you	Merci	mer-see
Excuse me	Excusez-moi	exkoo-zay mwah
Hello	Bonjour	boñzhoor
Goodbye	Au revoir	oh ruh-vwar
Good night	Bonsoir	boñ-swar
What?	Quel, quelle?	kel, kel
When?	Quand?	koñ
Why?	Pourquoi?	poor-kwah
Where?	Où?	oo

Useful Phrases

How are you?	Comment allez-vous?	kom-moñ talay voo
Very well,	Très bien,	treh byañ
Pleased to meet you.	Enchanté de faire votre connaissance.	oñshoñ-tay duh fehr votr kon-ay-sans
Where is/are…?	Où est/sont…?	oo ay/soñ
Which way to..?	Quelle est la direction pour..?	kel ay lah deer-ek-syoñ poor
Do you speak English?	Parlez-vous anglais?	par-lay voo oñg-lay
I don't understand.	Je ne comprends pas.	zhuh nuh kom-proñ pah
I'm sorry.	Excusez-moi.	exkoo-zay mwah

Useful Words

big	grand	groñ
small	petit	puh-tee
hot	chaud	show
cold	froid	frwah
good	bon	boñ
bad	mauvais	moh-veh
open	ouvert	oo-ver
closed	fermé	fer-meh
left	gauche	gohsh
right	droit	drwah
entrance	l'entrée	l'on-tray
exit	la sortie	sor-tee
toilet	les toilettes	twah-let

Shopping

How much is it?	Ça fait combien?	sa fay kom-byañ
What time…	A quelle heure…	ah kel urr
…do you open?	…êtes-vous ouvert?	et-voo oo-ver
…do you close?	…êtes-vous fermé?	et-voo fer-may
Do you have?	Est-ce que vous avez?	es-kuh voo zavay
I would like …	Je voudrais…	zhuh voo-dray
Do you take credit cards?	Est-ce que vous acceptez les cartes de crédit?	es-kuh voo zaksept ay leh kart duh krehdee
This one.	Celui-ci.	suhl-wee-see
That one.	Celui-là.	suhl-wee-lah
expensive	cher	shehr
cheap	pas cher, bon marché,	pah shehr, boñ mar-shay
size, clothes	la taille	tye
size, shoes	la pointure	pwañ-tur

Types of Shop

antique shop	le magasin d'antiquités	maga-zañ d'oñteekee-tay
bakery	la boulangerie	booloñ-zhuree
bank	la banque	boñk
bookshop	la librairie	lee-brehree
cake shop	la pâtisserie	patee-sree
cheese shop	la fromagerie	fromazh-ree
chemist	la pharmacie	farmah-see
department store	le grand magasin	groñ maga-zañ
delicatessen	la charcuterie	sharkoot-ree
gift shop	le magasin de cadeaux	maga-zañ duh kadoh
greengrocer	le marchand de légumes	mar-shoñ duh lay-goom
grocery	l'alimentation	alee-moñtasyoñ
market	le marché	marsh-ay
newsagent	le magasin de journaux	maga-zañ duh zhoor-no
post office	la poste, le bureau de poste, le PTT	pohst, booroh duh pohst, peh-teh-teh
supermarket	le supermarché	soo pehr-marshay
tobacconist	le tabac	tabah
travel agent	l'agence de voyages	l'azhoñs duh vwayazh

Sightseeing

art gallery	la galerie d'art	galer-ree dart
bus station	la gare routière	gahr roo-tee-yehr
cathedral	la cathédrale	katay-dral
church	l'église	l'aygleez
garden	le jardin	zhar-dañ
library	la bibliothèque	beebleeo-tek
museum	le musée	moo-zay
railway station	la gare (SNCF)	gahr (es-en-say-ef)
tourist office	l'office du tourisme	ohfees doo tooreesm
town hall	l'hôtel de ville	l'ohtel duh veel

Staying in a Hotel

Do you have a vacant room?	Est-ce que vous avez une chambre?	es-kuh voo-zavay oon shambr
I have a reservation.	J'ai fait une réservation.	zhay fay oon rayzehrva-syoñ
single room	la chambre à une personne	shambr ah oon pehr-son
twin room	la chambre à deux lits	shambr ah duh lee
room with a bath, shower	la chambre avec salle de bains, une douche	shambr avek sal duh bañ, oon doosh

double room, with a double bed	la chambre à deux personnes, avec un grand lit	shambr ah, duh pehr-son avek un gronñ lee

Eating Out

Have you got a table?	Avez-vous une table libre?	avay-voo oon tahbl duh leebr
I want to reserve a table.	Je voudrais réserver une table.	zhuh voo-dray rayzehr-vay oon tahbl
The bill please.	L'addition s'il vous plaît.	l'adee-syoñ seel voo play
Waitress/ waiter	Madame, Mademoiselle/ Monsieur	mah-dam, mah-demwahzel/ muh-syuh
menu	le menu, la carte	men-oo, kart
fixed-price menu	le menu à prix fixe	men-oo ah pree feeks
cover charge	le couvert	koo-vehr
wine list	la carte des vins	kart-deh vañ
glass	le verre	vehr
bottle	la bouteille	boo-tay
knife	le couteau	koo-toh
fork	la fourchette	for-shet
spoon	la cuillère	kwee-yehr
breakfast	le petit déjeuner	puh-tee deh-zhuh-nay
lunch	le déjeuner	deh-zhuh-nay
dinner	le dîner	dee-nay
main course	le plat principal	plah prañsee-pal
starter, first course	l'entrée, le hors d'oeuvre	l'oñ-tray, or-duhvr
dish of the day	le plat du jour	plah doo zhoor
wine bar	le bar à vin	bar ah vañ
café	le café	ka-fay

Menu Decoder

baked	cuit au four	kweet oh foor
beef	le boeuf	buhf
beer	la bière	bee-yehr
boiled	bouilli	boo-yee
bread	le pain	pan
butter	le beurre	burr
cake	le gâteau	gah-toh
cheese	le fromage	from-azh
chicken	le poulet	poo-lay
chips	les frites	freet
chocolate	le chocolat	shoko-lah
coffee	le café	kah-fay
dessert	le dessert	deh-ser
duck	le canard	kanar
egg	l'oeuf	l'uf
fish	le poisson	pwah-ssoñ
fresh fruit	le fruit frais	frwee freh
garlic	l'ail	l'eye
grilled	grillé	gree-yny
ham	le jambon	zhoñ-boñ
ice, ice cream	la glace	glas
lamb	l'agneau	l'anyoh
lemon	le citron	see troñ
fresh lemon juice	le citron pressé	see-troñ presseh
meat	la viande	vee-yand
milk	le lait	leh
mineral water	l'eau minérale	l'oh meeney-ral
oil	l'huile	l'weel

onions	les oignons	leh zonyoñ
orange juice	l'orange pressée	l'oroñzh presseh
pepper	le poivre	pwavr
pork	le porc	por
potatoes	les pommes de terre	pom duh tehr
rice	le riz	ree
roast	rôti	row-tee
salt	le sel	sel
sausage	la saucisse	sohsees
seafood	les fruits de mer	frwee duh mer
snails	les escargots	leh zes-kar-goh
soup	la soupe, le potage	soop, poh-tazh
steak	le bifteck, le steak	beef-tek, stek
sugar	le sucre	sookr
tea	le thé	tay
vegetables	les légumes	lay-goom
vinegar	le vinaigre	veenaygr
water	l'eau	l'oh
red wine	le vin rouge	vañ roozh
white wine	le vin blanc	vañ bloñ

Numbers

0	zéro	zeh-roh
1	un, une	uñ, oon
2	deux	duh
3	trois	trwah
4	quatre	katr
5	cinq	sañk
6	six	sees
7	sept	set
8	huit	weet
9	neuf	nerf
10	dix	dees
11	onze	oñz
12	douze	dooz
13	treize	trehz
14	quatorze	katorz
15	quinze	kañz
16	selze	sehz
17	dix-sept	dees-set
18	dix-huit	dees-weet
19	dix-neuf	dees-nerf
20	vingt	vañ
30	trente	troñt
40	quarante	karoñt
50	cinquante	sañkoñt
60	soixante	swasoñt
70	soixante-dix	swasoñt-dees
80	quatre-vingts	katr-vañ
90	quatre-vingt-dix	katr-vañ-dees
100	cent	soñ
1,000	mille	meel

Time

one minute	une minute	oon mee-noot
one hour	une heure	oon urr
half an hour	une demi-heure	urr duh-me urr
one day	un jour	urr zhorr
Monday	lundi	luñ-dee
Tuesday	mardi	mar-dee
Wednesday	mercredi	mehrkruh-dee
Thursday	jeudi	zhuh-dee
Friday	vendredi	voñdruh-dee
Saturday	samedi	sam-dee
Sunday	dimanche	dee-moñsh

Map Index